Truth and Irony

Terence J. Martin

Truth and Irony

Philosophical Meditations on Erasmus

The Catholic University of America Press
Washington, D.C.

The paper used in this publication meets the
minimum requirements of American National
Standards for Information Science—Permanence of
Paper for Printed Library Materials,
ANSI Z39.48-1984.
∞

Library of Congress
Cataloging-in-Publication Data
Martin, Terence J.
Truth and irony : philosophical meditations on
Erasmus / Terence J. Martin.
pages cm
Includes bibliographical references and index.
ISBN 978-0-8132-2809-9 (cloth : alk. paper)
1. Erasmus, Desiderius, –1536. I. Title.
B785.E64M333 2015
199'.492—dc23
2015030559

For Phyllis

Contents

Acknowledgments

THERE MAY SEEM to be something a bit foolish in dwelling at length over one's own folly, and yet that is exactly one of the cardinal invitations of Erasmus, and hence also the challenge of this book. And yet not to spend some time reflecting on and even marveling at human folly—at once so funny and wonderfully odd, yet often worrisome and quite savage, though occasionally elevated if still a little zany—is to miss something essential about our lives. Trying to understand something of the folly or madness of our lives, however, requires a remarkable manner of thinking, one that is capacious in its regard for the grand variety of experience; dexterous in its handling of the complexities of life; and agile in its ability to move about between opposing views, all the while preserving the unsettled and often unsettling irony that persists in the insight that emerges. It is this manner of thinking about our lives that Erasmus bequeaths to us, offering up a vivid model in his writings and posing an enduring challenge for us to follow suit. In this regard, I suggest, Erasmus teaches us to think better and hence to get at the truth about our lives in a way not possible by other means. For this legacy, I wish to acknowledge my thanks to Erasmus himself—in his memory, through his writings, and just possibly in our practice of this manner of thinking—so that we may learn, as Folly herself says in her closing toast in *The Praise of Folly*, to "live well," or perhaps just to live a little better, having come to know ourselves in an Erasmian manner.

My thanks go out to the living as well. I am grateful, in the first place, for the help of local friends and colleagues: certainly to John R. Shinners, with whom I have enjoyed countless rounds of talking and laughing at the full range and depth of human folly; to Phyllis Kaminski, for her good sense, abiding trust, and persistent encouragement to pursue this and other writing projects that give depth to the life of an undergraduate teacher; and to Herold Weiss, an invaluable colleague and trusted friend, with whom I have shared our respective work together over many years. As Horace reminds us, good thinking can be most honest, free, and fruitful when practiced among friends, and that holds just as much for the wider orbits in which my work has evolved. In this regard, I happily acknowledge my debts to Charles A. Wilson, Douglas Ottati, William Schweiker, and Richard B. Miller; we have been friends and allies in conversation for more decades than I wish to count, but how rich and how fertile have our annual gatherings been. I wish to thank as well Catherine Vanrie and Olivier Dodinot, whose natural hospitality, marvelous village, and charming *gîte* have provided a wonderful space in the Trièves for writing on Erasmus. I offer my thanks, finally, to the good people of the Catholic University of America Press for their help and support in bringing my project to publication.

Truth and Irony

Introduction

An Erasmian Manner of Thinking

WE HUMAN BEINGS are, to say the least, remarkably odd but interesting creatures. We have the ability to know a great deal about the world around us, and, too, we have the capacity to communicate the various things we come to know; and yet, somehow or other, we repeatedly find ourselves fooled by the way things appear and we habitually fail—either accidentally or intentionally—to say what we have in mind. We also have the talents and skills required to build communities and to manage organizations, thereby pulling together disparate individuals and binding together groups habituated to conflict; and yet, regrettably, our communities are prone to fracture and we have a terrible time trying to cope with differences of all sorts. Then, too, we by nature aspire to a wide array of goods and pleasures, the fruition of which might render us happy and just possibly fulfil our lives; and yet confusion abounds about what constitutes real or appropriate goods, some people aspiring to transcendent and spiritual goods, with others basking in the delight of pure sensuality, while most of us muddle along with varying degrees of relative satisfaction, never quite sure what will make for fulfilment. On each score it would seem that we come face to face with the oddity—and perhaps also the sadness—of our existence. Something is askew.

Looked at from another angle, however, the same points can be rendered more positively, at least to a point. We might say, for instance, that though our lives are infected with all kinds of illusions and though we suffer (and also practice) a great deal of deception, there is in us—both individually and collectively—a curiously resilient commitment to truth and honesty. Looked at from this perspective, we are a good bit more impressive, at least with respect to the persistence of our concern to distinguish what is real or true from what is not. And yet, one surely must add, what we all come to know eventually, that our grasp of reality is fleeting and our handling of truth is dubious. Much the same point can be said of our lives together: though dissension and conflict reign around the globe, tearing people apart over differences of every sort, there is ample evidence nonetheless that we human beings aspire—by nature, by habit, or by need—to the discovery and maintenance of communities founded on commonality and solidarity, even though these very social unities in turn engender yet further conflicts. What a fascinating mix of failure and aspiration this is, with the whole picture never quite being resolved into one side without the other—with gains in solidarity often giving rise to new traumas, and every new trauma inspiring yet renewed effort to secure common ground. Something similar can be said, finally, of the quest for fulfilment. Though confusion abounds about what good might render us happy, or, too, about what shape happiness might take, there is no getting around the fact that we human beings aspire—perhaps universally—for something that will complete our lives. Here again, however, this shared passion for fulfilment—indeed, a yearning for salvation of sorts—leads us (rather comically) into a whirligig of disparate and conflicting possibilities and leaves us (rather tragically) with the unsatisfying fray of contending parties.

My aim in these initial observations is to underscore the difficulties faced in the quest for self-knowledge. Knowing ourselves—what we are like, how we came to be this way, how we might be, and, too, how we should be—is extraordinarily difficult because we are such complex and confusing creatures. And yet, such knowledge is a perennial interest of those with a philosophical turn of mind, and for good reason, as insight on these matters might help us to enjoy richer and fuller lives. What I want to insist upon, at this juncture, is that a great deal depends on the kind of perspective we muster and the sort of tack we take to understand our lives. If it is the case that nothing about human existence is simple; or, more specifically, if it is the case—when it comes to questions of how people handle the truths they tell, how they manage relations between clans, tribes, and nations, and how they choose and arrange the goods they seek for fulfilment—that opposing claims can both be true enough, while neither is quite true when taken alone, even though the two together make for an unsettled combination; if things, once again, are this complex and confusing, then only an especially agile strategy of reflection will suffice. Put bluntly, to deal adroitly with the thin but crucial lines between honesty and deceit; to tend fairly to the odd but treacherous fusion of aspiration and failure in the relations between people; and to treat sensitively the curious but inescapably comical and tragic quality of the quest for happiness, these things require a very particular manner of thinking, one that is—in a nutshell—capacious and perceptive, flexible and maneuvering, and thoroughly ironic.

Much of this book is devoted to understanding and deploying the mode of thinking that—I am suggesting—is required to do justice to the complexities and oddities of human existence. For starters, however, it may be helpful to offer a rough sketch of what is involved, keeping in mind that the fine details will appear in due time. The first requirement would seem to be a vantage that combines distance and immediacy. To get a good sense of our lives, one needs a view from afar, not exactly from nowhere, but sufficiently distant to allow us to see ourselves as if from an alien angle, whereby all normal habits and everyday assumptions come to look different, perhaps small, now standing against the wider relief of usually unnoticed things. Without this wide-angle perspective, we may get an inflated sense of the importance of what is immediate; and yet, at the same time, without rich familiarity with the particular and the local, the view from afar will yield only a bloodless judgment.[1] The second requirement, I suggest, demands a perception which is especially agile, able to maneuver around from side to side, entertaining divergent perspectives; and, too, a perception which may playfully look at things inside and out, and perhaps, too, upside-down and then right-side-up. Such an approach—at once circumspect and yet flexible enough to hold opposites in tension—is inherently dialectical, meaning that it is able to glean the creative movement in the play of opposites and be sufficiently capacious to allow for a potentially unstable coincidence of opposites. What results is the material for a third requirement—namely, a ready comfort with nuance and a keen sense of irony. By irony here, I do not mean simply the knack for sensing witty turns-of-phrase, where what is meant is the opposite from what is said; but I mean, rather, the capacity for discerning the reversal of appearance and reality and for entertaining the coincidence of opposites; and, too, the experience of surprise, disruption, even shock at the incongruities unexpectedly encountered; and finally, too, the life and speech which provokes this experience through playful yet frank expressions.[2]

1. Thomas Nagel, *The View from Nowhere* (New York: Oxford University Press, 1986), 86.

2. Jonathan Lear, A *Case for Irony* (Cambridge, Mass.: Harvard University Press, 2011).

Self-knowledge, I have suggested, is important to living a full life, but it is difficult, and moreover, it must be this way since we are so complex and so odd. Perhaps the best evidence of this is the long list of competing claims about what makes us what we are. What is required, in turn, is a particular vantage point and tack, a way of proceeding in reflection informed by perspective and experience, developed with circumspection and dialectical agility, and characterized by nuance and irony. Much more of this manner of thinking will appear in the pages to follow, as each chapter takes up one of the issues mentioned—how we handle truth, the search for peace, and the quest for happiness. However, as always in philosophical matters, it is not easy to proceed alone, without a suitable model, absent a partner in conversation.

The Turn to Erasmus

In the pages that follow I want to suggest that the writings of Desiderius Erasmus of Rotterdam offer an excellent model for the kind of thinking just sketched. Born in Holland around 1467, the illegitimate son of Gerard (at some point, a priest) and Margereta (a widow and the daughter of a physician), the young Herasmus (as he was named) attended the local schools of Gouda and Deventer, and—upon the death of both parents—at 's-Hertogenbosch, where young boys received (as he would tell it much later) an assault on their "gifted minds" and plenty of pressure to join religious communities; but he would also receive—along the way—a taste of what he calls some literature of a "higher standard" and "a first taste of better teaching," which was circulating in the humanistic currents of the day. It was this literature and this learning which would become the focus of the entire life of Erasmus. As a young man, however, he succumbed to the pressure of his guardians and the lure of an old friend, or so he tells it in retrospect, to become the reluctant member of the Augustinian Canons of Steyn; though here, too, Erasmus would explore a good number of classical authors (in "furtive and nocturnal sessions"); and he would find outlets for lively conversations of a humanist bent. Despite these resources, or perhaps with their inspiration, Erasmus would seize the chance to leave the monastery in the service of the bishop of Cambrai; and he would spend many years defending his independence from the monastery, eventually receiving a series of papal dispensations from his vows.[3] He would become, in the ensuing years, a cosmopolitan scholar of great reputation, the leader of Christian humanism, counselor to royalty and correspondent with popes, and reformer of church and society.[4]

Recent studies on the life and work of Erasmus have done a great deal to flush out and focus the essential character of his achievement. Even just a brief scan of the literature, however, re-

3. For Erasmus's account of these years, see "A Brief Account of the Life of Erasmus of Rotterdam, Mentioned by Himself in the Preceding Letter," in *Collected Works of Erasmus: Correspondence*, vol. 4, trans. R. A. B. Mynors and D. F. S. Thompson (Toronto: University of Toronto Press, 1977), 403–10. The letter referred to in the title of the "Brief Account" is letter 1437 to Conradus Goclenius, dated April 2, 1524, to which Erasmus appended the "Brief Account." See *Collected Works of Erasmus: Correspondence*, vol. 10, trans. R. A. B. Mynors and Alexander Dalzel (Toronto: University of Toronto Press, 1992), 220–38. See also the extended letter to the fictitious "Lambertus Grunnius," where Erasmus tells in great detail the sad story of an "excellent young man" (with whom Erasmus coyly claims to be so familiar that he is "scarcely better acquainted" with himself) who is threatened by his guardians, cajoled by religious "body-snatchers," and seduced by an old friend to enter a religious community, where he "consoled himself with study" before escaping in the service of an "important bishop." Recounting the lad's permission from the pope to abandon his monastic garb, the letter proceeds to question the power of "monastic vows," which, as Erasmus observes, are neither biblical nor absolute. "To Lambertus Grunnius," CWE 4:6–32. On these events and the perceptions of Erasmus, see R. J. Schoeck, *Erasmus of Europe: The Making of a Humanist, 1467–1500* (Edinburgh: Edinburgh University Press, 1990), 26–120. First references to specific works of Erasmus and to individual volumes of the *Collected Works of Erasmus* give complete bibliographic information. Thereafter all references to individual works are given with a shortened title; and all references to volumes are given as CWE with volume and page numbers following.

4. See H. R. Trevor-Roper, "Desiderius Erasmus," in *Men and Events: Historical Essays* (New York: Hippocrene Books, 1977), 35–60.

veals a rich variety of accounts, as Erasmus is found to be—to select just a few epithets—"prince of humanists" (Schoeck); "tutor of Europe" (Margolin); "man of letters" (Jardine); "*humanist* theologian" (Boyle); "reformer" of theology, morals, and society (Olin); "committed pacifist" (Huizinga); and even "*enfant terrible*" (Febvre).[5] Complementing these portraits, others frame an image of Erasmus through the prism of specific texts. Then we meet the scholar of ancient languages and literature who concentrates his attention on the translation, annotation, and paraphrase of Christian scriptures, thereby setting theology on a renewed (and critically astute) biblical footing; or we encounter the compiler of the *Adages*, that multi-volume collection of some 4251 proverbs and sayings from the ancient world (both classical and biblical), presented anew to the modern world with interpretive and critical commentary;[6] and naturally we come across the satirist and playful humanist of the *Colloquies*, those charming and convivial dialogues where—as Erasmus puts it—he brings philosophy (and a bit of theology) into "games, informal conversations, and drinking parties";[7] but, too, in a more serious vein, we hear the champion of peace never miss-

5. R. J. Schoeck, *Erasmus of Europe: The Making of a Humanist, 1467–1500* (Edinburgh: Edinburgh University Press, 1990); and R. J. Schoeck, *Erasmus of Europe: The Prince of Humanists, 1501–1536* (Edinburgh: Edinburgh University Press, 1993). Jean-Claude Margolin, *Érasme: Précepteur de L'Europe* (Paris: Juliard, 1995); Lisa Jardine, *Erasmus, Man of Letters: The Construction of Charisma in Print* (Princeton, N.J.: Princeton University Press, 1993); Marjorie O'Rourke Boyle, *Erasmus on Language and Method in Theology* (Toronto: University of Toronto Press, 1977); John C. Olin, *Six Essays on Erasmus; and a Translation of Erasmus' Letter to Carondelet, 1523* (New York: Fordham University Press, 1979); Johan Huizinga, *Erasmus and the Age of Reformation* (New York: Harper and Row, 1957); and Lucien Febvre, *The Problem of Unbelief in the Sixteenth Century: The Religion of Rabelais*, trans. Beatrice Gottlieb (Cambridge, Mass.: Harvard University Press, 1982).

6. See Margaret Mann Phillips, "The Character and Growth of the 'Adages,'" in *The 'Adages' of Erasmus: A Study with Translations*, 3–165, ed. and trans. Margaret Mann Phillips (Cambridge: Cambridge University Press, 1964).

7. Erasmus, "The Usefulness of the *Colloquies*," in *Collected Works of Erasmus: Colloquies*, vol. 40, trans. Craig R. Thompson (Toronto: University of Toronto Press, 1997), 1103. Compare Erasmus to Johan von Vlatten, letter 1390, in CWE 10:97–98.

ing an opportunity to challenge anyone who will listen, including princes and popes, to abandon their militaristic policies;[8] and, most certainly, we discover the controversialist, taking on critics from both Catholic and Protestant parties, sometimes irenically, often with considerable ferocity; and then, finally, we hear the Erasmus of the correspondence, that collection of some sixteen hundred letters linking him in the give and take of ideas to a vast array of his contemporaries.[9] Plenty of evidence supports each of these portraits, and I have depended heavily on the scholarship on each.

The approach I want to take with Erasmus is somewhat different. What we have in Erasmus, I suggest, is a mind and pen at work, something wonderfully displayed in the portrait of Erasmus by Quentin Massys, and then again in Hans Holbein the Younger's 1523 painting of Erasmus at work, pen in hand.[10] Splendid as these paintings are, the mind of Erasmus is more vividly heard through his written words, as the inscription to Albrecht Dürer's engraving of Erasmus working at his desk explicitly states.[11] He appears alone in these works of art, at least as they now stand,[12] but of course he is not alone, as he could be composing one of the many letters to recipients across Europe; or, as is the case in the two paintings, he

8. See the helpful essay by José Chapiro, "Erasmus: Herald of a United World," in *Erasmus and our Struggle for Peace*, 3–122, ed. José Chapiro (Boston: Beacon Press, 1950).

9. See Wallace K. Ferguson, introduction to *Collected Works of Erasmus: Correspondence*, vol. 1, trans. R. A. B. Mynors and D. F. S. Thomson (Toronto: University of Toronto Press, 1974), ix-xxiii.

10. Quentin Massys, *Portrait of Erasmus of Rotterdam*, 1517, oil on panel, transferred to canvas, Galleria Nazionale d'Arte Antica, Rome, http://www.wga.hu/index1.html; and Hans Holbein, *Erasmus*, 1523, oil on wood, Musée du Louvre, Paris, http://www.louvre.fr/en/oeuvre-notices/erasmus

11. Albrecht Dürer, *Erasmus of Rotterdam*, 1526, engraving, National Gallery of Art, Washington, Web Gallery of Art, http://www.wga.hu/index1.html The inscription says that "a better portrait his writings show."

12. The portrait of Erasmus by Massys (also cited as Matsys or Metsys) originally was half of a diptych, with an opposing portrait of Peter Gilles. See Jardine, *Erasmus, Man of Letters*, 27–39.

is portrayed drafting commentary on biblical books. Through his pen and printers, Erasmus lived and worked in a vast network of correspondence and literary communication, by means of which his voice engaged those residing in church, university, and society. But while he may not be alone, even in his study, Erasmus was fiercely independent, and this freedom did not come easily. Indeed, as his correspondence makes clear, he carefully managed his financial resources (combining royal grants, remunerations from printers, payments for dedications, and the like); he juggled institutional ties (monastery, universities, and church); and he balanced his assorted political connections (princes, kings, and popes), all in a manner which would allow him to continue with his own course of thinking and writing, while still yielding him support without undesirable compromise or undue constraint. In each case he struggled to maintain his loyalties where due and to preserve his distance where appropriate, a tack which typically left him in the middle of dueling parties.

Erasmus most famously stands in the middle of the frequently hostile fray between Catholic theologians and Protestant reformers. What an odd position this is—to have sincere and thoughtful sympathies for both sides of this often virulent dispute; to have friends and confidants on both sides, many of whom urged Erasmus to stand with them, some of whom remained friends even when he resisted; and yet, too, to have adversaries in both parties, Catholics convinced he was Protestant, Protestants hostile because he was not. But how could he be both at the same time? Or how could he be neither? Without entering into the complex history of these matters, the substantive answer is that Erasmus was committed to the cause of education and intelligence in the service of a unified but reformed Christian community. But this left Erasmus even-handed over issues for which neither side could cotton balance or reserve. For the more strident on either side of the Reformation divide, the hesitation and equivocation of Erasmus appeared evasive and disingenuous, perhaps revealing a lack of nerve. Even allies were frustrated at times that Erasmus would not come clean with an unequivocal stand. Perhaps they were right on given occasions, maybe even many occasions; but, in any case, there is something more going on with Erasmus that they are missing—indeed, something essential about the workings of his mind that these suspicions ignore.

For my purpose, I want to suggest that there is a more positive explanation for the precarious independence of Erasmus; and that is, the very specific manner of thinking and writing that he cultivated led inexorably to his typically balanced positions. What we have in Erasmus is an especially perceptive, circumspect, and agile mind; one that naturally appreciates and savors the nuances and the ironies inherent in complex issues; and, thus, one that habitually enters disputed territories with an even-handed and balanced manner; and, too, a mind with the pen and the printers ready to express his insight and counsel with nuance and elegance. It is this quality of mind and this style of expression—that "mellow, balanced sanity," as Margaret Mann Phillips calls it—that gives his positions their typical mark of independence and reserve; but, of course, for those who demanded an unambiguous choice of sides, without hesitation or nuance, such characteristics could only appear as evasive and even disingenuous.[13]

The Erasmian manner of thinking offers a rich legacy for historical study; but it also yields an invitation for current thinking, and it is to this invitation that the meditations to follow respond. Though it is true that Erasmus never wished for an "Erasmian camp,"[14] a development which would have added only one more

13. Margaret Mann Phillips, *Erasmus and the Northern Renaissance* (New York: Collier, 1965), 206.

14. As he states it, "I am no 'Reuchlinist.' I belong to no man's party, and detest these factious labels. I am a Christian, and I know what 'Christian' means; I will not tolerate 'Erasmists,' and 'Reuchlinists' is not a word I know." Erasmus, "To

side to an age already wracked by raging and feuding sides, that does not rule out the enduring value of an "Erasmian" manner which—retaining the power to prod, stir, and unsettle—can yet be put to good use, perhaps not exactly in the way that Erasmus did for his age, but in a way that might strike similarly resounding chords in our time. We today, after all, face roughly the same difficulties in knowing ourselves—what we are like, how we came to be this way, how we might be, and, too, how we should be. And, too, we stumble over many of the same quandaries and we aspire to much the same kind of clarity when we pause to reflect on some very basic questions—how we handle truth, the challenge of peace, and the quest for happiness. No doubt historical differences affect these things and no doubt cultural variation shapes their expression, but these remain familiar and inescapable questions for all people. That being the case, I suggest that the Erasmian manner of thinking—with its rich percipience, its capacious sense of possibility, its dialectical agility, and, too, its appreciation of nuance and its eye for irony—is an excellent model and an ideal partner in conversation for approaching these questions. In this regard, it is well worth our while to follow the lead and respond to the challenge of the mind and the pen of Erasmus.

No doubt this will seem to be an unusual plan in our purportedly post-modern culture. Why be interested in a Renaissance humanist, someone certainly will be asking, when contemporary philosophy (at least certain strands of it) has overcome the anthropocentric biases of western humanism?[15] To some this will seem to be the height of naivete, almost as bad as trying to retrieve the

the Reader," letter 1041, in *Collected Works of Erasmus: Correspondence*, vol. 7, trans. R. A. B. Mynors (Toronto: University of Toronto Press, 1987), 129. This is not to say that Erasmus did not work avidly to promote the cause of "human studies." See, for example, Erasmus to Lorenzo Campeggi, letter 1062, CWE 7:195–201.

15. For a sweeping survey of the development of anti-humanist thought, including its earlier roots in France, see Stefanos Geroulanos, *An Atheism That Is Not Humanist Emerges in French Thought* (Stanford, Calif.: Stanford University Press, 2010).

European Enlightenment. In response, as Erasmus himself might ask, are not all those who see themselves triumphantly surpassing the illusions and foibles of past generations not worried by the passing of time? How long can one who takes pride in slaying one's intellectual parents expect to last, when a generation of new slayers wait in the wings? And, too, does not the self-certainty of philosophical fashions often belie a kind of shallow dismissiveness, a cocky narrowness, and a smug self-satisfaction? Can any genuine student of philosophy take pride in this? Then again, those who question the sense of retrieving the Erasmian should keep in mind what Erasmus certainly would tell them: that things are not always as they appear. Indeed, what seems like wisdom often turns out to be folly; and what is deemed old-fashioned and outdated may be—surprisingly—more lively and current than is thought. It is this surprise, I suggest, that is readily available in the works of Erasmus.[16]

The Praise of Folly

It is in *The Praise of Folly*, more so than any other of his works, that Erasmus gives the most complete performance of the qualities of mind just mentioned. And so it is in this work that we can most clearly pick up and tend to the invitation of Erasmus. Having said this, however, I must pause to acknowledge that Erasmus himself seems to downplay the importance of this work, suggesting to expected critics that he was simply amusing himself by playing with "trifles," as a child might ride a hobbyhorse. Then again, he adds, taking the opposite and ironic tack, students need some amusement, and all the better if "trifles lead to serious ideas" and if "frivolous subjects" are handled in such a way that a sensible reader

16. For a recent work running in parallel to the interests of these meditations—one that argues for the "restoration" of Erasmus and Voltaire—see Ricardo J. Quinones, *Erasmus and Voltaire: Why They Still Matter* (Toronto: University of Toronto Press, 2010).

will profit.[17] In the work that follows, Erasmus does both, and he knows it; and most surely he is delighted with the playful juxtaposition he manages, as he winds his way back and forth between the serious and the amusing. What we have here is a common gambit for Erasmus, one soaked in the playful irony of Horace, and one designed to fend off critics while signaling to friends to listen up carefully, though not too seriously, and certainly with a sense of humor.[18] Exactly the same ploy marks "The Antibarbarians," one of the earliest dialogues of Erasmus, where he presents three days of conversation spent in "pure amusement," though the dialogue does serious battle with the opponents of the humanities.[19] Or again, referring to the adage titled "A dung-beetle hunting an eagle," Erasmus admits wryly that he was "full of merry tricks," though he is writing about tyranny and terror.[20] In these and so many cases, Erasmus revels in the interplay of the grave and the comic, and in so doing, begins to initiate the reader into a manner of thinking that will be habitually agile and never flat-footed.

Erasmus sets to work on the reader's mind from the very start,

17. Desiderius Erasmus, "Erasmus' Prefatory Letter to Thomas More," in *The Praise of Folly*, trans. Clarence H. Miller (New Haven, Conn.: Yale University Press, 1979), 3–4.

18. Horace famously writes, "But tell me what law is violated if someone laughs while speaking truth? You know how teachers sometime give their pupils little cakes, to help them learn their ABCs. But I won't fool around, this is a serious discussion." *Horace's Satires and Epistles*, trans. Jacob Fuchs (New York: W. W. Norton, 1977), book 1, satire 1, lines 24–27. Erasmus returns to the Horatian fusion of the humorous and the serious in his famous letter "To Maarten van Dorp," letter 337, in *Collected Works of Erasmus: Correspondence*, vol. 3, trans. R. A. B. Mynors and D. F. S. Thomson (Toronto: University of Toronto Press, 1976), 115. For a perceptive discussion of this central feature of Erasmian thinking, see Walter M. Gordon, *Humanist Play and Belief: The Seriocomic Art of Desiderius Erasmus* (Toronto: University of Toronto Press, 1990), especially 81–98.

19. Erasmus, "The Antibarbarians," trans. Margaret Mann Phillips, in *Collected Works of Erasmus: Literary and Educational Writings*, vol. 23, ed. Craig R. Thompson (Toronto: University of Toronto Press, 1978), 23.

20. See "A dung-beetle hunting an eagle," in *Collected Works of Erasmus: Adages*, vol. 35, trans. Denis L. Drysdall (Toronto: University of Toronto Press, 2005), 178–214, adage III. vi. 1. The comment appears in Erasmus to Guillaume Budé, letter 531. See CWE 4:232.

as Folly announces her grand but audacious plan to sing her own praises to an ungrateful world. In the opening sentence, in fact, we are handed a glaring opposition: on the one hand, she concedes to having a bad reputation, "even among the biggest fools of all"; and yet, on the other hand, she boasts, it is Folly and no one else who pours forth "joy into the hearts of god and men alike." How are readers to take that? Is it possible to reconcile in one response both gratefulness for her benefaction and mistrust of her reputation? And what happens if we think both together? To help us out, Erasmus has Folly describe her audience's delighted response to her entry, thereby giving readers an invitation to follow suit. But it is not long before Folly addresses them (and possibly us) as "most foolish," a title of honor, she suggests, for the "initiates of her mysteries." So was that a compliment, and how should we take it if it was; or, for that matter, if it was not? For her part, Folly assures us that we can trust her, as she never wears "disguises," nor does she "say one thing and think another"; though in an interesting (and somewhat alarming) reversal, she tells us that she intends to "play the sophist," preferring the usually pejorative title of "sophist" to (what she surprisingly calls) the "infamous title of 'Sophi' (or 'wisemen')."[21] From the beginning, it would seem, Erasmus will not permit readers to become too settled, so he peppers us with tensions, has Folly say contradictory things, and makes us jump at unexpected reversals.[22]

As many scholars have noted, *The Praise of Folly* is broken into three discrete sections, and the medium and the message change as we move from one to the next. What readers encounter is an

21. Erasmus, *The Praise of Folly*, 9–17. On Erasmus's ambivalent regard for the ancient sophists, see Eric MacPhail, "Erasmus as Sophist," *Erasmus of Rotterdam Society Yearbook*, 26 (2006): 71–88.

22. Clarence Miller calls attention to several of Folly's tricks. Besides those just mentioned, Folly takes a jab at Erasmus himself, bragging that her speech will be "extemporaneous," unlike those who pretend that they dash off a long piece in a "couple of days," which is precisely what Erasmus claims to have done—tongue in cheek—in the prefatory letter to Thomas More. See Erasmus, *The Praise of Folly*, 9–17.

astonishing range and variation of types of folly; and, too, they face the incessant demand for a capacious and agile frame of mind to take in the myriad forms of folly described. In the first and longest section, we meet an assortment of happy fools: the newborn and the elderly man—equally bald and babbling—who charm the world with their toothless and witless manner; and between those ages, love-stricken men and women playing their wonderfully silly games of romance. What party, what friendship, and indeed, what marriage could thrive, Folly asks, without the dear quirks, the slight illusions, the fortunate oversights, the harmless lapses of memory, or, as Erasmus puts it, the "spice of folly," which makes life good and gives it cheer.[23] Indeed, she claims, nothing and nobody is "joyful or happy" without her good graces,[24] and that holds true for a wide range of innocent and contented fools, including—just to name a few—the "thick-skulled, lumbering louts" who happily march off to battle; the purblind scholars forsaking sleep for the sake of some imagined fame; the avid hunter who can think of nothing else; the religious nut fascinated with miracles and magic in the name of religion; the grandiose noblemen deluded with their fancy titles; and the happy idiot who treasures opinion over knowledge. All of these and more enjoy a "sort of continuous inebriation" thanks to Folly.[25]

While the happy madness of this first group of fools is handled with a comical touch and even a warm embrace, the fools of the second section are treated to a satirical bite, as their folly is consistently self-serving and frequently injurious to others. As Folly tells us, such fools are found "through all society from top to bottom." "What a theatre" it is, she exclaims, "how manifold the feverish fretting of fools."[26] From the common lot appear the crazed husbands, hypocritical mourners, self-destructive financial schemers, and conniving legacy hunters; each will spare no effort and

23. Ibid., 19–34.

24. Ibid., 28.

25. Ibid., 35–75.

26. Ibid., 76.

every principle to satisfy their greed at the expense of someone else. But while the gods (and readers) may enjoy their show, especially when the "tricksters" are outwitted by their "victims," it is the professional fools who put on the best (or rather the craziest) performance. And here, as the reader discovers, the list is long, as the range of madmen is wide indeed. It is an unsavory bunch, to say the least, including cut-throat merchants, domineering teachers, vain authors, pretentious lawyers, quarrelsome philosophers, ridiculous monks, arcane theologians, decadent princes, greedy bishops, and warlike popes.[27] Unlike the happy fools of the first section, this group proves more conniving than oblivious; their madness is less soothing than delirious; and, consequently, their folly is more destructive than convivial.

Everything changes, once again, as we meet the fools of the third part. Upon entering this section, however, the reader must jump yet again to make room for saintly types and religious ecstatics. Quoting scriptural texts—pretty much at random—Folly now praises those "fools for Christ's sake" who live a kind of blessed but odd life, abandoning property, ignoring injuries, and renouncing pleasures. These holy fools live so completely outside themselves that they seem to have been absorbed into that "Highest Good which gathers all things to Himself." As a result, Folly notes, they seem to have undergone "something very like madness." They are "completely beside themselves" and "they talk incoherently." Madder yet, they yearn to be "forever mad with this kind of madness."[28] By the time we reach this stage of the speech, the reader cannot help being amazed by the considerable landscape covered by Folly, and, too, by the huge differences between the fools residing in each section. To say the least, tending to these divisions and sampling the folly and the fools found in each section demands a capacious and wide-angle view of human life.

27. Ibid., 78–115.
28. Ibid., 115–138.

If moving across these divisions gives us a sense of the span of folly, and, too, of its ubiquity and its variation, we should notice as well the peculiar kind of perception at work in the steps and sections along the way. At times Folly invites us to look down upon the folly of human life from afar, as the gods are said to do when they lean over the edge of the heavens to watch the affairs of humanity, or as Menippus once did (in a dialogue of Lucian) when surveying human life from the vantage point of the moon.[29] When seen from the balcony of the gods, everything is shrunk, both in size and in significance. Everything can be caught in a single glance, so that nothing remains of what we took it to be. At so many other times, however, Folly treats us to vivid and detailed accounts of the folly of particular fools. Here we find the opposite percipience at work, inviting us to look at things close up, in living and familiar detail. And, as readers quickly learn, Folly knows her fools quite well. What is most impressive, however, and yet also most demanding for readers to follow, is that Folly sometimes does both together, juxtaposing a view from afar with close-up shots, or—more dramatically—alternating quickly from one to the other. In doing this, Folly moves abruptly from—what Clarence H. Miller calls—"stepwise analysis" of particular forms of folly to "large, kaleidoscopic scenes" focused on "swarming groups" of fools. She zooms in and then quickly zooms out, dragging the reader "down and [then] up," thereby (as Miller notes) keeping the reader "off balance," but also (more positively, I suggest) achieving a rare percipience that blends both a near- and a far-sighted focus. While the overall effect can be "dazzling" and "dizzying," its performance calls forth an especially agile and dialectical kind of perception.[30]

29. Lucian, "Icaromenippus, or the Sky-Man," in *Lucian*, vol. 2, trans. A. M. Harmon (Cambridge, Mass.: Harvard University Press, 1988), 267–323.

30. Clarence H. Miller, "The Logic and Rhetoric of Proverbs in Erasmus's *Praise of Folly*," in *Essays on the Works of Erasmus*, ed. Richard L. DeMolen (New Haven, Conn.: Yale University Press, 1978), 85–86.

The manner of thinking performed in *The Praise of Folly* is consistently capacious in scope and especially agile in focus. But it also is keenly ironic, and it is the relentless yet shifting sense of irony across the three sections that gives Erasmian thinking its characteristic power to unsettle and challenge our minds. The irony of the first section is funny and delightful, though indirectly disturbing. Here we find Folly cheerily standing everything on its head. As she tells it, the lot of these fools is preferable to the wise in every sphere of life. In the governance of states, for instance, leaders do not rely on serious "philosophical orations" to move an ignorant populace; much more effective, they know, are far-fetched tales, currying favor with fools, or conferring useless titles.[31] In social affairs, too, the wise man proves to be "more of a blockhead than a man," while the fool spices gatherings with "laughter, jokes, and witticisms."[32] Think as well about what makes personal relations lively and warm. It certainly is not the Stoic wise man who is "completely deaf to all human sentiment" and "untouched by emotion." Indeed, Folly quips, "what woman would consent to marry him?" Surely she would prefer "someone chosen at random from the mob of out-and-out fools."[33] Who, for that matter, better handles the miseries of life? Who faces death more nobly? Certainly not the wise with their infamous "weariness of life," but old men and old women—shriveled, doting, and white-haired—concealing their age with dyes and cosmetics, and throwing themselves into mad affairs with young lovers.[34]

With each of these examples, Folly leads us to the happy though unexpected conclusion—that the wise are miserable and worthless, while fools are happy and beneficial. While all this may "seem foolish," Folly gloats, it is "true as can be."[35] And it is true, we should note, by way of a genial and gentle form of irony in which

31. Erasmus, *The Praise of Folly*, 40–41.

32. Ibid., 30 and 39.

33. Ibid., 45–46.

34. Ibid., 47–48.

35. Ibid., 54.

the familiar is given an unfamiliar look. Standard assumptions—that the serious rationality of the wise is a great boon to life, while the idiocy of fools is to be shunned—are overturned and reversed; and the reader comes—surprisingly, and perhaps with an amazed grin—to embrace the happy fool. Though bolder forms of irony loom on the horizon, there is something dazzling in Folly's knack for allowing us to see the heretofore unacknowledged benefit of farce, illusion, and forgetfulness; though, too, we might wonder (and perhaps worry) if Folly's "fools, dolts, simpletons, [and] nincompoops" are not vulnerable in their careless joy to the mad schemes of more vicious fools.[36]

The irony of the second section turns to consider this more sinister type of fool. Now Folly's praise turns alarming and critical, and hence, it becomes threatening in its satire. For this very reason, in fact, most interpreters of *The Praise of Folly* do not find any irony in this section. But they are wrong, I suggest, as Erasmian satire clearly pivots on ironic contrasts. Folly's praise may sound a bit harsh, but it is hardly "merciless invective," as one critic calls it;[37] and, indeed, Erasmus is quite right to defend the tenor of his satire as relatively inoffensive.[38] The whole purpose of this section is to expose the self-aggrandizing and self-enriching inversion of

36. Ibid., 54.

37. Walter Kaiser, *Praisers of Folly: Erasmus, Rabelais, Shakespeare* (Cambridge, Mass.: Harvard University Press, 1963), 86. For a similar reading that magnifies the severity of Erasmian satire, see Constance M. Furey, "Invective and Discernment in Martin Luther, D. Erasmus, and Thomas More," *Harvard Theological Review* 98, no. 4 (2005): 479–83.

38. Though tough in criticism, the satire of Erasmus is measured and temperate. For his part, Erasmus insists that his jokes were gentle, not offensive. See "Erasmus' Prefatory Letter to Thomas More," *The Praise of Folly*, 4–5. See also Erasmus, "To make a display of pots," in *Collected Works of Erasmus: Adages*, vol. 33, trans. by R. A. B. Mynors (Toronto: University of Toronto Press, 1991), 94–95, adage II. ii. 40. Or again, as he writes to Martin Dorp, he assumes the "fictional and comic persona" of Folly in order "to admonish, not to sting; to help, not to hurt; to promote morality, not to hinder it." Those who are offended, he suggests, may well be guilty of the faults exposed. See Erasmus, "Letter to Martin Dorp," *The Praise of Folly*, 140–49.

values practiced so adeptly by the most respected elements of society, including princes and courtiers in the political sphere, and monks, theologians, bishops, and popes in the world of religion. Criticizing such hypocrisy, to be sure, can be done without irony, if the manner is direct and blunt. The Erasmian tack, however, is ironic, as Folly offers a mock praise of how these political and religious leaders stand the world on its head, while masking the whole affair with a veneer of nobility and sanctity. Things simply are not what they are made to appear to be, so Folly uncovers their pretense, thereby exposing their devious and treacherous form of madness. Doing this, of course, is bold and alarming, as it threatens the powerful players in the worlds of politics and religion. But the irony embedded in the satire of Erasmus becomes even more unsettling when it becomes apparent that Folly's exposure includes such a wide swath of the political and religious elite. Such madness is so rampant, in fact, that it becomes difficult not to ask some truly disturbing questions: is any of this madness Christian? Or, with a more uncanny hint, is this in fact what Christianity really is all about? And if the latter is the case, does that not mean that Christianity—ultimately and curiously—is not Christianity, if anything is? Erasmus himself does not explicitly ask these questions, as he almost always hopes that things might go better with the Christian world; but the questions are there for the asking, and—as we will see later, where Erasmus does ask these questions—they are some of the most potent thrusts of Erasmus's irony.

The irony of the third section, finally, is uplifting and inspiring, but also more than just a little baffling. Here, too, some interpreters have not sensed the irony of this final form of folly, though a few have rightly noted the ironic point of this apparently ideal form of folly.[39] Christ is the biggest fool of all, Folly tells us, with ample help

39. Kaiser calls it a "simpler, quieter variety of irony." Kaiser, *Praisers of Folly*, 88. Clarence Miller also finds this section to be "equally ironic." See the introduction to Erasmus, *The Praise of Folly*, xvii.

from the letters of Paul: "Though he was the wisdom of the Father, [he] became somehow foolish in order to relieve the folly of mortals when he took on human nature." Madder yet, he proceeds to "heal" mortals "through the folly of the cross."[40] In imitation of these absurdities, would-be Christians are called to an utterly senseless life:

> They throw away their possessions, ignore injuries, allow themselves to be deceived, make no distinction between friend and foe, shudder at the thought of pleasure, find satisfaction in fasts, vigils, tears, and labors, shrink from life, desire death above all else—in short, they seem completely devoid of normal human responses, just as if their minds were living somewhere else, not in their bodies.

How crazy is this? Or, as Folly asks, "can such a condition be called anything but insanity?"[41]

To say the least, these images and these questions confront readers with a breathtaking irony. Is Jesus really "beside himself," perhaps fit to be chained, as his family supposedly thought in the third chapter of the Gospel of Mark? And is Christian life really to be so bizarre? Though these images are presented as something ideal, as a kind of "wise folly" or "sagacious madness," it is hard not to be amazed and baffled at their oddness.[42] Minimally it should be said that such a life will be perceived as mad, which is how Erasmus explains the family's sense that Jesus "was not in control of his mind."[43] The irony is far bolder, however, where Erasmus refrains from diluting the idea that a Christ-like life is—in fact—"a certain kind of madness and folly." Then Christians appear to be quite mad,

40. Erasmus, *The Praise of Folly*, 130. On Christ as "divine madman," see M. A. Screech, *Laughter at the Foot of the Cross* (Boulder, Colo.: Westview, 1999), 84–89.

41. Erasmus, *The Praise of Folly*, 132.

42. Erasmus, "Letter to Martin Dorp," 157.

43. Erasmus, "Paraphrase on Mark," trans. Erika Rummel, in *Collected Works of Erasmus: New Testament Scholarship*, vol. 49 (Toronto: University of Toronto Press, 1988), 51–52. Erasmus writes, "those who spurn all earthly things, even life itself, and embrace the heavenly philosophy with all their heart appear insane to those who have a taste only for earthly things destined to perish."

like the crazed escapee in Plato's myth of the cave who returns from the outside to tell those trapped inside that he had "seen things as they truly are," and hence, that they have been "deceived" in thinking that the "wretched shadows" are real.[44] Certainly this fellow will be seen as crazy, but perhaps in another sense he actually is out of his mind; his world truly is backwards from anything he has known. In the same vein, though this section may be a "holy eulogy" of an ideal type of Christian life, its irony carries the uncanny possibility that the ideal (even as it may be ideal) is—in fact—quite insane.[45] For his part, Erasmus assuredly senses the crazed quality of this ideal, when he observes that such people shun all thoughts of pleasure, shrink from life, and are "bitterly hostile to literature," none of which could be attractive to Erasmus.[46] As with the earlier sections, the irony of the third part stirs and agitates the mind, thereby inviting readers to practice a kind of thinking which recognizes and reacts to the unexpected surprises of a world come to be seen in inverted fashion.

Everything gets more complicated, and indeed more mind-twisting, when we back away and consider the rolling irony across the types of folly. Indeed, as Miller puts it, "the experience of the book is to play off one irony against the other."[47] Doing so, however, makes everything more complicated and more perplexing, leaving readers to think apparently incompatible, if not contradictory, thoughts. It is here that Erasmian irony becomes truly unsettling and at times even eerie. In moving from the first to the second section, folly as genial and beneficial gives way to folly as vicious and destructive; and the alert reader must adjust to the strange idea that

44. Erasmus, *The Praise of Folly*, 133–34. Erasmus defends this analogy with Plato in "Letter to Martin Dorp," 158.

45. Erasmus, "Letter to Martin Dorp," 158. On the veritable madness of the ecstatic and the enraptured, see M. A. Screech, *Erasmus: Ecstasy and the Praise of Folly* (London: Penguin, 1980), 128 and 193.

46. Erasmus, *The Praise of Folly*, 132.

47. Miller, "Introduction" to Erasmus, *The Praise of Folly*, xvii.

folly devours folly, or in other words, that innocent folly becomes vulnerable to the schemes of treacherous folly. What seemed so genial and what was handled so comically comes face to face with a treacherous madness tragically bent on the destruction of the natural pleasures of innocent folly.[48] In straddling the second and third parts, a glaring abyss opens between the actual functionaries of religion and society and an apparently ideal model of Christ-like existence. At this point Erasmus leaves readers in a lurch, intentionally, it would seem. Do these forms of life have anything at all in common? Does "Christian" have any coherent meaning in the face of these opposing examples? The "sharp contrast" sounded in these questions gives the book its "reform thrust," as John C. Olin rightly observes; but it also heightens the uncanny possibility that the word "Christian" might be incurably ambiguous.[49]

In her closing words, Folly says that she hates a listener with a memory; but if we take that as a cue to remember what came before, then one might wonder how the holy fools of the third section stand with respect to the happy ones of the first. It would seem that the third type has transcended the first altogether, but then again, the praise of natural folly seemed genuine, so was none of that true? Walter M. Gordon offers a qualified response to this question, suggesting that the "benign foolishness" of the first part serves as an "analogue for and introduction to the final vision of celestial ecstasy," and hence that natural folly finds "its true fulfilment in the folly of Christ and his followers" in the third section.[50] In this reading, therefore, natural folly provides a springboard for leaping beyond itself into the heavenly folly of the final section. The alternative ap-

48. As Wayne E. Rebhorn puts it, "man cannot sustain the illusion of comedy when the waking nightmare of tragedy continually thrusts itself before his dazzled eyes." Wayne E. Rebhorn, "The Metamorphoses of Moria: Structure and Meaning in *The Praise of Folly*," *Publications of the Modern Language Association of America* 89, no. 3 (May 1974): 471.

49. Olin, *Six Essays on Erasmus*, 53.

50. Gordon, *Humanist Play and Belief*, 198 and 210.

proach, as Miller nicely observes, is to see how Erasmus has Folly lead us "to find opposite positions equally plausible," without compromise to either option. Thus, for example, "only the worldly fool is happy, only the otherworldly fool is happy"—both make sense "while Folly concentrates on it, but how can we believe both?"[51] How, in fact, can we entertain both at once, as the happiness each promises—one natural and one mystical—would seem to stand opposed to one another? In following this reading, we are led to a kind of ironic coinciding of opposites, where the tension between the poles remains unresolved, and the mind-spinning challenge is to accommodate their difference without reduction and without conflation.[52]

The more one tends to the rolling irony in the work of Erasmus, however, the more puzzling the whole project becomes. Folly keeps praising things, but the sum of what she says cannot be true, as the forms of life she praises are irreconcilable, or so it would seem. How, in short, can the innocent, the vicious, and the saintly each be praised? Granted, Folly does distinguish between the destructive folly of the second part (the kind that stirs people to greed, lust, and war) and the more pleasant folly of the first section (the kind that "relieves the heart from its anxieties" and "soothes it with the balm of manifold pleasures"); and, too, she signals the transition from what has become a satire to an authentic encomium in the third part.[53] In both passages, however, she continues with her praise as if nothing had changed, still claiming those described as her loyal followers. But does that make any sense? Where, in

51. Clarence Miller, "The Logic and Rhetoric of Proverbs in Erasmus's *Praise of Folly*," 93.

52. In this regard, Erasmus appears to echo Nicholas of Cusa by entertaining a coincidence of opposites. Indeed, as Kaiser writes, "whether those opposites are jest and earnest, praise and censure, or wisdom and folly, it is the *coincidentia*—the synthesis, the equipoise, the concord—which produces the quality of irony." Kaiser, *Praisers of Folly*, 24. On connections to the work of Nicholas of Cusa, see Kaiser, *Praisers of Folly*, 9–12.

53. Erasmus, *The Praise of Folly*, 58 and 115.

the end, is the unity of this work? How do the disparate characters hang together? One solution is topical—in short, that Erasmus is juggling different ways of being human (naive, cunning, and ecstatic); or, more specifically, different ways of being a Christian (superstitious, corrupt, and saintly); or, finally, as he writes in an adage, different ways of going "mad."[54] Spotting this unity of topic helps a bit, but only just that, as the raging variation undercuts whatever coherence the topic may provide. How, for instance, can the name "Christian" be anything but equivocal—and thus have any unified meaning—given the disparate forms of madness affecting people of this religion? In the end, it would seem, the coherence (if one may call it that) lies in the irony, though Erasmian irony—as we have seen—is inherently unsettled and unsettling, dialectically calling forth a coincidence of opposites which push and strain against each other, dynamically yielding insights that can only be called paradoxical.[55]

The temptation for readers, therefore, is to find a settled position in one of the three sections, and, thereby, to resolve the paradoxes, to find a firm conclusion, and to grasp a point where Erasmus finally is serious. Such a move has proved too enticing to resist for most interpreters of Erasmus's work. But succumbing to this temptation means side-stepping the full challenge of Erasmian thinking; and, consequently, it means missing the full impact of his irony. One option is to locate a serious (and non ironic) moment in the spiritual fulfilment of the third section. Léon-E. Halkin, for instance, insists that it is this "mystical ecstasy"—the "highest of follies"—which Erasmus exalts in *The Praise of Folly*.[56]

54. Erasmus, "Not everyone is mad in the same way," CWE 35:396–97, adage III. x. 97.

55. On paradox in Erasmus and the Renaissance, see Rosalie L. Colie, *Paradoxia Epidemica: The Renaissance Tradition of Paradox* (Princeton, N.J.: Princeton University Press, 1966).

56. Léon-E. Halkin, *Erasmus: A Critical Biography*, trans. John Tonkin (Oxford: Blackwell, 1993), 85–87.

Rebhorn argues, similarly, that the mystical section is the "serious and unironic" climax, providing a "sure direction" and a "foretaste of the true," for the process which leads "from comedy to tragedy and then beyond."[57] And, most certainly, M. A. Screech has argued with great thoroughness that the heart of the theology of Erasmus is to be found in the "witty, erudite, sustained and moving praise of a form of religious ecstasy which is indistinguishable from a bout of temporary madness."[58] A second option is to focus on the more serious (and indignant) voice of reform in the second section. No doubt both reformers and those stung by the satire in Erasmus's day would deem this section to be the serious and firm voice of its author; and this view has been given fresh life by A. E. Douglas, who faults Erasmus for allowing his own critical voice to override that of Folly.[59] Fewer scholars have stressed the serious claims of the first section, though it is the most charming part of Erasmus's work; and, as we will see in the third meditation, there is plenty of supporting material in other works of Erasmus. Not without reason, therefore, has Peter G. Bietenholz emphasized the enduring importance of simple and natural pleasures—the Epicurean note, as it were—in the work of Erasmus.[60] Each of these readings has some evidence behind it, and yet in laying stress on one section, and moreover by insisting that this constitutes the serious point of the work, each cuts short the unsettling work of Erasmian irony.

57. Rebhorn, "The Metamorphoses of Moria," 471–73.

58. Screech, *Erasmus: Ecstasy and the Praise of Folly*, xvii.

59. See A. E. Douglas, "Erasmus as a Satirist," in *Erasmus*, ed. T. A. Dorey (Albuquerque, N.M.: University of New Mexico, 1970). Erasmus enlarged the satirical material in the editions of 1514 and 1516. See James D. Tracy, *Erasmus of the Low Countries* (Berkeley, Calif.: University of California Press, 1996), 48.

60. Peter G. Bietenholz, "Erasmus, His Mistress Folly, and the Garden of Epicurus," in *Encounters with a Radical Erasmus: Erasmus' Work as a Source of Radical Thought in Early Modern Europe*, ed. Peter Bietenholz, 108–40 (Toronto: University of Toronto Press, 2009).

But what would happen if we avoided the temptation to tame the irony and resolve the paradoxes? What if we accept the idea that the unifying purpose of *The Praise of Folly* lies in the endless wheel of irony? Or, again, what if we come to terms with the most unsettling proposal of all—to wit, that there is no firm conclusion or resting point in this work, and that to insist upon one is to miss altogether (what Walter Kaiser calls) its "delicate balances" and "subtleties of flavor?"[61] Doing this, I suggest, is precisely what is required to think along with Erasmus, and hence, to think in an Erasmian manner. And, in fact, careful readers will find that they have no choice but to be tossed from one form of folly to another, since Folly's praise of folly is—as Miller has it—ceaselessly "self-affirming" (building up one form of folly) and "self-negating" (calling forth an opposing form of folly).[62] As Kaiser puts it,

> The truth [Folly] derives from polar opposites is the dynamic truth Erasmus believed in, and her irony is the logical mode of expression both for a quality of mind that perpetually perceived the qualifying *but* to any argument and for an empathy of heart that participated actively in all aspects of being without committing itself exclusively to any one.[63]

The irony of Erasmus, in other words, issues from the capacious sensibility (there are always others sides and rival angles) and the agile percipience (blending perspective and familiarity) which are so evident in the movement of Folly's speech. Thinking along with Erasmus, therefore, means entering a "vertiginous semantic labyrinth" (to quote Kaiser, once again) that leaves us (sadly enough) in a state of "permanent uncertainty," but also leads (more pleasantly) into an unending horizon of possibility.[64] Such is the challenge of the irony of Erasmus.

61. Kaiser, *Praisers of Folly*, 91.
62. Miller, "Introduction," *The Praise of Folly*, xvii.
63. Kaiser, *Praisers of Folly*, 93.
64. Ibid., 36.

The most serious alternative to an ironic reading of *The Praise of Folly* is to be found in Walter Gordon's argument that the work be read as a kind of mystical allegory. Unlike others who find the book's culmination in the mystical ending, Gordon grants that Folly leaves the opposition of the first and third parts "open-ended"; and, too, he admits that the "struggle" of the natural and the mystical is "not settled in the end," at least in print. He counters, however, that Erasmus himself is not "indifferent" about which form of folly is chosen, and indeed, Gordon writes, "one folly or other has to be chosen."[65] Taking his cue from a comment Erasmus makes to Martin Dorp, Gordon advises us to heed the "paradoxical usage of language" whereby "base imagery"—calling Christ a robber, adulterer, drunkard, or heretic—is "meant to prod the soul to reach beyond the humble, earthen reality towards the heavenly." In the same manner, Gordon argues, *The Praise of Folly* "celebrates a festive madness of intemperate and mindless enjoyment only to have this image serve as an analogue for and introduction to the final vision of celestial ecstasy."[66] What an "arresting idea," Gordon comments, that the crazed loss of self-control in part one, the way in which these fools go out of their minds with "their lovemaking, their drunkenness, and their recklessness" anticipates the "amatory, ecstatic, and self-forgetting" quality of "celestial madness" in part three.[67] What a wild allegory, indeed; but it is one, Gordon suggests, that gives *The Praise of Folly* its purpose and coherence.

The problem with this reading, I suggest, is that it neutralizes the haunting juxtaposition of opposites in the Erasmian theater of folly; and, hence, it arrests the ongoing motion of Erasmian irony. One should remember, for starters, that there is no reason to think that Folly has stopped playing the sophist in the closing sec-

65. Gordon, *Humanist Play and Belief*, 183 and 198–99.
66. Ibid., 210.
67. Ibid., 217.

tion. What she does, after all, is to mount an extended argument from authority—just as "picayune lawyers" do, we are told—citing a number of biblical texts, apparently at random and without concern for whether or not they are connected; and, too, she defends her forced and sometimes twisted exegesis as something that should be allowed to her, just as it is to "great masters of divinity."[68] But this hardly gives confidence that the proposals to follow are serious and trustworthy. After this, Folly fires off a hodgepodge of classical proverbs to establish—in very slippery and dubious fashion—the value of folly. Since, she says, everyone knows that "in the absence of the reality, the appearance of it is the best thing," folly must be an "enormous advantage," as schoolboys are taught "to pretend to be foolish when the case requires." Folly is of such value, apparently, that even a "deceptive shadow" of it deserves praise. Then, too, she quotes Cicero, entirely out of context (of course), as saying, "Everything is full of folly." Armed with this blanket claim, she concludes to the excellence of folly, as (again appealing to proverbial wisdom) "who does not know that the more widespread any good thing is, the more excellent it is."[69] As we will see in the first meditation, however, Erasmus is a staunch critic of deception by pretense; and, too, in contrast to what Folly claims here, he insists that "what is excellent in any way is always the least showy," and thus conversely, that the worst of things are always the most showy, and for that reason, the most popular.[70] So are we supposed to trust this goddess? Or should we not be on guard, as we have been throughout the work?

More specifically, should we readily embrace her proposal that the Christian religion—in its very ideals and in the happiness it

68. Erasmus, *The Praise of Folly*, 177 and 127. Gordon asserts that Folly has "long ago abandoned the role of the Sophist." Gordon, *Humanist Play and Belief*, 195.

69. Erasmus, *The Praise of Folly*, 117–18.

70. Erasmus, "The Sileni of Alcibiades," in *The 'Adages' of Erasmus*, 274, adage III. iii. 1. See *The Praise of Folly*, 69.

promises—is "something very like madness," such that its adherents are "completely besides themselves," talking "incoherently," "making sounds without sense," and "repeatedly" changing the "entire expression of their faces"—"now happy, now sad; now crying, now laughing, now sighing."[71] Gordon refers to the folly of this section as "Christian foolishness," and on this score he is not alone, as most interpreters assume this folly to be "Christian" and many regard it as the ideal form of Christian life.[72] We should not overlook the fact, however, that there are Christians residing in all three sections of Erasmus's book—some superstitious, many corrupt, and a few who are ecstatic. So it is not so obvious that the third section holds the key to what Erasmus thinks of Christian life; it is possible, after all, that he regards the several senses of "Christian"—the innocent, the vicious, and the mystical—as enduring forms of life that continually offset each other. Given Folly's ongoing sophistic performance, in fact, is it a wise assumption to put so much emphasis on the ecstatic mystic? No doubt this is a form of Christian life, and it would seem, too, that the intense love it entails is especially noble; but it nonetheless is—to say the least—a particularly bizarre form of behavior. Is it really beyond doubt that speaking in tongues and frenzied changes of expression are the unqualified ideal toward which Erasmus seriously points? In so many other works of Erasmus, after all, we discover a very different portrait of the ideal life—one that is simple and unpretentious, intelligent with a zest for conversation, and, too, humane to others and committed to the cause of peace. So is all this to be swept away in the move toward mystical felicity? Or are those who stress the mystical allegory being taken in by a sophist?

My suggestion is that there is more at stake in *The Praise of Folly* than the allegorical movement from natural to mystical folly; and,

71. Erasmus, *The Praise of Folly*, 137.

72. Gordon, *Humanist Play and Belief*, 197.

indeed, that the text demands (and deserves) a reading which preserves the enduring cross-currents of coinciding opposites, and one therefore that faces the unsettling dialectics of Erasmian irony without recourse to a final resolution. To be sure, one of Gordon's best examples for the allegorical reading is the way in which imagery of wine and intoxication—"not infrequent in the Bible"—signals the allegorical relationship between the first section's "festive language, which threatens to violate all decorum, and the essence of its spiritual utterance" in the third part. As Gordon reminds us, the "cup flows generously" in the first section—from the drunken revelry of the gods to the rowdy parties of Folly's tipplers.[73] What is the life of fools, Folly exclaims, except a "sort of continuous inebriation which fills the mind with joy, delight, and exquisite pleasure?"[74] Folly's parting salute, therefore, where she encourages us to "drink your fill," may be read either naturally or mystically. As Gordon puts it, her words "may be understood sacramentally as a behest to partake in the drink that leads to the fulness of life or as invitation to lift the cup of good red wine."[75] In Gordon's reading, however, we are invited and prodded to take the leap beyond the emptiness (the "mere vacuity") of natural existence for the fulness of heavenly life.[76] While there may well be something to this, the consistently ironic reading I am proposing insists that natural existence remains a vital counterpoint to other-worldly madness. Life does not end, after all, and fine Burgundy wine remains a source of delight and comfort, as Erasmus often attested.[77] Indeed, the the-

73. Ibid., 211–12.

74. Erasmus, *The Praise of Folly*, 73.

75. Gordon, *Humanist Play and Belief*, 198.

76. Ibid., 198–99 and 212. For a similar reading of Folly's encouragement to drink up, see Rebhorn, "The Metamorphoses of Moria," 473. The passage also has been read as a creative christening of the symbolism of ancient mystery cults. See Marjorie O'Rourke Boyle, *Christening Pagan Mysteries: Erasmus in Pursuit of Wisdom* (Toronto: University of Toronto Press, 1981), 46–49.

77. Erasmus treasured his supply of Burgundy wine, and certainly not for sacra-

ater of human existence is not a "deserted stage," as Gordon's reading suggests, but one filled with worldly goods and festive pleasures.[78] Readers of *The Praise of Folly*, therefore, would be wise to consider the possibility that natural folly constitutes an enduring foil to the mystical; just as the vicious poses a never-ending threat to the innocent; and, too, just as the mystical offers a striking correction of the corrupt; and perhaps, as well, as Gordon argues, the mystical promises a heavenly fruition of the natural.

In sum, *The Praise of Folly* offers both a distinctive manner of thinking and an exemplary display of human self-understanding; and, as we have seen, it cannot achieve the latter except by means of the former. Quite rightly does James D. Tracy describe this book as a work of "extraordinary complexity"; and in saying this he echoes Cornelis Augustijn, who claims that there is "no more subtle book than this."[79] Equally correct, Anne Reeve calls *The Praise of Folly*

mental purposes. See Erasmus to Marcus Laurinus, letter 1342, in *Collected Works of Erasmus: Correspondence*, vol. 9, trans. R. A. B. Mynors (Toronto: University of Toronto Press, 1989), 382–383. As Tracy notes, Erasmus regarded such wine as an "antidote to the stone," which is why he would declare that his "hope for prolonging life" rests in securing a new supply of wine. See Erasmus to Herman Lethmaet, letter 1359, CWE 10:8. See Tracy, *Erasmus of the Low Countries*, 129. Though Erasmus attributed medicinal value to the wines of Burgundy, he clearly also possessed a discriminating palate, as he instructs Ferry de Carondelet that he would prefer a cask of wine which was "a light ruby in colour, not too fiery, but of good quality, though it should be well aged." See Erasmus to Fery de Carondelet, letter 1749, in *The Collected Works of Erasmus: Correspondence*, vol. 12, trans. Alexander Dalzell, (Toronto: University of Toronto Press, 2003), 354. Showing an even more discriminating fondness for fine wine, Erasmus inserts frequent praise of Beaune wines in the *Colloquies*—where, in fact, one likeable but raucous character claims that wine from the Beaune region is just like the Gospel: "It makes a new man of you." See Erasmus, "Cyclops, or the Gospel-Bearer," in CWE 40:867.

78. For a fuller and more ironic reading of Folly's farewell, see Kaiser, *Praisers of Folly*, 65–68. I will return to the ironic tension of mystical and natural pleasures in the third meditation.

79. Tracy, *Erasmus of the Low Countries*, 47; and Cornelis Augustijn, *Erasmus: His Life, Works, and Influence*, trans. J. C. Grayson (Toronto: University of Toronto Press, 1991), 69.

"one of the world's great funny books."[80] Indeed, as the preceding pages have shown, it is an especially rich, yet exasperating work; at once so rewarding when read well, and yet so very difficult to read well, and thus—sadly enough—so easy to misread. What a rare work: capacious and agile, inherently dialectical and dynamic, relentlessly ironic, it is an intellectual display rarely found in literature and never repeated so fully in other works of Erasmus. As scholars have noted, by proceeding in this manner Erasmus taps into a long tradition of fools and folly in popular culture and literature; there are many fools and worlds of irony behind the text of Erasmus.[81] And yet, more important for my purposes is the manner in which Erasmus creatively recasts these sources, thereby challenging and inviting centuries of readers to take up and practice this distinctively Erasmian manner of thinking. The real force of Erasmian irony, I suggest, belongs in the reception and the reflection of later readers, where the Erasmian tack can be deployed profitably in pursuit of self-knowledge.

Meditation and Dialogue

The following chapters are exercises in philosophical meditation. My aim, in brief, is to recover the intellectual posture and manner of thinking found in the works of Erasmus, to think along with him as he addresses key issues concerning human existence, and then to deploy this Erasmian approach in dialogue with other voices. I will ask with respect to Erasmus—as Edmund Husserl did with his

80. *Erasmus' Annotations of the New Testament: The Gospels*, ed. Anne Reeve (London: Duckworth, 1986), xi. Giving the humor of Erasmus a more specific quality, Mikhail Bakhtin calls *The Praise of Folly* "one of the greatest creations of carnival laughter in world literature." Mikhail Bakhtin, *Rabelais and His World*, trans. Helene Iswolsky (Bloomington, Ind.: Indiana University Press, 1984), 14.

81. On the medieval and renaissance traditions of fools and folly, especially the *sottie* and the *sermon joyeux* performed by the *sociétiés joyeuses* of France, see Miller, "Introduction," *The Praise of Folly*, xix–xx; and, too, Barbara Swain, *Fools and Folly during the Middle Ages and the Renaissance* (New York: Columbia University Press, 1932).

meditations on Descartes—whether these are "still such thoughts as might infuse our times with living forces?"[82] I will reply, as Husserl did with Descartes, that there most certainly are enduring forces in Erasmian thinking—notably the acuteness of his perception, the boldness of his criticism, the agility of his dialectics, and the unsettling impact of his irony. When Husserl worked with Cartesian texts, he insisted that his aim was "not to adopt their content but, in *not* doing so, to renew with greater intensity the radicalness of spirit, the radicalness of self-responsibility, to make that radicalness true for the first time by enhancing it to the last degree."[83] In large part the same purpose applies to my work here with Erasmus. I have no intention of uncritically adopting Erasmian positions on specific issues, though I do seek to recover and to rekindle the "radicalness of spirit" at play in *The Praise of Folly* and other works of Erasmus. For there is something truly radical and worthy of retrieval in both the playful dialectical agility and the haunting questions of Erasmian irony. But I will not be so bold—or so presumptuous—as to suggest that I will make this "radicalness true for the first time"; for that I gladly defer to Erasmus, as his writings most certainly achieved their claim to truth without my help.

These Erasmian meditations emulate Husserl's method, therefore, though only to a point, whereupon the differences become significant and telling. What they share is the task of retrieving the "living force" of a great thinker, trying thereby to revive and amplify his claim to say something true about our lives and world. They differ, however, in what they take to be the philosophical task at hand, what Husserl calls the responsibility we have to ourselves. As Husserl sees it, his task is to reawaken the fundamental "impulse" of Descartes's philosophy by seeking to achieve "the ultimate conceivable freedom from prejudice," something Descartes famously

82. Edmund Husserl, *Cartesian Meditations: An Introduction to Phenomenology*, trans. Dorion Cairns (The Hague: Martinus Nijhoff, 1970), 4.

83. Ibid., 6.

sought through exercises in radical doubt, in order to secure (what Husserl calls) "an absolute grounding of science" in the "ultimate evidences" of the "transcendental ego."[84] How different is the work of Erasmus, and hence also of philosophical meditations on the work of Erasmus. Indeed, what we have in Erasmus is not an effort to ground anything, but rather a critical unsettling of dogmatic thinking and formal constraints, and thus an ironic disruption of the customary grounds on which we stand. These meditations also differ in genre from those of Husserl. Whereas Husserl follows the lead of Descartes by turning inward in solitary reflection, these meditations on Erasmus cannot ignore the penchant for the dialogue in Erasmus—a genre to which he makes a singularly creative contribution by fusing the Socratic interest in drawing out the truth with the eclectic, down to earth, and leisurely style of Ciceronian conversation, topped off with the wit and bite of Lucianic irony.[85] While I will not write in the form of a dialogue—a task far more difficult than the easy flow of the dialogues of Erasmus suggests—the meditations to follow will seek to retrieve the living force of Erasmian thinking by engaging a variety of voices in critical conversation.

As indicated at the start of this introduction, these meditations concern key matters of human self-knowledge. Important as these questions are for orientation in the world, they are notoriously difficult because—as said earlier—we are so complex, so odd, and—as Erasmus might say—so wonderfully full of folly. But they must be asked, and they must be pursued. Consider, therefore, to take but one example, how Immanuel Kant poses the questions in his *Logic* of 1800. Kant asks, "What can I know? What ought I to do? What

84. Ibid., 6–7.

85. See Terence J. Martin, *Living Words: Studies in Dialogues about Religion* (Atlanta: Scholars Press, 1998), 249–316. For a study of the dialogue form in the *Colloquies*, see Jacques Chomarat, *Grammaire et rhétorique chez Erasme*, vol. 2 (Paris: Belles Lettres, 1981), 849–930.

may I hope for?"[86] Each of these questions is asked—in one way or another—by philosophers of all times and all stripes. That includes the ancients, who often privilege metaphysical concerns over anthropological questions; and it includes those of recent times, who variously displace anthropological questions altogether. But there is no compulsion to approach such questions in the metaphysical terms of the ancients, under the rubric of the True, the Good, and the Beautiful; neither is it necessary to make the critical turn to the structures of subjectivity, as a modern such as Kant did; nor finally is it helpful to renounce these questions by dismantling their intelligibility, as various post-modern writers are wont to do. These are questions that are fundamental to human existence, though to be sure they must be asked naturally and freshly, reflecting with full honesty and genuine perplexity the urge to understand how it goes with human life.

It is precisely this honesty and this freshness that I find in the works of Erasmus; and it is with his casting of these questions that I will begin these meditations. The first meditation deals generally with issues of honesty and deceit in human speech, but focuses more specifically on the tension between irony and sophistry. Since neither the ironist (a Socrates, for instance) nor the sophist (such as Gorgias) mean exactly what they say and are the way they appear, the question arises whether either is honest, or perhaps, whether both are liars. Taking its bearings from an adage titled "The Sileni of Alcibiades," this meditation offers an Erasmian defense of ironic truth-telling in critical conversation with Gorgias and Jacques Derrida. The second meditation addresses the fact of war and the challenge of peace. Tapping into a number of Erasmian texts, this meditation takes up the arguments of Erasmus for peace and pits them against various efforts to find moral justifica-

86. Immanuel Kant, *Logic*, trans. Robert S. Hartman and Wolfgang Schwarz (Indianapolis, Ind.: Bobbs-Merrill, 1974), 29.

tion for war. In doing so, it entertains and pursues the unsettling questions and eerie proposals that arise from the Erasmian line of thinking—to wit, that war has become a natural feature of civilized life; that its practice and its justification are part and parcel of Christian culture; but that no rational and sane people can—in the face of the ghastly consequences of warfare—so eagerly seek to justify its practice unless they have a latent enthusiasm or even a love for war. The third meditation, finally, returns to the debate about the relative balance of mystical delights and everyday, earthly pleasures in *The Praise of Folly*. Rejecting unrestrained hedonism, but also dissenting from the long Christian diatribe against natural life in the name of ascetic spirituality, this meditation takes up the bold but odd suggestion made by Erasmus in "The Epicurean" that "there are no people more Epicurean than godly Christians."[87] Following the trajectory set in *The Praise of Folly*, as well as in many of the *Colloquies*, it affirms the Erasmian move to dialectically offset mystical felicity with the natural pleasures of everyday human life.

It is my hope that the three meditations to follow will shed some light on the areas of inquiry so commonly found in the quest for self-knowledge. They certainly do not cover all that could be addressed, nor do they pretend to do so. But if they manage to stir some thought and provoke some conversation, then they will have been worthwhile. Then, again, it is my hope that the deployment of Erasmian thinking in these meditations might prompt someone to return for a fresh reading of Erasmus. What they will find, I suggest, is a towering intellectual of his day and his culture; but they also will discover—should they read with humility and openness—a manner of thinking and writing with the power to stir and prod reflection in our own period, even with its very different problems and sensibilities. Indeed, I hope that it will become apparent in the following meditations how the dialectical agility and

87. Erasmus, "The Epicurean," CWE 40:1075.

unsettling irony of Erasmian thinking can hold its own in conversation with both the giants of classical thought and the celebrities of current philosophy. In each meditation, I will begin with what Erasmus has to say on the matter in question, taking up his line of thinking, but also—in the process—his manner of thinking, attempting as the meditation evolves to play out the trajectory of the Erasmian tack in dialogue with other voices, even if the result goes a bit beyond Erasmus's own words.

First Meditation

Irony and Deceit

IT IS PLATO who has the drunken Alcibiades warn that the whole life of Socrates is ironic.[1] He is like one of those statues of Silenus found in "any shop in town": on the outside they appear plain or even grotesque, but when opened up they reveal the radiant figure of a god inside.[2] Socrates is

1. Plato, *Symposium*, trans. Alexander Nehamas and Paul Woodruff (Indianapolis, Ind.: Hackett, 1989), 216e.

2. Plato, *Symposium*, 215b. Plato here taps into the tradition of Silenus in classical myth and art. The guardian of Dionysius and his frequent companion, Silenus is the hero of wine and dance. Often linked in tradition with the satyrs, he sometimes is pictured with the ears of a horse and a tail. As an individual figure, however, he generally appears as a fat and jovial old man, drunk and stumbling about, relying on other satyrs for support. See the marvelous collection of images at http://warburg.sas.ac.uk/vpc/VPC_search/subcats.php?cat_1'5&cat_2'184 In the *Symposium*, Plato plays on the ambiguity attributed to satyrs in ancient tradition. They are said to be both "grotesque hedonists and yet the immortal companions of a god, cruder than men and yet somehow wiser, combining mischief with wisdom, lewdness with skill in music, animality with divinity." Richard A. S. Seaford, "Satyrs and Silenus," in *The Oxford Classical Dictionary*, 3rd ed., ed. Simon Hornblower and Antony Spawforth (Oxford: Oxford University Press, 1996), 1361.

just like that, Alcibiades complains; he is not what he appears to be. In his bearing he appears a bit dazed and claims to be ignorant of everything, but when one looks beneath the surface, one finds a "sober and temperate man."[3] His manner of speaking, too, appears at first to be "totally ridiculous"—at once plain, repetitive, and laughable—but if anyone bothers to open up his arguments and get "behind their surface," they will find they are sensible, even divine, and filled with virtue.[4] But, oddly enough, much the same thing can be said of the sophists, only in reverse: those who, having studied the art of speech-making with Gorgias,[5] know how to make most anything sound good, though when opened up with a few questions they often are found to be shallow and self-serving. The sophists, too, are not what they appear to be.

Erasmian Variations

Gifted with a keen sense of irony, Erasmus takes up this double-sided perception and plays it out in the world of philosophy and religion. In one of his Adages, aptly titled "The Sileni of Alcibiades," Erasmus surveys the classical philosophers and biblical figures who—like the little wooden sileni—are unassuming and unimpressive on the outside, but wise and virtuous when examined more closely. The "most extraordinary Silenus of all," Erasmus contends, is Christ: "in such service to mankind, there is a pearl of great price, in such humility, what grandeur! in such poverty, what riches! in such weakness, what immeasurable strength!"[6] But, Erasmus laments, today "the greater part of mankind are like Sileni inside out." Now applying the ironic perception critically, he

3. Plato, *Symposium*, 216d–e.

4. Ibid., 221d–222a.

5. Reference is made to the fifth century orator and teacher of rhetoric in Plato, *Symposium*, 198c. Plato has Socrates call attention to the fact that Agathon's speech in praise of love imitates the style of Gorgias.

6. Erasmus, "The Sileni of Alcibiades," in Phillips, *The 'Adages' of Erasmus*, 272, III. iii. 1.

observes how "the people who claim to be most religious"—the priests, theologians, bishops, and popes—are "the furthest from true religion," even as they present themselves with pomp, power, and splendor. Open up these figures, Erasmus observes, "and you will find nothing but a soldier, a trader, or finally a despot."[7] And the same treacherous reversal also "brings about a reversed use of words," so that what is meant by love or peace is turned inside out and used as a cover for enmity and war.[8] So much human language does not mean what it says; and, once again, things are not as they appear.

It is little wonder that Erasmus excuses himself for comparing Christ with Silenus. Though he insists the comparison is appropriate—what glory and wisdom rest beneath this obscure and lowly life, one finally "despised and rejected of men"—he is well aware that Christians will "shrink from this picture," preferring instead a more august, and certainly more robust, figure for their savior.[9] And, too, Erasmus knows a thing or two about "ridiculous old Silenus," the tutor of Dionysius and a wild dancer, often drunk, a freakish but still amiable creature. Not exactly the image people want for their Christ. But what Erasmus seeks in the legends of Silenus is the famous incongruity of the rough, untamed, and

7. Ibid., 273–74.

8. Ibid., 279.

9. Ibid., 272. Erasmus defends the analogy in his "Letter to Martin Dorp," arguing that the words will only be "intolerable" to the "malicious critic" who reads the comparison in a "scanty and perfunctory fashion" in order to put them in "the worst possible light." However, he suggests, "if a holy and fair-minded man should read what I wrote, he would approve of the allegory." See the "Letter to Martin Dorp," 159. Elsewhere Erasmus employs roughly the same contrast, but without reference to the figure of Silenus. Unlike the world, he writes, "when we see [Christ] from far off, the prospect seems somewhat dour, as we look at the crosses and the contempt for pleasures and for life. Yet anyone who in trust throws himself completely on Christ will find that nothing is more pleasant, more beneficial, or more delightful." Erasmus, "Homily on the Child Jesus," in *Collected Works of Erasmus: Literary and Educational Writings*, vol. 29, ed. Elaine Fantham and Erica Rummel (Toronto: University of Toronto Press, 1989), 67.

even mischievous figure who, when pressed—as Silenus was by the shepherd boys of Virgil's sixth *Eclogue*—delivers a song of wisdom, precisely the kind of startling contrast he finds, once again, in Alcibiades's raving praise of Socrates.[10] As Erasmus retells Alcibiades's eulogy, Socrates had "a yokel's face, with a bovine look about it, and a snub nose always running; you would have thought him some stupid, thick-headed clown." But, as with Silenus, if you get behind the appearances, "you find a god rather than a man, a great, lofty and truly philosophic soul."[11] What is remarkable, however, is how this pattern of incongruity—something splendid and valuable hidden behind lowly and plain appearances—shows up across human life and culture: in philosophers, in biblical figures, in books of all sorts, and finally in natural phenomena. In each of these cases, Erasmus observes, "the most excellent things are the deepest hidden."[12] Whoever seeks the treasures of wisdom and virtue, therefore, will have to dig deeply in the most unex-

10. See Virgil's sixth "Eclogue," in *The Eclogues and Georgics of Virgil*, trans. C. Day Lewis (Garden City, N.Y.: Doubleday, 1964), 45–47.

11. Erasmus, "The Sileni of Alcibiades," 270.

12. Ibid., 276. "The writings of all the poets and the Platonist philosophers belong to this category," Erasmus observes, "but especially the sacred Scriptures, which like those images of Silenus mentioned by Alcibiades enclose unadulterated divinity under a lowly and almost ludicrous external appearance." Erasmus, "The Handbook of the Christian Soldier," trans. Charles Fantazzi, in *Collected Works of Erasmus: Spiritualia*, vol. 66 (Toronto: University of Toronto Press, 1988), 67–68. Good reading of these texts, therefore, requires one to "open the Silenus" (to "crack open the nut") in order to discover with delight and astonishment the "divine wisdom" resting beneath the surface. Literal reading of historical narrative, therefore, often must give way to figurative interpretation. See Erasmus, "An Exposition of Psalm 33," trans. Emily Kearns, in *Collected Works of Erasmus: Expositions of the Psalms*, vol. 64, ed. Dominic Baker-Smith (Toronto: University of Toronto Press, 2005), 278–82 and 301. In parallel fashion, Erasmus notes, proverbs or adages—brief and trivial though they may seem—reveal "sparks of that ancient philosophy" for the one who looks "closely and deeply." *Collected Works of Erasmus: Adages*, vol. 31, trans. Margaret Mann Phillips (Toronto: University of Toronto Press, 1982), 14. On the manner in which adages both conceal and reveal truth, see William Barker, "Implied Ethics in the *Adagia* of Erasmus: An Index of *Felicitas*," *Renaissance and Reformation; Renaissance et Réforme* 30, no. 1 (2006): 87–102.

pected places, and, in any case, probe thoughtfully to get a glimpse beneath the surface.

But, as Erasmus sadly observes, there are very few "hidden good Sileni" in the world; in fact, as we have heard him say, "the greater part of mankind are like Sileni inside out."[13] Thus, to take some religious examples, priests with their "tonsure" appear holy, but "if you look into the Silenus," Erasmus suggests, "you will find them worse than laymen." Monks, too, look so pious, with their "flowing beards, pale faces, hoods, bowed heads, girdles, and proud truculent expressions"; but "open them up, and you find mere buffoons, gluttons, vagabonds, [and] libertines."[14] Theologians, as well, could be taken for "wisdom's peak," when decked out with "their grand titles, learned bonnets, splendid sashes"; in fact, Erasmus quips, you may find more "authentic wisdom in one obscure individual, generally thought simple-minded and half-crazy," whose mind has been taught by the "heavenly spirit of Christ," than in "the many strutting characters acting the theologian, three or four times Doctor So-and-so, blown up with their Aristotle and stuffed full of learned definitions, conclusions, and propositions."[15] Bishops, finally, could easily be taken "to be divine beings" when seen capped with a "mitre gleaming with jewels and gold" and armed with a "crozier likewise encrusted with gems"; but, counters Erasmus, "open the Silenus, and you will find nothing but a soldier, a trader, or finally a despot, and you will decide that all those splendid insignia were pure comedy."[16] In these and all such examples, Erasmus concludes, everything is inside-out; an appropriate estimate of things is "utterly reversed," so that "what we should particularly honour passes without a word and what we should strive for with all our might is regarded with contempt."[17] None of these people are what

13. Erasmus, "The Sileni of Alcibiades," 273.

14. Ibid., 277.

15. Ibid., 274.

16. Ibid., 277.

17. Ibid., 279. Alternative imagery for these twisted figures includes Paul's reference

they seem; and their dissemblance is self-aggrandizing and treacherous.

The ultimate scoundrels, as Erasmus tells it, are those who veil their poisonous speech under the guise of sanctity; and precisely this well-studied deception, he laments, is at work "through the whole Christian community."[18] As he observes in his own day, calumny is all too common in Christian life: monks draft "defamatory caricatures," theologians fire off "scandalous pamphlets," and still others level "false ascriptions" of heresy; and each does so with "weapons dipped in hellish poison."[19] And yet, Erasmus notes with an ironic eye, things will appear to be otherwise, for these people have "discovered the art of concealing their hatred" by seeming to be "models of Christian religion and honour."[20] What a grand deception, this is! They speak with venomous tongues, yet disguise "their devilish malice with the pretext of religion."[21] They "call themselves preachers," all the while hiding "their daggers beneath their holy robes."[22] They "profess the simplicity of the gospel," and

in Acts 23:3 to the "false and pretentiously dressed high priest Ananias" as a "whited wall," because "inwardly he was far different from what [he appeared to] be outwardly." Or again, Erasmus notes, there is the Jesus of Matthew 23:27, lambasting the scribes and Pharisees as "whited sepulchres," as they "sparkle on the outside" but are "full of the bones of the dead" on the inside. See Erasmus, "A whited wall," CWE 35:136, III. vi. 23. And, too, there are the "colossi of Myron and Praxiteles," which as Lucian notes, outwardly "gleamed with much ivory, flashed with much gold, and were bright with diverse colors," while on the "inside there was nothing but pitch, nails, spiders, mice and other such rubbish which corresponded not at all the exterior image." See Lucian, "The Dream, or the Cock," *Lucian*, 2:223.

18. Erasmus, "The Tongue (*Lingua*)," trans. Elaine Fantham, in CWE 29:353. Margaret Mann Phillips calls "The Tongue" a "complete example of the Erasmian approach," and it certainly is that, only now applied to the uses and abuses of language. See Phillips, "Erasmus on the Tongue," *Erasmus of Rotterdam Society Yearbook* 1 (1981), 125. On the ambiguity of language for Erasmus, see Laurel Carrington, "Erasmus' *Lingua*: The Double-Edged Tongue, *Erasmus of Rotterdam Society Yearbook* 9 (1989), 106–18.

19. Erasmus, "The Tongue," CWE 29:348–49.

20. Ibid., 352–53 and 314.

21. Ibid., 349.

22. Ibid., 353 and 350.

yet "they bear on their tongue the cunning of the devil."[23] Like the sileni of old—*only turned inside out*—what appears and what is heard are twisted reversals of what rests within—their actual motives and their real agenda. Such "artful pretense," Erasmus quips, has become something of a "sport with monks."[24] But when what they say is "at variance with their mind" and when what they do is contrary to their hearts, then their entire lives are "nothing but a lie."[25]

With this charge we arrive at a critical thrust of Erasmus's work on the human tongue, and it involves a double-indictment built upon an ironic perception. The root target is the venomous speech or the corrupted lives; but to get at these, the concealment by pretense—*the lie*—must be exposed and challenged. And the sileni inside-out are highly proficient in concealing their intentions and purposes. With artfully crafted disguises, everything is reversed, so that self-promotion appears as humility, deviousness comes to look like sincerity, and maliciousness seems kind.

Initial Questions

It is easy to sympathize with Erasmus's satirical exposure of fakes and frauds. Pretense and posturing, duplicity and hypocrisy, deceit and treachery—these have always been worthy targets for satiric criticism. However, it is somewhat more difficult to know what to say of the authentic sileni, for they, too—after all—are not what they appear to be. And the key question to be pursued in the next pages is why this is the case? If sileni inside-out are not what they appear to be because they dissemble in a deceptive manner, then

23. Ibid., CWE 29:358.

24. Ibid., 328 and 316.

25. Ibid., 315. Indeed, he adds, "they do not only lie in their speech, … but even in their feigned countenance, their portentous apparel, their diets, titles, and ceremonies; they lie before the whole world, bringing great damage to the religion which they dishonestly profess." Ibid.

why are sileni right-side-out not what they appear to be; are they similarly dissembling, and just possibly deceptive as well? A few examples will yield an initial sense of the suspicions at work in these questions.

When it comes to the Silenus of ancient legend, he had no choice about his appearance, as he was grotesque by nature. And yet, it seems that people had to snare him in order to hear his wisdom, sometimes by getting him drunk and then binding him after he passed out.[26] This would suggest that—in some way—he held back his wisdom, allowing his odd appearances to convey the impression that he was just a fat old drunk with donkey ears. If this is a fair reading of the traditions, then a certain dissemblance is implied. In other cases, a wise silenus might deliberately avoid ostentatious display, opting instead for something simpler and less showy. According to Paul's letter to the Philippians 2:6–8, Christ did something like this, when emptying himself of the "form of God," he took on the "form of a servant" to live among human beings. In the context of the letter, this term seems to extol humility with a divine example. But it is not hard to see how such language would give rise to docetic readings of the Christ-figure, where the divine reality is veiled by a thin layer of physical life; and here we have the roots of a christology of divine dissemblance.

Interestingly enough, a similar kind of dissemblance appears in some of the best-known works of Erasmus himself—*The Praise of Folly*, for instance, where he poses as a foolish goddess; or the *Colloquies*, which he coyly defends as simple exercises in grammar and manners for schoolboys; or even an essay on deception in the guise of an adage.[27] It is hard to see any sinister motives in these works, though many of Erasmus's critics thought otherwise; but, regardless, these genres certainly do involve a kind of artful,

26. For a compendium of references to Silenus and the sileni in the ancient Greek traditions, see http://www.theoi.com/Georgikos/Seilenos.html

27. Erasmus, "The Usefulness of the Colloquies," CWE 40:1097–98.

literary pretense. Finally, to take an authentic silenus mentioned by Erasmus—Diogenes of Sinope—it is interesting to note that the ancient collections give mixed signals on this character's character. On the one side there are the bizarre tales of Alexander the Great admiring the utter freedom and frankness of a crusty old man in a tub, while, on the other side, there are the detractors (including Plato, reportedly), suspecting that the Cynic's rustic lifestyle and unbridled bluntness were a fabricated cover for hidden conceit.[28] The former trusts and admires the appearances, while the latter suspects outright deceit from this silenus.

With these examples in mind, it is worth returning briefly to Erasmus's account of the silenus right-side-out. When writing on language, for instance, Erasmus reacts to hypocrisy and deceit with an imperative to honesty. Drop all pretense, he exhorts his readers, and "let the tongue be at one with the heart."[29] The natural purpose of the human tongue, he tells us, is to be the "messenger" of one's "mind and intentions." Assuming, therefore, that someone has wisdom in their mind and love in their heart, then it is "fitting"—Erasmus insists—that what is said or done "match" what is thought or felt.[30] At a minimum this would seem to rule out ignorant statements and hateful actions; and the person who spoke or acted ignorantly or hatefully would come under suspicion of not being wise or loving in the first place. That an ignorant or vicious person would speak or act ignorantly or viciously would curiously—be an instance of ingenuous behavior, and thus it would be a case of an ignorant or vicious life—very curiously—where there was at least one virtue—honesty. Such a possibility, however, falls

28. Diogenes Laertius, *Lives of Eminent Philosophers*, vol. 2, trans. R. D. Hicks (London: William Heinemann, 1925), 23–85, classical pagination. To Alexander's offer of anything Diogenes wants, the philosopher—having been resting in the sun—responds, "stand out of my light." See *Lives*, 38. For examples of spats with Plato, see *Lives*, 25–26 and 58.

29. Erasmus, "The Tongue," CWE 29:409.

30. Ibid., 314.

outside the purview of Erasmus; he, no doubt, would be more concerned with the ignorant or vicious person speaking or acting as if they were wise or virtuous, and this—as we have seen—is the target of his satire. The question at hand, however, has to do with the sileni right-side-out, since by definition they also are not what they appear to be. So, if the ideal is one of honesty, then how is it that the authentic silenus ends up looking and speaking (on the outside) differently from the way they truly are (on the inside)? Why the incongruity? How is this not another case of pretense? Or at least of dissemblance? And possibly of deception?

Erasmus offers a number of answers. For starters, he suggests, the sileni right-side-out simply are not concerned with appearance or show. They are not trying to make their way in life by means of image and status; so, by neglecting showy display, they come off as lowly or unimpressive, the opposite of what they really are, were they opened up. If this holds, then the incongruity in a figure like Socrates is explained by his neglect of show, not by manipulation of appearances. The fact that common consciousness is so thoroughly addicted to flashy display also helps to explain why no one bothers to open up an authentic silenus. People purportedly flock to hear Diogenes whistling—what a show!—but they ignore him entirely when he speaks to them of serious matters.[31] Were someone to stop and listen to what he was saying, they might wonder why they never noticed him; but the fault would be the crowd's inattentiveness, not the philosopher's dissemblance. When it comes to the silenus who deliberately chooses an unassuming façade—like the Christ of Philippians—the incongruity of reality and appearance might be justified by noble intentions, where the wise condescends out of humility—though this response, interestingly, does not deny the dissemblance. The same thing might be said of Erasmus's account of his own literary pretense. Tapping some lines

31. Diogenes Laertius, *Lives of Eminent Philosophers*, 27.

of Horace, Erasmus insists that he wrote *The Praise of Folly* "under the guise of pleasure," since a "bitter-dose of truth, if sugar-coated goes down readily"; and the *Colloquies* were composed in a simple and playful manner in order to help young people learn their lessons.[32] Here, too, the pretense is not denied, but justified as innocent for pedagogical reasons.

Not everyone, however, has trusted these kind of explanations, and understandably so. The last two reasons for the gulf between appearance and reality concede dissemblance, only suggesting that it is driven by noble motives, not sinister ones. But that defense already acknowledges that the authentic and the reversed sileni are both intentionally not who they seem to be. Though one may be virtuous and the other vicious, both are dissemblers, and that seems to collapse the original distinction, leaving both kinds of sileni on the same footing, at least in this respect. Many, too, have doubted the first two explanations—one based on disregard for appearances, the other rooted in people's oversight. Is the Silenus of old not deliberately profiting from the concealment offered by his odd exterior? Is it possible that all the startling public antics of Diogenes the Cynic—walking around the crowded market in the daylight with a lantern, looking for a human being—are not a bit of staged lunacy, disguising an astute observer of human existence? And, as supporters and adversaries of Jesus might have wondered, is there not an agenda—heretical and dissident or prophetic and apocalyptic—hidden behind this character's well-choreographed public shows? And, lastly, as admirers and enemies of Erasmus certainly suspected, is there not a trenchant critic working behind the clever literary guises he assumes?

Each of these suspicions—in one way or another—lead straight to Erasmus's darkest and most unsettling proposal—and that is,

32. Erasmus, "The Usefulness of the Colloquies," CWE 40:1097–98. Erasmus alludes to Horace's advice to fold laughter into serious discussion. See *Horace's Satires and Epistles*, book 1, satire 1.

that "every mortal is a liar."[33] Given the prevalence of deceit in human affairs, Erasmus can sound remarkably pessimistic when he frankly concedes that—at least at some level—no one is entirely free from pretense.[34] If this is true, however, then the original distinction of the kinds of sileni collapses entirely, so that every Silenus—both right-side-out and inside-out—is a trickster at heart. In that case, everyone is a liar. As we will see, however, Erasmus refuses to embrace this option. Indeed, he argues, the cultivation of an intelligent and humane tongue remains an ideal worthy of steadfast hope and diligent aspiration, and that goal includes maintaining the distinction between honesty and deceit. If someone fashions themselves a Christian, for instance, then their faith should find clear and honest expression in a modest, healing, and mild manner of speaking.[35] "Pretense does not suit the children of light," he insists.[36] One would think, therefore, that the authentic sileni—Silenus, Socrates, Diogenes, and Jesus—would be similarly honest. The sileni right-side-out, after all, is a figure whose wisdom and virtue find natural expression in an unadorned tongue, one that is simple, but wise, and most likely—in the eyes of most people—a bit foolish. But, as we have seen in the questions and doubts raised above, this has proved to be a precarious proposal. None of these figures are exactly what they appear to be; and what they say is not always

33. Erasmus, "The Tongue," CWE 29:332. The language used by Erasmus is taken from Romans 3:4, where Paul underscores the faithfulness of divine promises over and against the human capacity to lie. As Erasmus writes on this passage, "God cannot be deceived and he cannot deceive. But man, inasmuch as he is man, is capable of both." See Erasmus, "Paraphrase on Romans," in *Collected Works of Erasmus: New Testament Scholarship*, vol. 42, trans. John B. Payne, Albert Rabil Jr., and Warren S. Smith Jr. (Toronto: University of Toronto Press, 1984), 23. Erasmus's critical comments on this text are more muted. See *Collected Works of Erasmus: New Testament Scholarship*, vol. 56, trans. John B. Payne, Albert Rabil Jr., Robert D. Sider, and Warren S. Smith Jr. (Toronto: University of Toronto Press, 1994), 92–93.

34. Erasmus, "The Tongue," CWE 29:332.

35. Ibid., 406.

36. Ibid., 315.

what they mean. So is there, in the end, any difference between the sileni right-side-out and the sileni inside-out?

This question—and the insistence of Erasmus that there is a distinction between authentic and inauthentic sileni—will comprise the focus of the meditation to follow. What better place to start than to examine how fragile this distinction has proven to be with respect to the character of Socrates—something already at play in Plato's ambiguous handling of Socrates, and something still at work in later receptions of this philosophical silenus.

Platonic Doubts about Socrates

Consider, once again, the testimony of Alcibiades in Plato's *Symposium*. What we find—not surprisingly—is ample material to support the idea of Socrates as an authentic Silenus. On the outside, Alcibiades observes, Socrates appears to be "crazy about beautiful boys"; and, too, he "likes to say he's ignorant and knows nothing." "Once you have looked inside," however, he is seen to be a "sober and temperate man"; and, indeed, it turns out that he could care less whether someone is "beautiful, or rich, or famous in any other way that most people admire." What this silenus "keeps hidden within," Alcibiades marvels, is practically "godlike—so bright and beautiful, so utterly amazing."[37] The same pattern holds for his words and arguments, as well. On the surface his language is ordinary and even laughable; indeed, he is "always making the same tired old points in the same tired old words." But, Alcibiades notes, if one listens carefully and goes "behind their surface," one finds the most splendid insights, something "truly worthy of a god." In fact, he marvels, if one manages to get beneath the appearance of Socrates's speech, one will find that "no other arguments make any sense."[38] Socrates is, in sum, exactly like the statues of Silenus: his

37. Plato, *Symposium*, 216d–217a.

38. Ibid., 221e–222a.

words and wisdom are not anything like they appear to be on the surface; they are far richer and more splendid.

At the same time, however, the speech of Alcibiades is laced with undercurrents, which leave the issue a good bit murkier than it may seem at first glance. It turns out, he tells the others, that Socrates harbors certain magical powers beneath his rough exterior. In this regard, he suggests, Socrates is more like the satyr Marsyas, whose flute playing (at least as Alcibiades tells it) has the power to "possess" people. Unlike Marsyas, however, Socrates puts his "spells" on people with "words alone," leaving those who listen to him "astounded and possessed."[39] And this is, Alcibiades complains, exactly what he suffers when conversing with Socrates. In fact, he exclaims, when Socrates speaks to him he is completely "beside" himself: his "heart starts leaping," tears stream down his face, and even "the frenzied Corybantes" will seem sane in comparison. No other great speaker, not even Pericles has ever had such an effect on him. Only Socrates, it seems, wields the power to confront Alcibiades with the shallowness and pointlessness of his public career. It is hardly surprising, therefore, that he responds by stopping up his ears and making a quick escape from the company of Socrates.[40] What this intensely dramatic testimony shows is that beneath the surface of Socrates's lowly appearance is a man with the extraordinary power to unsettle a successful man's life. That this is the case does not, of course, undermine the comparison of Socrates with Silenus, but it does suggest that it may not be such a good idea to open up this very peculiar silenus. The impact could be overwhelming.

Continuing along these same lines, there is plenty of evidence in Plato's text suggesting that what we have in Socrates is a silenus whose interior wisdom is so profoundly heavenly that he is unable

39. Ibid., 215c–d. For a compendium of ancient sources on Marsyas, see http://www.theoi.com/Georgikos/SatyrosMarsyas.html

40. Plato, *Symposium*, 215e–216c.

to pass on what he knows to others. Indeed, he seems to be a tragic silenus—someone whose message inevitably ends up twisted or aborted in its recipients. The force behind this proposal takes its start from the two main pillars of Socrates's speech under the guise of Diotima. In the first place, Diotima advises, one must ascend a kind of staircase of loves—rising above sexual desire for particular bodies to an aesthetic appreciation of the beauty of bodily form; and from there to the higher love for personal character and social values; until one reaches the highest level, where one gazes with love upon "the Beautiful itself, absolute" and "not polluted" by anything physical or transient.[41] But, in the second place, because such love wants to "possess the good forever," aspiring for a certain "immortality" in love, it hopes to "give birth" to "offspring" who live on into the future.[42] Only upon the vision of Beauty itself, she says, "will it become possible for him to give birth … to true virtue."[43] A philosopher might give birth to "ideas and arguments" in another by means of conversation, though "the greatest and most beautiful" offspring is the "moderation and justice" required for the "proper ordering of cities and households."[44] In either case, the transcendent vision should bear very practical fruit.

By this measure, however, Socrates is a colossal failure. Many of the things Alcibiades says of Socrates, in fact, suggest that while he may have ascended to the vision of absolute Beauty, this has turned him into an utterly "bizarre," almost superhuman figure.[45] When serving with the Athenian army, for instance, he supposedly stood up to hardship and hunger better "than anyone in the whole army"; and, so too, we are told, he was immune to the fiercest winter weather, having trudged through snow and ice in "bare feet."[46] Strangely enough, nothing physical seems to affect him, so he is unaffected by sexual arousal; he can drink anyone "un-

41. Ibid., 211e.

42. Ibid., 206a, 208b, 207a, and 209d.

43. Ibid., 212a.

44. Ibid., 209c and 209a.

45. Ibid., 221d.

46. Ibid., 219e–220b.

der the table," though "no one ever saw him drunk"; and, in the midst of deadly battle, he remains calm and brave.[47] Odder yet are the reports from other soldiers that—when "thinking about some problem or other"—he "stood outside ... glued to the same spot," for the entire day, and the night, "until dawn."[48] Something similar happened on the way to Agathon's house for the banquet, when Socrates loses himself in thought, standing "motionless" on the neighbor's porch; this is just "one of his habits," Aristodemus assures the others, "so don't disturb him."[49] What strange behavior all this is—so aloof, so unnatural, so completely transcendent of the ordinary limits of human experience, or so it would appear.[50] And yet, it should not be forgotten, how much the Socrates of Plato's dialogues loves the company of others, and that he never seems more content than in conversation with others.

So the question has to be settled. Has this strange man who Plato depicts through his character's words as a marvelous Silenus—at once frumpy, comical, but sociable on the outside, and yet when opened up and examined more closely, strangely super-human, almost divine in his wisdom on the inside—has this remarkable man, who just may have ascended to a vision of the Beautiful itself, successfully managed to pass his wisdom on to offspring? The evidence in the *Symposium*, which of course is shaped by Plato, is decidedly negative. The students of Socrates either do not understand or cannot digest what he attempts to convey to them. Aristodemus, who followed Socrates to the banquet, as he followed him most everywhere, had a notoriously bad memory, making him an unlikely candidate for a successful student.[51] Apollodorus, who

47. Ibid., 219b–c, 220a, and 221a–c.

48. Ibid., 220c–d.

49. Ibid., 174d–175b.

50. See Martha C. Nussbaum, "The Speech of Alcibiades: A Reading of the *Symposium*," in Martha C. Nussbaum, *The Fragility of Goodness; Luck and Ethics in Greek Tragedy and Philosophy* (Cambridge: Cambridge University Press, 1986), 183–84 and 191.

51. Three times it is noted that Aristodemus—a "runt of a man" who was "ob-

narrates the speeches on love which he received from the absent-minded Aristodemus, is a complete failure. Having tasted a little philosophy from Socrates, he is convinced that he and he alone knows what is "important" in life, while everyone else is mired in "trivial" matters.[52] Without doubt, however, Alcibiades is the most dramatic, but also the most interesting, failure among the students of Socrates.[53] Unlike the others in attendance, Alcibiades has looked beneath the surface of this silenus, and he seems to have understood his challenge. What makes Alcibiades so interesting is that while he has come to understand that his "political career is a waste of time" and that he should be tending to his "personal short-comings" and doing something about his way of life, he nonetheless cannot help but return to his "old ways"—working to "please the crowd"—the minute he leaves Socrates's side.[54] Though one cannot blame a teacher for the ineptitude of students—one would hope—it is hard not to notice that Plato is raising serious questions about the character of his teacher Socrates. Has he not failed the test of what is ostensibly his own speech—to bear fruit in the lives of others? Is what we have in Socrates a silenus right-side-out who is unable to convey his transcendental wisdom through simple and unadorned conversation? Is Socrates the silenus tragically flawed?

Plato's suspicions about Socrates, however, appear to go even deeper than this. Plato seems, in fact, to deliberately blur the lines between philosophy and sophistry; and, by so doing, begins to undermine the difference between a silenus right-side-out and a silenus inside-out. In what is often taken to be the deciding moment

sessed with Socrates" (173b)—could not remember everything that happened at the gathering at Agathon's house. Plato, *Symposium*, 178a, 180c, and 223d.

52. Ibid., 173c–d.

53. On the character of Alcibiades, see Nussbaum, "The Speech of Alcibiades," 165. See also James A. Arieti, *Interpreting Plato; The Dialogues as Drama* (Savage, Md.: Rowman and Littlefield, 1991), 109–10.

54. Plato, *Symposium*, 216a–b.

of the dialogue—the brief interlude following Agathon's flamboyant performance—Socrates confesses how "ridiculous" he had been to agree to a competition in praise of love with those trained by the sophist Gorgias. For his part, he knows nothing of "this business" of praising something with "the grandest and the most beautiful qualities," whether or not they are true. In what appears to be an open and clear break with sophistry, Socrates declares that he will "tell the truth" about Love.[55] At this juncture there appears to be a parting of the ways between a silenus right-side-out (who will tell the truth honestly) and the sileni inside-out (who play the sophistic game of dissemblance). After a brief exchange with Agathon, where the latter is forced to admit that he does not really know what he is talking about, Socrates launches into his own performance under the guise of a holy woman named Diotima. His way of telling the truth, it turns out, involves—in the manner of Greek theater—donning a spectacular mask and speaking through the fictional disguise of a goddess; and, moreover, the divine persona he assumes is portrayed as someone with great wisdom on ultimate questions. To say the least, this is no longer the simple facade of a silenus right-side-out; he no longer speaks in the "same tired old words," as reported by Alcibiades. When Socrates concludes the speech, moreover, the others burst into applause at the fine performance. Apparently his show was quite extraordinary.[56]

What a strange turn of events this is. But there is more. When earlier declining to participate in the sophist's game of praising something regardless of its truth or falsity, Socrates had quoted Euripides, declaring that his "tongue" had promised to participate in the round of speeches, but "the mind" had not.[57] In the context, this could be taken to be an acknowledgment that he had spoken incorrectly by agreeing to give a speech praising love, since he had

55. Ibid., 199b.

56. On Socrates's prevarication as Diotima, see Arieti, *Interpreting Plato*, 105.

57. Plato, *Symposium*, 199a.

not fully understood the sophistic nature of the event. If he had known this with his mind, he seems to be saying, then he would not have agreed with his tongue. Given the guest list assembled by Plato, however, this is hard to believe. Phaedrus is a well-known lover of works composed by the speechwriter Lysias; Pausanias is a student of the sophist Prodicus; Agathon is a student of the sophist Gorgias; Aristophanes is a famous writer of comedies; and so on. Socrates must have understood the nature of Eryximachus's proposal for a competitive round of speeches in honor of love. If this is correct, and it would be understood in this sense by any readers in Plato's day, then in quoting Euripides, Socrates has said one thing (promised with his "tongue") and meant or thought another (with his "mind"); but this is very much the kind of dissemblance practiced by trained sophists.[58] That he now promises with his "tongue" to tell the truth about love, only to proceed with an elaborate performance in disguise, seems to reverse course again, now apparently following through with the kind of show which is sure to please the others. The best that can be said at this point is that it is not so clear what Socrates is up to, or rather, what Plato is having him be up to. Is he making a clean break with the sophists or is he in fact one with them?

The *Symposium* is a truly complicated dialogue, and the points and counterpoints running through this text are a credit to Plato's literary finesse in presenting a complex figure in a nuanced and uncertain manner. We meet with a Socrates who commits himself to telling the truth about love; and then, soon after, we encounter an Alcibiades who twice declares—in a clear echo of Socrates—that he will "only tell the truth" about Socrates.[59] As if to reenforce this claim, Plato has Alcibiades insist that he is "going to show you what he really is," a promise which itself is bolstered by the fact that there is "truth in wine," and there is a good deal of wine in

58. See Arieti, *Interpreting Plato*, 104.

59. Ibid., 214e and 217b.

Alcibiades.[60] Four times, therefore, we are told by Plato that Alcibiades is a truth-teller, at least in this drunken state. What we are told of Socrates, in sum, is that he is a remarkable silenus, whose Marysias-like powers are dangerous, and thus someone who—in the end—is tragically incapable of transmitting his wisdom in a practical manner. And, to cap it off, we are urged not to "believe a single word Socrates said."[61] In presenting Alcibiades in this manner—as a truth-teller telling the truth about a would-be truth-teller—has Plato told us the truth about Socrates? And if he has, what exactly is that truth?

In a word, we are told by Plato to beware—that is, to meet the words of others carefully and cautiously, no matter how polished or how simple they appear to be. This is true of the sophists, some of whom make a living from deception, but all of whom are accomplished in moving an audience by crafting a captivating display; but it also is true of the philosophers whose claim to not be sophists—the very thing endlessly repeated in philosophical textbooks and reverently embraced by straight-laced Platonists—may not be as ironclad as often thought. Plato knows, after all, that not all sophists are alike. Some—like Tisias and Gorgias—vainly pride themselves on being able to "make trifles seem important and important points trifles by the force of their language."[62] Another sophist—Prodicus of Ceos—is famous for his insistence on the precise use of words,[63] a concern very much shared by Socrates in Plato's dialogues, though Socrates complains—in jest—that he would be much wiser if he could have afforded Prodicus's fifty-drachma course on "knowledge of names."[64] And Plato knows, too,

60. Ibid., 216d and 217e.

61. Ibid., 214d.

62. Plato, *Phaedrus*, 267a, in *The Complete Dialogues of Plato*, ed. Edith Hamilton and Huntington Cairns (Princeton, N.J.: Princeton University Press, 1973).

63. Plato, *Protagoras*, 341a–b; and *Charmides*, 163d, *The Complete Dialogues of Plato*.

64. Plato, *Cratylus*, 384b, *The Complete Dialogues of Plato*.

that there are independent writers—someone like Isocrates—who seem to be neither sophists nor philosophers, but rather, what Prodicus called the "frontiersmen between philosophy and politics." We should "not be hard on them," Socrates counsels respectfully, as they "come near to wisdom."[65] As we have seen in the *Symposium*, moreover, Plato knows full well that a figure like Socrates is not without artifice, so the lines distinguishing a philosopher from a sophist are far from clear.

And yet, importantly, Plato does not entirely collapse the distinction. Socrates, for instance, is said to be "crazy about beautiful boys," chasing after them in a "perpetual daze." But much to the dismay of Alcibiades, the interests of Socrates are not sexual; indeed, he seems to want these young men to become thoughtful and virtuous. Pausanias, alternatively, is very much interested in sex with boys, and Agathon is his darling; though, Pausanias insists—in the sly manner of the worst kind of sophist—that, unlike the "common" pederast, his interest in teen boys is a socially-approved "heavenly" love which will make the lads "better in wisdom" and "virtue."[66] Though Socrates might appear lecherous, he actually is committed—or so we are told—to the young lads' personal growth; while Pausanias insists that his interests are for the boys' personal growth, but in reality he is lecherous.[67] No doubt the parents of Athens who "hire attendants" to guard their sons had trouble seeing the difference between Pausanias and Socrates.[68] And that is precisely where Plato leaves us as well—with a real but tenuous distinction between the philosopher and the sophist.

Much the same point is made in a lighter and even comedic manner by the cast of characters assembled by Plato, as well as their shared habit of depicting "Love" in their own image. To say the least, this is a very odd collection of characters put together

65. Plato, *Euthydemus*, 305c and 306c, *The Complete Dialogues of Plato*.

66. Plato, *Symposium*, 180c–185c.

67. See Arieti, *Interpreting Plato*, 101.

68. Plato, *Symposium*, 183c.

by Plato; any readers in his own day (and, of course, there could not have been many) would have living memories of these individuals, and they either would be aghast or in stitches laughing at the very thought of such men having anything worthwhile to say about love. For starters, Phaedrus, Eryximachus, and Alcibiades were accused of vandalizing the "Herms" of Athens—those sacred border-markers, replete with extruding male genitals, and thought to bring good fortune to those who rub them. For his part, moreover, Alcibiades would be remembered for betraying his city while assisting the Spartans in their triumph over Athens. Others were less notorious, though their reputations were checkered. Agathon was a renowned but typical celebrity; Aristophanes was a famous, but feared, comedian; and Pausanias, at least as a character, was a slick-talking sexual predator. And then there is Socrates, who would have been remembered as the convicted and executed corrupter of Athenian youth. What a strange lot of characters assembled by Plato; and, most importantly, Socrates is placed right in the middle of this group. He is not—as the philosopher—somehow of better repute; he is one of them, plain and simple.

So, too, there is a recurrent pattern of self-projection throughout the speeches. Each character who speaks portrays Love in his own image; essentially, therefore, each speaker praises himself.[69] Phaedrus's portrait of love is simple and one-dimensional, reflecting what we know of his character; the speech of Pausanias depicts love (like himself) as a heavenly pederast; Eryximachus the physician describes the ultimate lover as one who reconciles opposing forces, something (he claims) that is best evident in his "own field, the science of medicine";[70] Aristophanes creates a masterful myth of human origins, one that asks people—not surprisingly—to look at their lives from a comic angle; Agathon, who has studied

69. See Arieti, *Interpreting Plato*, 102 and 107.

70. Plato, *Symposium*, 186a.

the correct "method" for praising something, extols the beautiful young poet, a mirror-image of himself. Significantly, Socrates is no exception to this pattern. Toward the beginning of the speech of Diotima, for instance, he engages in exactly the same laughable exercise of self-adulation: love, we are told, is "tough and shriveled and shoeless and homeless, . . . always living with Need"; but it also is "brave, impetuous, and intense . . . always weaving snares, resourceful in his pursuit of intelligence, a lover of wisdom through all his life."[71] What a vivid image of Socrates as the silenus right-side-out, straight from the mouth of Socrates—or should it be Diotima's, which, of course, actually is Plato's. With this pattern of self-projection in mind, it seems that what Plato has done in the *Symposium* is to assemble a notorious cast of characters engaged in praise of themselves. It is, in this regard, a comic study of human existence, in light of which Socrates the silenus is just as laughable as everyone else.

A Fragile Distinction

Though the *Symposium* of Plato is the primary classical source from which Erasmus draws the imagery of the Silenus, the very character of a silenus right-side-out (that is, in this case, of Socrates) already is in question within Plato's text. In the closing scene of the *Symposium*, we hear that—as others were nodding off—Socrates was "trying to prove to them that authors should be able to write both comedy and tragedy." If the preceding discussion is correct, then Plato has managed to do precisely that with respect to the character of Socrates: he is laughable in the company he keeps and in his self-projection; he is a tragic failure at transmitting whatever wisdom he has managed to achieve; and to cap it off, despite his protests, it is difficult to distinguish him clearly from the sophists.[72] To say

71. Ibid., 203d.

72. Ibid., 223d. On comedy and tragedy in the *Symposium*, see Arieti, *Interpreting*

the least, these suggestions seem to call into question the Erasmian portrait of Socrates as an authentic silenus—one who is simple and unassuming on the outside, but filled with wisdom and virtue beneath the surface.

Socrates's history of reception in western intellectual culture does little to bolster Erasmus's contention; but it also—significantly—is not without its points of support. Frankly, the question seems to be right where Plato left it.[73] Thus, for instance, though Enlightenment authors such as the Marquis de Condorcet champion Socrates's opposition to the sophists, Jeremy Bentham regards Socrates as a sophist "talking nonsense under pretense of teaching wisdom and morality."[74] Or again, while Michel de Montaigne celebrates Socrates's utterly natural and honest manner, the Baron de Montesquieu complains of the "tissue of sophisms" in the thought of Socrates and Plato.[75] And, oddly enough, roughly the same uncertainty appears entirely within the work of Voltaire, who notes that while Socrates perished for his opposition to the sophists, there is nonetheless "something of the quack in Socrates."[76] In short, the Socrates received from Plato remains a slippery figure as he passes through the history of interpretation. Indecision reigns with respect to Socrates being a philosophical truth-teller or an out-and-out sophist.

Additionally, only a few readers of Plato have made much of the comparison of Socrates with Silenus, or, more generally, put much emphasis on the ironic structure of a simple and rough exterior concealing an interior of wisdom and virtue. Not surpris-

---

Plato, 110. For a different reading of how the *Symposium* incorporates both comedy and tragedy, see Nussbaum, *The Fragility of Goodness*, 171.

73. See Herbert Spiegelberg, "Introduction" to *The Socratic Enigma: A Collection of Testimonies through Twenty-Four Centuries*, ed. Herbert Spiegelberg (Indianapolis, Ind.: Bobbs-Merrill, 1964), 3–20.

74. Spiegelberg, *The Socratic Enigma*, 193 and 83.

75. Ibid., 169 and 180.

76. Ibid., 181 and 183.

ingly, however, Montaigne treasures the unadorned naturalness of Socrates's humanity, while hinting at the remarkable wisdom hidden beneath the common appearance and familiar analogies. As Montaigne puts it, he "wanted neither to be nor to seem anything else" than a human being living and speaking "in conformity with its natural conditions."[77] And yet, Montaigne observes, the wisdom and virtue of Socrates will be missed entirely by those who fail to look behind the surface. Indeed, "we should never have picked out the nobility and splendor of his admirable ideas" under "so mean a form," "we who consider flat and low all ideas that are not raised up by learning, and who perceive richness only in pomp and show."[78] Even at his trial, Montaigne suggests, Socrates refused to renounce "truth and sincerity" in order to make his plea "with the make-up of the figures and fictions of a memorized oration."[79] He remained, in short, plain and common on the outside, yet noble and admirable within, an authentic silenus through and through.

After Montaigne, it is above all Søren Kierkegaard who admires the value of Socratic irony. When it comes to Socrates, Kierkegaard writes, "the outer was not at all in harmony with the inner but was rather its opposite, and only under this angle of refraction is he to be comprehended."[80] What Kierkegaard notes first about the appearance of Socrates is the utter simplicity—that "touching

77. Michel de Montaigne, "On Some Verses of Virgil" (III. 5) and "Of Repentance" (III. 2), in *The Complete Works of Montaigne*, trans. Donald M. Frame (Stanford, Calif.: Stanford University Press, 1957), 681 and 614. For precisely this reason, Montaigne confesses, that "nothing is so hard for [him] to stomach in the life of Socrates as his ecstasies and possessions by his daemon." Montaigne, "Of Experience," in *The Complete Works of Montaigne*, III. 13. 856.

78. Montaigne, "Of Physiognomy," in *The Complete Works of Montaigne*, III. 12. 793.

79. Ibid., 807.

80. Søren Kierkegaard, *The Concept of Irony with Continual Reference to Socrates*, trans. Howard V. Hong and Edna H. Hong (Princeton, N.J.: Princeton University Press, 1989), 12.

simplicity," indeed, a "sublime simplicity."[81] Behind and beneath this lowly exterior, however, is an admirable wisdom—that he recognized his own "ignorance"—and this ironic insight is what gives Socrates "his elevation over the world's shabbiness."[82] And it is the greatness of Socrates, as Kierkegaard tells it, that he was able to "express [this] ignorance" with "cunning dialectical simplicity"—that is, without show or grandeur, but in such a disarmingly plain manner that he could "catch the shrewd" in their false claims to knowledge, while at the same time prompting his would-be followers to come to terms with themselves rather than become reliant on the master. In Kierkegaard's words, Socrates's simple but odd appearance—so "very ugly . . . [the] clumsy feet, and, above all, a number of growths on the forehead and elsewhere. . ."[83]—all this kept the "learner at a distance," throwing students (like Alcibiades) back on themselves, rather than forming a relationship based on admiration and imitation.[84] "What the world now needs," Kierkegaard concludes, and indeed what the Christian world needs—confused as it is by [so] much knowing"—is "a Socrates," that "noble simple wise man of ancient times."[85]

But clearly not all readers have been such admirers, and the counter-currents of suspicion concerning Socrates—and notably, concerning Socratic irony—run strong. Friedrich Nietzsche deserves pride of place among those who suspect that there is something devious and perhaps even decadent in this ancient Athenian

81. Søren Kierkegaard, *Christian Discourses*, trans. Walter Lowrie (New York: Oxford University Press, 1961), 245–46.

82. *Søren Kierkegaard's Journals and Papers*, vol. 4, trans. Howard V. Hong and Edna H. Hong (Bloomington, Ind.: Indiana University Press, 1975), 213–14.

83. *Kierkegaard's Concluding Unscientific Postscript*, trans. David F. Swenson (Princeton, N.J.: Princeton University Press, 1968), 222.

84. Ibid.

85. Søren Kierkegaard, *Fear and Trembling and The Sickness Unto Death*, trans. Walter Lowrie (Princeton, N.J.: Princeton University Press, 1954), 223; Kierkegaard, *Christian Discourses*, 245.

buffoon. Though at times Nietzsche can sound quite positive about Socrates, more often than not he regards him pejoratively as "the shrewdest of all deceivers."[86] As Nietzsche puts it in the *Twilight of the Idols*, "everything about him is exaggerated, buffo, caricature, [but] everything is at the same time hidden, reserved, subterranean."[87] On the outside, Nietzsche observes, Socrates fascinated people with his "fear-inspiring ugliness"; and, too, he "exercised fascination" over others with his "dialectical manner" of conversing, by which he "seemed to be a physician, a saviour."[88] Both the physical appearance and the rhetorical manner, however, conceal the subterranean "*ressentiment* of the rabble."[89] His notorious ugliness should have been an indication that he "was rabble," since such an appearance—as Nietzsche tells it—is a sure sign of "thwarted development, a development *retarded* by interbreeding."[90] And the dialectical manner, Nietzsche argues, by which Socrates laughed at the "awkward incapacity of his noble Athenians ... to give an account of the reason for their actions,"[91] is the "last-ditch weapon in the hands of those who have no other weapons left."[92] With a "divine directness and sureness," therefore, a "deep-seated illusion" is first found "manifested in Socrates," the "illusion that thought ... might plumb the farthest abysses of being."[93] At that point, Nietzsche notes, "the one noble and truly human occupation" is to separate "true knowledge from illusion and error";[94] and with that, the dialectic cunning of the rabble defeats

86. Friedrich Nietzsche, *Twilight of the Idols and The Anti-Christ*, trans. R. J. Hollingdale (Middlesex, England: Penguin, 1968), 34.

87. Ibid., 31.

88. Ibid., 33.

89. Ibid., 32.

90. Ibid., 30.

91. Friedrich Nietzsche, *Beyond Good and Evil*, trans. Walter Kaufmann (New York: Random House, 1966), 104, section 191.

92. Nietzsche, *Twilight of the Idols*, 31–32.

93. Friedrich Nietzsche, *The Birth of Tragedy and The Genealogy of Morals*, trans. Francis Golffing (New York: Doubleday, 1956), 85 and 93.

94. Nietzsche, *The Birth of Tragedy*, 94.

the "*nobler* taste" and a life of healthy instinct.[95] The ironic life of Socrates, in the end, is not to be trusted.

The distinction between philosopher and sophist finally collapses in the work of Jacques Derrida, or so he would have it seem. At the root of Derrida's work on these issues is the notion that speech is a *pharmakon*—an "an inherently two-pronged drug," which can function as either a medicine or a poison.[96] In a word, speech can heal or it can maim—depending on who is wielding the power of speech, with what skill, and for what ends. It is Derrida's contention that there is an "analogy" (he means, really, an equivalence) between the "socratic *pharmakon*" and the "sophistic *pharmakon*." In fact, he observes, the two seem "proportioned" to each other, making us go back indefinitely from one to the other, without any clear difference.[97] Picking up on the fact that Diotima's portrait of love (*eros*) is also (as we saw earlier) a portrait of Socrates, Derrida proceeds to accent the magical qualities of Socrates's discursive life. Since (as Diotima argues) love hovers and moves with yearning "between" ignorance (a lack of something) and wisdom (a fulfilment of that lack), it is personified as something of a "great spirit," neither god nor mortal, but like "messengers who shuttle back and forth between the two," conveying prayers from people to the gods and bringing people divine commands and "gifts in return for sacrifices." Indeed, we are told, it is through such messengers that "all divination passes," as well as the "art of priests in sacrifice and ritual," but also the works of "enchantment, prophecy, and sorcery."[98] Connecting this language explicitly to Socrates, Diotima says, he is—"though all his life"—"resourceful in his pursuit of intelligence, a lover of wisdom"; but in all of this, too, he is a "ge-

95. Nietzsche, *Twilight of the Idols*, 31.

96. See Martin, *Living Words*, 350.

97. Jacques Derrida, *Dissemination*, trans. Barbara Johnson (Chicago: University of Chicago Press, 1981), 119.

98. Plato, *Symposium*, 202e.

nius with enchantments, potions, and clever pleadings."[99] In short, Derrida concludes, Socrates has the "face of a *pharmakeus*"—he is a verbal magician, a rhetorical sorcerer.[100]

No wonder, therefore, that Agathon would complain that Socrates is trying to "bewitch" him; and, how fitting is Alcibiades's comparison of Socrates with Marsyas—as one who can "cast his spells" with "words alone."[101] Then, too, there is the warning from Alcibiades that the words of Socrates are like the bite of a poisonous "snake."[102] Indeed, like a "viper's venom," Derrida suggests, "Socrates' words" have the "ability to penetrate and make off with the most concealed interiority of the body or soul"; his speech seizes its listeners with a "dionysian frenzy and philosophic mania."[103] In this regard, Derrida asks, is not Socrates "the spitting image of a sophist? a *pharmakeus*? a magician? a sorcerer? even a poisoner?" "How can they be distinguished?"[104] His reply is that they cannot.

The force of Derrida's proposal rests with a direct comparison of Socrates as a "master of the *pharmakon*" and what Gorgias says about the powers of speech in the *Encomium of Helen*.[105] The latter work is a "display speech," a kind of showcase for the talents of Gorgias as a speaker and writer, in which he seeks to exonerate Helen from the charge that she is guilty for her abduction and seduction by Paris, and hence, too, for the ensuing Trojan War. In an initial statement of Gorgias's case, he notes that "speech is a powerful lord"—it can stop fear and banish grief and create joy and nur

99. Ibid., 203d.

100. Derrida, *Dissemination*, 117.

101. Plato, *Symposium*, 194a and 215c–d.

102. Derrida, *Dissemination*, 118. Plato, *Symposium*, 217e.

103. Derrida, *Dissemination*, 118. See Plato, *Symposium*, 218b.

104. Derrida, *Dissemination*, 117 and 119.

105. Gorgias, "Encomium of Helen," trans. George Kennedy, in *The Older Sophists: A Complete Translation by Several Hands of the Fragments Der Vorsokraticker*, ed. Rosamond Kent Sprague (Columbia, S.C.: University of South Carolina Press, 1972), 50–54.

ture pity." Thus, he suggests, "if it was speech which persuaded her and deceived her heart," she is not necessarily to blame.[106] Gorgias then presses his argument further. In an apparent indictment of sophistic persuasion, delivered to exonerate the victim of sophistic sorcery, Gorgias observes that "all who have and do persuade people of things do so by molding a false argument."[107] Relying on "opinion" (which is "slippery") rather than knowledge (which presumably would be firm), people (like Helen) "come under the influence of speech, just as if ravished by the force of the mighty."[108] Like "sacred incantations," the words of the persuader merge "with opinion in the soul"; and by that means, the "power of the incantation is wont to beguile it and persuade it and alter it by witchcraft."[109] Here, precisely, is the kind of language Derrida finds so prevalent in descriptions of Socratic speech: with its "spellbinding powers of enchantment," it is "kin to witchcraft and magic."[110]

In making his case, Derrida observes, "Gorgias indicts *logos* in its capacity to lie."[111] But that is not entirely correct. While he indicts the slippery and even false designs of persuasive speech in order to exonerate Helen, in fact Gorgias is praising—putting on display, celebrating, even advertising—the rhetorical skills that he sells as a professional sophist. How very slippery *his* speech is, as he indicts slippery speech in order to defend Helen of the charges against her. Much the same point is made where Gorgias compares speech to a drug (*pharmakon*). As he tells it, "the effect of speech upon the condition of the soul is comparable to the power of drugs over the nature of bodies." As with drugs, so too in the case of speeches: "some distress, others delight, some cause fear, others make the hearers bold, and some drug and bewitch the soul with a kind of evil persuasion."[112] In these terms, Gorgias argues, persua-

106. Gorgias, "Encomium of Helen," 8 (using classical pagination).

107. Ibid., 11.

108. Ibid., 11–12.

109. Ibid., 10.

110. Derrida, *Dissemination*, 115.

111. Ibid., 116.

112. Gorgias, "Encomium of Helen," 14.

sive speech "constrained the soul, persuading it which it persuaded, both to believe the things said and to approve the things done." Reversing the charges against Helen, Gorgias concludes, it is "the persuader [Paris], like a constrainer, [who] does the wrong and the persuaded [Helen], like the constrained, in speech [who] is wrongly charged."[113] In the end, if Helen "was persuaded by speech she did not do wrong but [simply] was unfortunate"[114]—that is, she was unfortunate to meet up with a smooth-talking and seductive persuader. Here again, Derrida might say, Gorgias indicts *logos* in its capacity to mesmerize. Once again, however, this is not entirely correct. While he indicts the drug-like effects of persuasive speech in order to exonerate Helen, in fact Gorgias—as a wielder of the *pharmakon* and as the purveyor of rhetorical drugs—is marketing his wares to potential students.

When it comes to Socrates, Derrida observes, there is little if anything to distinguish him from Gorgias. Socratic "irony"—the fact that he appears one way on the outside while being something else on the inside, or again, that his speech sounds so simple and unimpressive while being astute and wise when examined closely—all this, Derrida insists, "does not consist in the dissolution of a sophistic charm or in the dismantling of an occult substance or power through analysis and questioning."[115] The approach of Socrates is not that straightforward. Nor, Derrida continues, does it "consist in undoing the charlatanesque confidence of a *pharmakeus* from the vantage point of some obstinate instance of transparent reason or innocent *logos*." Socrates is neither transparent nor innocent. Rather, "Socratic irony precipitates out one *pharmakon* by bringing it in contact with another *pharmakon*."[116] It is one sorcerer casting his spells on another sorcerer; they are combatants in the same magical spectacle. The result, Derrida

113. Ibid., 12.

114. Ibid., 15.

115. Derrida, *Dissemination*, 119.

116. Ibid.

concludes, is that Socrates's *pharmakon* "reverses the [sophistic] *pharmakon*'s power and turns its surface over"—as Socrates does with Agathon, when the latter is forced to admit that—impressive as his speech was—he really did not know what he was talking about. The reason Socrates can do this, Derrida suggests, is that "the *pharmakon* properly consists in a certain inconsistency, a certain impropriety, this nonidentity-with-itself always allowing it to be turned against itself";[117] or, more plainly put, every claim contains within itself a negative feature which can be reversed or turned upside-down with an ironic shift of perspective and a bit of clever cross-questioning. But, of course, Gorgias would agree entirely with this, since he well knows that "what is incredible and unclear" can be made to "seem true to the eyes of opinion"; and, no doubt, he would enjoy the opportunity to make what seems true suddenly appear incredible and unclear as well. In this task, however, he would expect to be joined by another *pharmakeus*—namely, Socrates.

Maintaining the Distinction

Derrida leaves us, curiously, with the darkest proposition entertained by Erasmus—to wit, that everyone is a liar; or, as Gorgias might add, that everyone is either a liar or the victim of a liar. But, as we have seen, this is a proposition ultimately rejected by Erasmus. The possibility of critically challenging pretense, fraud, and treachery requires an alternative ideal—a manner of speaking which is genuine, honest, and trustworthy; and this is the manner Erasmus finds at work in those rare but authentic sileni right-side-out. That distinction, however, has proven precarious—already questioned in Plato, despite the support of Montaigne and Kierkegaard, under suspicion by Nietzsche, and most boldly threatened by Derrida. For the latter, the truth-telling philosopher and

117. Ibid.

the deceitful sophist are equally sorcerers and snakes; they both charm, bewitch, and mesmerize. They are contestants in the same match of words, using the same spells and the same poisons. Not surprisingly, that is exactly the stance of Gorgias in the *Encomium to Helen*. In his eyes, persuasion takes different forms, but it is the same art in each case. The sophist can "make what is incredible and unclear seem true to the eyes of opinion"; while the orator can—with words "written with art but not spoken with truth"—bend "a great crowd"; and the philosophers—in their "verbal disputes"—make "the belief in an opinion subject to easy change" by means of the "swiftness of thought."[118] There is, finally, no distinction to be made between the cunning sophist, the manipulative orator, and the swift-talking, dialectical philosopher. Everyone is a liar, or the victim of a liar.

So the question comes down to this: is there no way forward? Can the Erasmian distinction be maintained? If sileni inside-out are not what they appear to be because they dissemble in a deceptive manner, then why are sileni right-side-out not what they appear to be; are they similarly dissembling, and just possibly deceptive as well? Are Gorgias, Nietzsche, and Derrida right? Or is there really a difference between a philosopher who claims to tell the truth and a sophist who deceives? Is there a difference between a silenus right-side-out and a silenus inside-out, or are they all fundamentally tricksters, sorcerers, and snakes? Is there anything left to the Erasmian ideal, or must we surrender to Gorgias's judgment—that everyone is either a liar or the victim of a liar?

As a first response, one must concede some of the complexities in these questions. Since not all sophists in Plato's day are deceitful and exploitative, and not all philosophers are so transparent, there is plenty of overlap between the two. And even with respect to a more exploitative sophist like Gorgias, Derrida is right to say

118. Gorgias, "Encomium of Helen," 13.

that "the threads of these complicities are almost impossible to disentangle."[119] Gorgias certainly knows how close the swift-talking philosopher is to his own art; and Plato does not have his characters attribute so much language of magic and sorcery to Socrates without being aware of the apparent linkage. Certainly it is hard —after all these questions and suspicions—not to grant a certain dissemblance on the part of Socrates, even if this is due to neglect of appearance; but, then again, it surely must be admitted that this kind of passive dissemblance seems to be studied and well-practiced. Much the same point must be granted with respect to books written by clever authors. The *Symposium*, for instance, appears simple enough at first glance, but—as we saw earlier—there are so many layers and levels of meaning buried beneath the surface of the text; and behind all that is a very clever author who, with literary finesse, is making things seem one way, but then subtly suggests that they might be altogether different. The same thing applies, of course, to one of Erasmus's finest and most famous works, *The Praise of Folly*, where he speaks through the persona of a goddess to deliver his take on human life. Surely this, too, involves a kind of literary dissemblance on Erasmus's part. But having granted the passive dissemblance of a Socrates or the literary dissemblance of an Erasmus, does this mean that either is deceitful or devious?

To defend both against this charge, consider the possibility that both Gorgias and Derrida are over-confident in the magical powers of persuasive speech. For his part, Gorgias sounds cocksure that Helen was bewitched by the beguiling influence of Paris's words. Indeed, Gorgias declares, she was swept away as surely by the power of seductive speech, "as if ravished by the [physical] force of the mighty."[120] What a rare bit of braggadocio this is! And,

119. Derrida, *Dissemination*, 117.

120. Gorgias, "Encomium of Helen," 12.

as Erasmus's goddess would no doubt add, what a pure expression of a sophist's "self-love"—no doubt rendering himself "most happy," as self-love is meant to do, while attracting clients in the process.[121] But the professional conceit of Gorgias blinds him to another possibility—to wit, that Helen may not have been deceived by the bewitching charm of a seducer's appeal. Perhaps, as Sappho claims, it was neither physical force nor a persuasive spell that made her leave her noble husband and family; perhaps, rather, as Folly might suggest, it was the "madness" of her own love—that she loved so "intensely" that she no longer lived in herself, "but rather in that which she loves."[122] Though renowned for her beauty, she emptied herself of her exalted status and became the tramp for the love of another. Of her husband and child, Sappho writes, "she forgot them all, she could not remember anything but longing."[123] What absolute madness, what wild folly, but then again—strangely—how noble, under the sordid exterior of a runaway wife.[124] Yet it is precisely this possibility that Gorgias overlooks. His professional folly, as Erasmus would no doubt have Folly say, traps him in a very narrow and distorted judgment—where everyone is either a liar or the victim of a liar; and this, regrettably, is why Gorgias is so completely certain that Socrates is as deceptive as he is.

Derrida also is over-confident, though in a different sense than Gorgias. Strange as it may sound, Plato's Alcibiades is something like Helen. Like her, his famous good looks and widely esteemed political stature are all but abandoned, as he throws himself madly

121. Erasmus, *The Praise of Folly*, 68–69.

122. Ibid., 136.

123. *The Poetry of Sappho*, trans. Jim Powell (New York: Oxford University Press, 2007), Fragment 16, 6–7.

124. The nobility of Helen's love is nicely portrayed in Guido Reni's *Abduction of Helen* (1631), where Helen is led away—hand upon hand—by Paris, as she gazes calmly forward. See http://www.wikigallery.org/wiki/painting_230660/Guido-Reni/The-Abduction-of-Helen,-1631-2

at Socrates. What a scene this is, and what a slut he has become! He tries exercising with Socrates, but "got nowhere" with that; so he takes to direct pleading, saying, "you can have me, my belongings, anything my friends might have."[125] When rebuffed, he cuddles up with Socrates, spending "the whole night next to him." But nothing works. It is fascinating, indeed, to hear the extent of Alcibiades's madness: he is beside himself with yearning, totally helpless, with no other "purpose in life"—in fact, a complete "slave" to the object of his love.[126] While it seems true—at least by the accounts from Alcibiades—that Socrates had bewitched him, driving him mad for philosophy, he responds with dramatic—and quite unphilosophical—self-abandonment, as he offers himself sexually to the ugliest man in Athens.

Unlike the story of Paris and Helen, however, in this case the lover meets rejection. "In spite of all my efforts," he complains, "this hopelessly arrogant, this unbelievably insolent man he turned me down!"[127] It turns out that Socrates is not who he seems to be, and he apparently has not been using his bewitching manner to gain sexual advantage. Had Socrates been that kind of wizard, then Alcibiades would have been a prize addition to his stable of boys. So, we might ask Derrida, what kind of magician is this? If Derrida claims that Socrates and the sophists share an equivalent talent for rhetorical sorcery, then the example of Alcibiades may not be as well-suited to Derrida's case as he would like to think. It is an odd, even misbegotten power, after all, which sets out to prompt the reflective life, only to produce a kind of sexual frenzy. No sophist would be proud of that result. Derrida, therefore, either is over-confident as to the power of sophistic magic, or he is wrong to attribute it to Socrates. Apparently Socrates is a different kind of lover and speaker—strangely neither self-promoting, nor

125. Plato, *Symposium*, 217c and 218d. Compare Plato, *Protagoras*, 310c–e.

126. Plato, *Symposium*, 219b–e.

127. Ibid.

domineering, nor exploitative. And that is precisely what Derrida overlooks.

The underlying difference becomes clearer when directly comparing the outcomes of philosopher and sophist. Choosing this measure for comparison, of course, is exactly what someone of a sophistic turn of mind would want, since good speech for them (as for Derrida) is defined by successful persuasion. On this scale, to be sure, the sileni right-side-out rarely amount to anything; indeed, they have a consistently poor record when it comes to achieving their intended results. In fact, those who claim to get their message often (perhaps, usually) do not get the point at all, which is why Erasmus so regularly satirizes the self-promoting, hypocritical, and exploitative lives of would-be Christians, and why he consistently ridicules the lifeless lives of self-styled philosophical wisemen.[128] As we saw earlier, Plato seems to call attention to exactly this—rather tragic—quality of Socrates's life, as none of his students can digest what he has to say; and, no doubt, much the same could be said for other authentic sileni.

Moreover, in the speech of Diotima, the most concrete practical "offspring" of the transcendental vision of Beauty itself is said to be the "proper ordering of cities and households"; but this is, oddly enough, the ideal standard of outcome set by Isocrates in "Antidosis."[129] Certainly one of the most noble sophists, Isocrates insists that anything worthy of the name "philosophy" must surely "enable us to govern wisely both our own households and the commonwealth."[130] So Plato seems to be suggesting—rather

128. On Erasmus's spoofs on the Stoic wiseman, see Erasmus, *The Praise of Folly*, 45–48.

129. Plato, *Symposium*, 209a. See Isocrates, "Antidosis," in *Isocrates*, vol. 2, trans. George Norlin (London: William Heinemann, 1928), 285.

130. As Isocrates puts it, true philosophy must be practical, for "likely conjecture about useful things is far preferable to exact knowledge of the useless." Isocrates, "Helen," in *Isocrates*, vol. 3, trans. by LaRue Van Hook (London: William Heinemann, 1928), 5. Clearly responding to Isocrates, Plato has his characters in the *Symposium*

bluntly, but also ironically—that Socrates fails the test of proper outcomes maintained by the best of sophists; but, then again, that failure should not be surprising if he is not setting out with sophistic aims. Conversely, sophists like Gorgias are far more successful in life, as their students go on to successful careers in business and politics, while the sophists themselves become rich in the process—and, not insignificantly, they never are forced to drink lethal poison. Much the same thing can be said for the cast of professional fools satirized by Erasmus in *The Praise of Folly*—the cut-throat merchants who seek "the meanest goal by the meanest methods"; the ever-flattering courtiers who will say anything needed to assure their decadent lives; or the hypocritical bishops who cast "their nets for money" under the cover of pastoral sanctity.[131] In all of these cases, it is the one who manages the appearances the most persuasively who prospers; or, to use the words of Gorgias, it is the one who can "make what is incredible and unclear seem true to the eyes of opinion."[132] By this measure, however, authentic sileni are miserable failures—and, ironically, that may be a good thing.

Using the sophists' measure of success, in fact, helps to reestablish the distinction between sileni right-side-out and sileni inside-out, since there are good reasons why one succeeds and the other does not. It is the folly of human life, Erasmus observes, that when it comes to the performances of "actors, singers, orators, and poets," "the less skillful anything is, the more admirers it obtains, according to the rule that the worst things usually please most people."[133] Along with the low standard of common taste, he adds, it also holds that "the human mind is so constituted that it

reject an evening of conversation on "useless" things (the "usefulness of salt," for instance), preferring to spend their time talking about something truly useful—the nature of love. See, too, "Helen," 12. It should be remembered, however, that in the ancient world salt most certainly was something very useful.

131. Erasmus, *The Praise of Folly*, 77, 109, and 110.

132. Gorgias, "Encomium of Helen," 13.

133. Erasmus, *The Praise of Folly*, 69.

is far more taken with appearances than reality."[134] If this is the case, however, then it is easy to see why a cunning merchant or an exploitative priest—much less a master sophist like Gorgias—will reap great rewards, since they know how to bend common opinion with an outward show of credibility, sanctity, or honesty. And, moreover, it matters little for the sileni inside-out whether they actually are sincere, holy, or honest, since (as Folly quips in sophistic fashion) "in the absence of the reality, the appearance of it is the [next] best thing."[135] If one is intent on self-promotion or plotting exploitation, then this surely is the way to go. In such cases, Erasmus likely would conclude, the worst of things is always the most showy. But this is, as we have seen, the exact opposite of the authentic sileni figures. They, too, are not the way they appear to be, and yet their dissemblance is remarkably ill-suited to sway an audience; in fact, we have seen—in the case of Socrates—how bad they are at moving others, as the least showy is so often ineffectual. These odd creatures are, in a word, very bad sophists; and the reason for that is that they are driven neither by self-promotion nor by design to take advantage of others. In this regard, Erasmus observes, "it is always the same: what is excellent in any way is always the least showy."[136] Their excellence, however, rests within—so one must look behind the plain facade to see what they have to offer.

Early in *The Praise of Folly*, Erasmus has Folly suggest that "all human affairs" are a bit like the Sileni of Alcibiades—what "appears 'at first blush'" will, when examined "more closely," turn out to be the opposite. So, for example, "beauty will become ugliness; riches will turn to poverty; notoriety will become fame; learning will be ignorance." "In brief," Folly notes, "you will find everything suddenly reversed if you open the Silenus."[137] Though in this context, too, Erasmus takes up the Silenus image in order to fo-

134. Ibid., 71.

135. Ibid., 117.

136. Erasmus, "The Sileni of Alcibiades," 274.

137. Erasmus, *The Praise of Folly*, 43.

cus on the differences and reversals of appearance and reality, it now is meant to apply to everyone, not just to select figures such as Socrates. Indeed, as Erasmus has Folly argue in the first part of *The Praise of Folly*, "the whole life of mortal men" is "but a sort of play" in which people wear costumes and don masks to play their roles.[138] At this point in the book, therefore, Erasmus celebrates the innocent masks and ubiquitous folly which makes human life so odd and yet so rich. Or, as Folly puts it, though "all these images are unreal," the "play cannot be performed in any other way."[139] Some lies, therefore, are innocent.

But then, Erasmus interjects, what if someone should dare to strip away the costumes from the actors, so they were suddenly seen for who they really are? Suddenly everything would look different: "the actor just now playing a woman would be seen to be a man; the one who had just now been playing a young man would look old; the man who played the king only a moment ago would become a pauper," and so on. If this happened, Folly asks, "wouldn't all the spectators be right to throw rocks at such a madman and drive him out of the theater?"[140] By destroying the "illusions," he would have spoiled the whole play; and, what is key for theater as for life generally, Folly suggests, is "this deception, this disguise," since this is "the very thing that holds the attention of the spectators."[141] What false wisdom, what "perverse prudence," this would be, to rip away the masks; and with good reason, Folly quips, everyone would take such a person "for a raving lunatic."[142] Far better to let the play be a play, and neither challenge the deception nor contest the disguise. Life runs on costumes and disguises.

No doubt Gorgias and Derrida would agree with Folly on this point. Life is filled with lies, Gorgias would say, so learn to lie well or become the victim of better liars. But Erasmus sees it differ-

138. Ibid., 43–44.

139. Ibid., 44.

140. Ibid., 43.

141. Ibid., 43.

142. Ibid., 44.

ently; and he is able to see things differently because he is able—unlike Gorgias and Derrida—to maintain distinctions between various combinations of appearance and reality. *The Praise of Folly*, as we saw in the introduction, covers three forms of folly, and the dividing lines are opaque but significant. When Folly speaks of the theater of life, where appearances are not to be disturbed, Erasmus comically celebrates the ubiquity of innocent folly. If a bald man wears a toupee, a woman paints her face, or a husband (mistakenly) believes his wife to be the most beautiful woman in the world, then these little illusions (based on false appearances) harmlessly bring happiness to life. If, as Folly notes, someone were to strip away these little lies, then people would be quite right to think him crazy. When it comes to the professional fools, however, all of whom—in one way or another—are self-aggrandizing and exploitative, then it is Erasmus himself who "drops down direct from heaven"—so to speak—to expose their pretentiousness and to satirize their viciousness.[143] The masks of these figures—these sileni inside-out—are not innocent in the least, and their deception is treacherous. How different, finally, are the fools praised at the end of *The Praise of Folly*, those mad creatures who, in taking so little care with reputation, titles, and status—in short with their external and social appearances—"ignore injuries, allow themselves to be deceived, make no distinction between friend and foe."[144] Can such a condition be called anything but insanity, Folly asks? Certainly Gorgias and Derrida would ask the same thing.

In the end, none of these Erasmian distinctions find a place in the world of Gorgias and Derrida, since both, in their respective manners, fold distinct forms of dissemblance into a single mold. For his part, Erasmus has a finer ear for the variations on a common theme—to wit, that there are different forms of folly, different

143. Ibid., 44.
144. Ibid., 132.

ways of going mad, and finally, different ways of dissembling. In a word, appearances and reality are combined and held in different ways in human life and speech, and these differences are philosophically and morally significant. The latter difference, in fact, makes all the difference in the world inasmuch as some forms of dissemblance pack the potential for speaking the truth, while others serve the interests of deceit. Gorgias and Derrida are wrong, therefore, to conflate the ironic philosopher and the crafty sophist. As they see things, once again, everyone is a liar or the victim of a liar. For Erasmus, however, while most everyone dissembles, that does not make everyone a liar. Not all dissemblance is a lie; and, indeed, as we will now see, the dissemblance of the authentic silenus is uniquely and powerfully fit for speaking truthfully about our lives.

Erasmian Proposals

By insisting on the deep and abiding difference between a silenus right-side-out (a figure like Socrates) and a silenus wrong-side-out (a sophist like Gorgias), Erasmus magnifies the way in which dissemblance—being one way but seeming another, or saying one thing but meaning another—can express two fundamentally different forms of existence: one, as we have seen, unpretentious and unimpressive in appearance but genuine and wise at the core, the other ostentatious and dazzling in public but disingenuous and devious behind the scenes; one curiously bent on finding and conveying truth, the other persistently set on deceit at the expense of others; and one frequently ineffectual though potentially unsettling, the other highly successful, often entertaining, and likely reassuring. The latter character is common, familiar, and celebrated; they are at home in the world and they prosper. The former, quite clearly, are odd and rare, even elusive, often irritating, and yet very intriguing. How then is this strange form of existence to be understood? If authentic sileni are not sophists, then who exactly are they?

In a word, the authentic silenus is a figure for whom the capacity for irony has become a human excellence. As Jonathan Lear might put it, such a person has the unique ability to occasion an ironic experience in themselves or someone else. In his actions and expressions, and indeed in his very comportment, a silenus like Socrates lays open a "gap" between a particular form of life and the "aspiration or ideal" which it claims to embody.[145] In Lear's terms, however, irony is not merely critical reflection of the way in which something falls short of its ideal, as such reflection is commonplace in most social worlds. Irony involves, rather, the exposure and display of the yawning "abyss" between the way a world has come to be and the way it aspires to be; and it does so in a manner that is meant to "grab" and shake those who will listen.[146] The experience of irony, consequently, entails an unsettling "disruption" of normalcy and a halting sense of "disorientation"—something plainly evident in the tossing and turning of Alcibiades in response to conversation with Socrates.[147] Authentic sileni manage to instigate these experiences because they are both committed to the ideals in question (being a human being, being a citizen, being a Christian, and the like) and yet—in their character, their actions, and their words—they are strangely the reversed image of the way the world has come to work. Little wonder, therefore, that Alcibiades warns that the life and words of Socrates are not what they appear to be, and, too, that his strange existence harbors magical powers. The time spent in conversation with this ironic figure, it turns out, opens up a massive fissure in the middle of Alcibiades's self-image, leaving him with the uncanny sense that what had seemed so "familiar" (his career and his fame) comes to seem strange and "unfamiliar" (empty and worthless).[148]

The authentic silenus, in short, is a kind of oracle with a unique-

145. Lear, *A Case for Irony*, 11.

146. Ibid., 15 and 13.

147. Ibid., 16.

148. Ibid., 19.

ly powerful and unsettling manner of telling the truth about human life. Like an oracle, though not necessarily with an appeal to an external spirit, the authentic silenus discloses who we are in terms that seem "alien and enigmatic," but which when faced squarely and digested, give rise to—what Lear calls—a "more or less massive disruption" of personal identity.[149] What is important to stress, in the first place, is that this form of irony constitutes an especially bold form of "truthfulness" leading to unanticipated self-knowledge. As Lear puts it, the ironic experience involves a "moment of excruciating self-conscious awareness" wherein the individual gets a "glimmer" of how so much of life "falls wildly short" of the ideal professed.[150] It is the truth, after all, that rattles the otherwise self-assured Alcibiades. And yet, in the second place, none of this could happen without an underlying commitment to the intended ideal. In Lear's words, someone like Alcibiades undergoes ironic disruption precisely because the values Socrates proposes matter to him, though they stand in glaring contrast to the life he cannot help but lead. Neither the instigator of irony (Socrates) nor the one undergoing its disruption (Alcibiades) stands aloof and between competing "final vocabularies" (as Richard Rorty would have it), as the capacity for irony (again in Lear's terms) is "partially constituted by an openness to getting rattled by one's own commitments."[151] Then again, in the third place, there is no escaping that the oracle's truth usually falls on deaf ears. In fact, resistance to irony is pandemic in most social worlds. Authentic sileni—like Socrates, Christ, and Diogenes—are no match for the deceptive but alluring force of sophistic persuasion.

It would be a stretch to place Erasmus in the same class with

149. Ibid., 15–16.

150. Ibid., 95 and 100.

151. Ibid., 119; see also 37–39. For Rorty's portrait of the independent and detached ironist, see Richard Rorty, *Contingency, Irony, and Solidarity* (Cambridge: Cambridge University Press, 1989), 73.

these three figures, though *The Praise of Folly* and some of the works to be discussed in the next two meditations go a long way toward excellence in the deployment of irony. In his literary performances, quite clearly, Erasmus displays an enormous capacity for ironic truth-telling. But while Lear focuses on what he calls a "robust form of irony," where the individual undergoes a massive disruption of normalcy, Erasmus entertains a broader spectrum of ironic experiences.[152] At times, as we have seen, Erasmus playfully stands things on their head (fools are happy and the wise are miserable); or he satirically reverses the twisted reversals of powerful people (bishops are fishing for wealth not souls). At these points the ironic experience is marked less by anxious disruption than by head-turning surprise; but even this gentler form of irony is designed to grab the attention of readers, perhaps triggering a sense of shock or sparking a hearty and knowing laugh. More potently, as we have seen from *The Praise of Folly*, Erasmus will capitalize on the ambiguity of a term—the meaning of "Christian," for instance—thereby confronting readers with an eerie coincidence of opposites. The ambiguity of the name—Christian as superstitious fools, as treacherous madmen, or as crazed lovers—strikes up an uncomfortable or unsettled feeling for those who care about being Christian. As Lear puts, such a juxtaposition yields the "haunting" and even "uncanny" question as to whether Christianity lacks coherence altogether.[153] Taking one more step, finally, Erasmus raises the kind of limit questions that Lear identifies as calling forth the most robust experience of irony. This happens, in Lear's words, when a form of life is "interrogated" as to "whether it has anything to do with" the form of life "it purports to be." What, for instance, happens if no one "actually fits the bill?"[154] Or, in the terms of this meditation, what if everyone really is a liar? What if no one is tell-

152. Lear, *A Case for Irony*, 16.

153. Ibid., 95.

154. Ibid., 23.

ing the truth? It is at these points that Erasmus flirts with the most uncanny possibility, bringing us face to face with the potential collapse of the difference between truth-telling and deception.

The reason Erasmian irony is so powerful is that he faces the possible collapse of truth-telling without flinching, even while it matters to him greatly that the distinction between honesty and deceit be maintained. It is an unsettling prospect, indeed, and the prevalence of deceit in human affairs—then, now, and always—lends a good deal of support to the idea that no one whatsoever is telling the truth. Perhaps, as social anthropologist F. G. Bailey argues, society—as the political contest for power by means of self-interested persuasion—"requires for its survival the practice of deceit."[155] Consistent with Bailey's line of thinking, though not his ultimate conclusion, one might appeal to the crafty counsel drawn from Machiavelli, that the prudent prince must learn how to be a "great simulator and dissimulator"—playing the "fox" with others and addling "the brains of men with trickery."[156] Might this be the secret code of all political agents? Perhaps, as evolutionary theorist Robert Trivers suggests, all of this is the inevitable result of evolutionary processes, which give biological advantage to the "practitioner of self-deception." As he puts it, "we deceive ourselves [fool ourselves] the better to deceive [or fool] others." Deception occurs at all levels of life, he argues—from gene to cell to individual to group," so there is "neither point nor possibility to escaping its practice."[157] None of these observations would rattle a sophist such

155. F. G. Bailey, *The Prevalence of Deceit* (Ithaca, N.Y.: Cornell University Press, 1991), 27.

156. *Machiavelli: The Chief Works and Others*, vol. 1, trans. Allan Gilbert (Durham, N.C.: Duke University Press, 1989), 64–65. In a letter from late May 1521, Machiavelli proposes a contest in lies, as he is confident of victory. As he puts it, "for a long time I have not said what I believed, nor do I ever believe what I say, and if indeed sometimes I do happen to tell the truth, I hide it among so many lies that it is hard to find." *Machiavelli: The Chief Works and Others*, vol. 2, trans. Allan Gilbert (Durham, N.C.: Duke University Press, 1989), 973.

157. Robert Trivers, *The Folly of Fools: The Logic of Deceit and Self-Deception in*

as Gorgias, as he expects nothing less from well-trained speakers; and it probably would not surprise Derrida either, as he regards the magic spell of someone like Socrates as the flip side of the sorcery of a sophist like Gorgias. But it is something that shakes Erasmus, precisely because (as Lear notes) what is at stake matters to him greatly; and it is something that should disturb the rest of us because the alternative is a world given over to the sophists and the tyrants. His response, as we have seen, is to speak truthfully about deceit, but to do so with the dissembling posture of the authentic silenus, in a manner designed to surprise, to shock, and to disrupt readers from their easy acquiescence to a world of lies. What we receive, in the end, is an ironic defense of ironic truth-telling.

Not surprisingly, however, the choice of irony as a form of truth-telling puts Erasmus on a collision path with another group—those of a more "rigorist" or "purist" mind-set who deplore all forms of dissemblance as lies. This objection, oddly enough, returns us to the point where this meditation began—that is, wondering if there is any significant difference between the silenus right-side-out (a truth-teller who dissembles) and the silenus inside-out (an outright deceiver). In the lifetime of Erasmus, it is Alberto Pio, the diplomat and conservative Catholic, who accuses Erasmus of—among many other things—holding that lying was permissible and beneficial.[158]

Human Life (New York: Basic Books, 2011), 1–28. Thus, Trivers argues, "deceiver and deceived are trapped in a coevolutionary struggle that continually improves adaptations on both sides." Importantly, Trivers allows for "mechanisms for the correct apprehension of reality" running side by side with "mechanisms of self-deception." Ibid., 28.

158. In Pio's words, Erasmus holds that "lying is not only permitted according to circumstances and times, but that it is even beneficial." See Erasmus, "The Apology of Desiderius Erasmus of Rotterdam against the Patchworks of Calumnious Complaints by Alberto Pio, Former Prince of Carpi," trans. Daniel Sheerin, in *Collected Works of Erasmus: Controversies*, vol. 84, ed. Nelson H. Minnich (Toronto: University of Toronto Press, 2005), 352, footnote 1429. Erasmus cites this accusation almost verbatim in "The Apology of Desiderius Erasmus of Rotterdam," CWE 84:356, only adding that he is being accused of holding that such lies are "without sin." For an extended dis-

Behind Pio stands the classical figure of Augustine, who famously argues that lies of all sorts—whether to preserve bodily chastity, to ensure a person's safety, or even to save someone's life—are sinful actions.[159] Lying is not permitted, he insists, even to advance religious truth against lying heretics—like the Priscillianists, who were said to counsel dissimulation in the face of adversaries.[160] Augustine's stance on deceit is classically expressed in his reading of Paul's public reprimand of Peter at Antioch for "simulating" his approval of Jewish dietary laws in Galatians 2:11–14. In his *Commentary on Galatians*, Augustine uses the episode to stress the "great example of humility" evident in Peter's acceptance of the pubic censure by a "junior shepherd."[161] Elsewhere, however, Augustine goes to great lengths to deflect any suggestion that Paul himself was simulating to please his Gentile audience (in Antioch) or in retelling the story in Galatians.[162] As Augustine writes to Jerome, "if we once admit in that supreme authority even one polite lie, there will be nothing left of those books."[163] Martin Luther follows Augustine's reading of Galatians in exonerating Paul of any dissemblance, though—not unexpectedly—he champions Paul's "unbending" challenge to Peter (despite the latter's "high prestige") for "endangering the majesty of the doctrine of justification."[164] Together, Augustine, Pio, and

cussion of the controversy between Erasmus and Pio, see Nelson H. Minnich, "Introduction," CWE 84:xv–cxli. See also Erika Rummel, *Erasmus and His Catholic Critics, 1523–1536, vol.* 2 (Nieuwkoop: De Graaf, 1989), 115–23.

159. Augustine, "Lying," trans. Mary Sarah Muldowney, in *Treatise on Various Subjects*, ed. Roy J. Deferrari (New York: Fathers of the Church, 1952), 53–110. For Augustine, a lie is a "false statement made with desire to deceive." Augustine, "Lying," 60.

160. Augustine, "Against Lying," trans. Harold B. Jaffee, in *Treatise on Various Subjects*, 125–57.

161. Eric Plumer, *Augustine's Commentary on Galatians: Introduction, Text, Translation, and Notes* (Oxford: Oxford University Press, 2003), 145–47.

162. See Augustine, "Against Lying," 157–60.

163. Augustine to Jerome, letter 28, in *Saint Augustine: Letters*, trans. Sister Wilfrid Parsons (Washington, D.C.: The Catholic University of America Press, 1964), vol. 1, 96.

164. *Luther's Works: Lectures on Galatians, 1535*, vol. 26, chapters 1–4, ed. Jaroslav

Luther cast doubt on the veracity and the virtue of innocent dissemblance; and in so doing, they undercut the kind of ironic truth-telling defended by Erasmus by collapsing the distinction between innocent and deceptive dissemblance.

At this point, however, one has to wonder at the odd cross-currents forming around these questions. Derrida and Gorgias, as we have seen, argue that there is no difference between the ironic philosopher and the sophist: both are deceptive. But then, too, the rigorists argue that there is no difference between the ironist and the sophist: the dissimulation of both is nothing but lies. What an odd convergence this is, between those who refine the art of lying because they doubt that anyone is telling the truth and those who demand pure truth and abhor all dissimulation of whatever sort. In the middle stands the ironic truth-teller, who like the sophist dissembles but like the rigorist hopes to tell the truth. And it is that dexterity and sense of nuance, as well as that commitment to telling the truth about our lives that marks the Erasmian contribution to the quest for self-knowledge. That possibility, however, is precisely what the rigorists reject. Both Pio and Luther complain that Erasmian irony is cagey and deceptive. But would it not startle Pio (the loyal defender of Roman theology) to learn that Martin Luther (the father of the Protestant Reformation) agrees with him and that they both agree with Augustine? They agree with Augustine in seeing Peter as a liar, and they agree with each other in thinking that Erasmus is no better than Peter. But would it please Luther to find himself allied with Pio? And could Pio tolerate being associated with Luther? What brings these two together is their shared fondness for Augustine's insistence on the purity of truth and their mutual distrust of Erasmus's handling of truth; neither

Pelikan (St. Louis, Mo.: Concordia Publishing, 1963), 106–20. For a discussion of Augustine and Luther's treatment of deception in the context of Galatians, see Perez Zagorin, *Ways of Lying: Dissimulation, Persecution, and Conformity in Early Modern Europe* (Cambridge, Mass.: Harvard University Press, 1990), 20–25 and 33–34.

can countenance a crack in the bulwark of authority—scriptural for Luther and ecclesial for Pio.[165] Truth as they believe it to be must be absolute, yet curiously, they do not mean the same truth and they do not defend the same authority. Their apparent alliance depends entirely on the formal demand for certainty narrowly defined and confirmed by firm authority; however, even on their own terms, both cannot be right.

Following the Erasmian line of thinking yields a more capacious sense of the possibilities of human communication, and hence, also, a more nuanced account of truth-telling than is possible for either the sophist or the rigorist. In his response to Pio, for instance, Erasmus points out the shades and degrees of pretense and deception which are distinct from outright lies.[166] And in place of Augustine, Erasmus follows the exegesis of Jerome, who in reading Galatians 2:11–14 suggests that Peter and Paul knowingly staged a kind of "holy quarrel" in order to assuage the fears of their respective communities.[167] Unlike Augustine, Jerome stresses the pious pre-

165. Nelson H. Minnich rightly notes the irony of Luther and Pio finding "some agreement" in their shared criticism of Erasmus, when they were vehemently opposed to each other on the disputed questions of the day. See Minnich, "Introduction," CWE 84:cxxviii.

166. As Erasmus puts it, "truth … is not always the opposite of lying." Erasmus, "The Apology of Desiderius Erasmus of Rotterdam," CWE 84:357; and compare with Erasmus, "Wine speaks truth," in *Collected Works of Erasmus: Adages*, vol. 32, trans. R. A. B. Mynors (Toronto: University of Toronto Press, 1989), 76, I. vii. 17. It should be noted that Pio also acknowledges there are "non-sinful uses of various sorts of deceit," and hence that "figurative expressions," for instance, or "metaphorical expressions" are not lies strictly speaking. See CWE 84:352, footnote 1430; 356, footnote 1454; 357, footnote 1461. At the same time, Erasmus observes, critics such as Pio continue to brand *him* as the "advocate of lying," even though they too concede that "not every lie is a capital crime" (CWE 84:355–56). It is curious, therefore, that Pio links Erasmus with the "orators"—someone like the sophist Gorgias, presumably—who "lie whenever it is useful in advancing the cause which they are supporting," thereby missing the effort of Erasmus to defend the truth-telling capacity of the sileni right-side-out as fundamentally distinct from the crafted disguises and artful deceptions of the sileni inside-out. See CWE 84:353, footnote 1437.

167. *St. Jerome's Commentaries on Galatians, Titus, and Philemon*, trans. Thomas P.

tense of Paul. In changing his voice for the occasion, Jerome suggests, "it is not that he was pretending to be what he was, but that he merely seemed to be what would have helped others."[168] Erasmus agrees entirely, marveling at how "skilful and slippery" Paul is when addressing the Corinthians. Indeed, he is like a "chameleon" or a "Proteus," "turning himself into every shape that he may shape them anew in Christ."[169] This is not to say that Paul is playing the sophist, as his rhetorical dexterity is not a symptom of deceit but a virtuous means of conveying the truth appropriately and effectively. As Erasmus famously puts it, "a prudent steward will husband the truth"—bringing it out appropriately, in a timely manner, in the dose that is required. Christ does as much when he "attuned himself" to the sensibilities of different groups, varying his words to each group with "courtesy and meekness."[170] Paul does the same when with "courteous language" he "twists" the inscription on the altar to an "unknown god" into "evidence for their faith," with the

Scheck (Notre Dame, Ind.: University of Notre Dame Press, 2010), 100. On the dispute between Jerome and Augustine as source for sixteenth century thought, see Perez Zagorin, *Ways of Lying*, 15–24. The correspondence between Augustine and Jerome vividly illustrates the larger issues at stake. See *Saint Augustine: Letters*. See also Erasmus's rendering of Galatians 2:11–14, in "Paraphrase on *Galatians*," 42:104–5.

168. *St. Jerome's Commentaries on Galatians, Titus, and Philemon*, 182. Jerome cites several examples where Paul "became a Jew to the Jews in order to gain the Jews" (1 Corin 9:20). As Paul says of his methods, "just as I please everyone in all things, not seeking what is useful to myself, but what is useful to the many, that they may be saved" (See 1 Corin 10:32–33).

169. See the remarkable passage on Paul's agility in communication in Erasmus to Erard de la Marck, letter 916, in *Collected Works of Erasmus: Correspondence*, vol. 6, trans. R. A. B. Mynors and D. F. S. Thomson (Toronto: University of Toronto Press, 1982), 248–49. As Erasmus writes, "this Paul of ours is always skilful and slippery … a squid, such a chameleon—he plays the part of Proteus or Vertumnus … turning himself into every shape that he may shape them anew for Christ; with such freedom does he himself twist and turn like a man who threads the windings of a maze, and appearing to us in a fresh guise every time." Interestingly, these qualities are precisely what Luther hurls as charges against Erasmus.

170. Erasmus to Justas Jonas, letter 1202, in *The Collected Works of Erasmus: Correspondence*, vol. 8, trans. R. A. B. Mynors (Toronto: University of Toronto Press, 1988), 203. See Bietenholz, *Encounters with a Radical Erasmus*, 141–48.

simple "alteration and omission of several words."[171] Even Augustine showed "gentleness in teaching" and "prudence in husbanding the word of God" when dealing with Donatists and the Manichaeans.[172] And Plato, too, did "not disapprove of pretense and concealment of the truth in a philosopher who has to govern the commonwealth, provided he uses these tricks for the good of the people."[173] So, Erasmus observes, nuance and candor in telling the truth has ample backing in biblical and classical traditions.

What is needed to speak the truth well, Erasmus contends, is a "sort of holy cunning"—or, what amounts to the same thing, an ironic manner of telling the truth.[174] This is not—I must stress—an endorsement of lying and deceit, as the opponents of Erasmus (such as Luther and Pio) contend. It means, rather, that telling the truth is not as simple as the rigorists suggest, nor is it as impossible as the sophists pretend. On one level, this take on truth issues in a general ethic of the tongue. As we saw earlier, much of the energy of Erasmus in this regard centers on the "deadly sickness of a malicious tongue" that has "infected the whole world with its awful venom"—a malady evident in the "indiscreet chattering, headlong lying, [and] bitter quarreling" so common in human affairs; but he also—more constructively—exhorts readers toward a thoughtful, gentle, and irenic tongue.[175] Along the way, however, Erasmus also

171. Erasmus to Justas Jonas, letter 1202, 8:204. See also *Collected Works of Erasmus: New Testament Scholarship*, vol. 50, ed. John J. Bateman, trans. Robert D. Sider (Toronto: University of Toronto Press, 1995), 108.

172. Erasmus, To Justas Jonas, Letter 1202, CWE 8:204.

173. Erasmus, To Justas Jonas, Letter 1202, CWE 8:205. Erasmus refers to Plato's *Republic* 3, 389B and 459C-D. See *The Republic of Plato*, trans. Francis MacDonald Cornford (New York: Oxford University Press, 1945), 78 and 158. Erasmus stresses the necessity of the ruler's genuine beneficence. Compare with Erasmus, "The Apology of Desiderius Erasmus," CWE 84:353–54.

174. Erasmus to Justas Jonas, letter 1202, CWE 8:210. See Jean-Claude Margolin, "Dire et ne pas dire: La pratique Érasmienne du sous-entendu," in *Les Normes du Dire au XVIe Siècle*, Actes du Colloque de Rouen, November 2001, ed. Jean-Claude Arnould and Gérard Milhe Poutingon (Paris: Honoré Champion, 2004), 125–43.

175. See Phillips, "Erasmus on the Tongue," 113–25.

flushes out what it might mean to "husband the truth" in everyday matters. What Erasmus seems to have in mind in these passages is not so much "cunning," as a sense of tact, civility, and timing. It is a good idea, he advises in a letter on the art of writing letters, to use a little "charm" or "pretense" when asking to borrow money.[176] Or again, very innocently, an Erasmian character makes space for civil turns of speech—calling someone "best of friends" when it is not the case—as something very different from lying for profit.[177] A bit more strategic, but still morally legitimate for Erasmus, it may be "expedient" or "lawful" to "conceal the truth," especially if blurting out the truth will not do any good.[178] Along the same lines, he notes, when "the truth of itself has a bitter taste for most people," it is wiser to "soften" the "painful subject by the courtesy of one's handling than to pile one cause of hatred on another."[179] Or with virtuous dissemblance, Erasmus insists, one may practice "well-meant deception" for someone's good, which is not the same as "wilful deception."[180] On another level, however, the praise of "holy cunning"

176. Erasmus, "On the Writing of Letters," trans. Charles Fantazzi, in *Collected Works of Erasmus: Literary and Educational Writings*, vol. 25 (Toronto: University of Toronto Press, 1985), 75.

177. Erasmus, "The Liar and the Man of Honour," in *Collected Works of Erasmus: Colloquies*, vol. 39, trans. Craig R. Thompson (Toronto: University of Toronto Press, 1997), 344–48. See also Erasmus, "Things and Names," in CWE 40:812–13.

178. See Erasmus's advice to this effect in Erasmus to Lorenzo Campeggi, letter 1167; Erasmus to Luigi Marliano, letter 1195; and Erasmus to William Blount, Lord Mountjoy, letter 1219, in CWE 8:113, 173, and 262.

179. Erasmus to Justas Jonas, letter 1202, CWE 8:203. In sum, Erasmus writes that while "a Christian … ought to be free of all pretense," there remain occasions "when it is right for truth to remain unspoken, and everywhere the time, the manner and the recipients of its publication are of great importance." See Erasmus to Jonas, CWE 8:205.

180. "An Admonition against Lying and Slander," trans. Peter Matheson, in *Collected Works of Erasmus: Controversies*, vol. 78, ed. James D. Tracy and Manfred Hoffmann (Toronto: University of Toronto Press, 2011), 388–89. We find Erasmus at his most slippery in this piece. See Johannes Trapman, "Erasmus on Lying and Simulation," in *Truth and Honesty: Principles and Strategies of Fraud and Deceit in the Early Modern Period*, ed. Toon van Houdt et al. (Leiden: E. J. Brill, 2002), 33–45.

leads directly back to the ironic figure of the authentic silenus. The true silenus, as we saw at the start of this meditation, is the embodiment of this kind of virtuous irony. Plain and unimpressive in appearance and speech, the silenus right-side-out speaks the truth by means of a kind of holy dissemblance—in the manner, once again, of an oracle—confronting those willing and able to listen with the unsettling and even eerie truth about our lives.

With this point we come to the heart of the Erasmian proposal. What we have, on the one hand, is an ironic account of deceptive speech—one that capitalizes on the playful inversion of appearance and reality embodied by the authentic silenus, in order to expose the deceptive ways of sophists and their defenders. It is the truth about lies told with dissemblance, in a manner designed to undercut the bleak prospect that everyone is a liar. On the other hand, we have an ironic account of truth-telling—one that embraces and deploys the resources of dissemblance in order to expose the narrowness of those who demand one pure truth. It is the truth about truth-telling told by means of dissemblance, in a manner meant to shatter the arrogant self-certainty of the rigorists. On both sides, therefore, Erasmus works to carve out legitimate space for ironic truth-telling, but, of course, neither Gorgias and Derrida nor Pio and Luther allow for such a posture or manner. In this regard, the Erasmian line of thinking constitutes an independent track for telling the truth; and in the context of this meditation, that means telling the truth about how we handle language—whether honestly or with deceit. The force of Erasmian irony—in short, the truth of such irony—resides in the unsettling of confidence and the shattering of assumptions about matters important to our lives. However, since diehard rigorists and cunning sophists are largely immune to having their convictions rattled, the force of such irony falls upon those of us not yet entirely under the rigorous sway of an absolute authority or not yet completely seduced by the charming suasion of the sophist. We are led by the haunting questions and provocative proposals of the ironists to a kind of self-knowledge, one that involves a shaking of certainties in a manner that leaves us humbly loyal to the quest for truth.

The ironic existence of the authentic silenus is something very rare. What philosopher, for instance, approximates the ironic existence of Socrates? And what Christian's life, for that matter, truly resembles the life of Christ? It is not—strictly speaking—a normative ideal against which to measure our lives, much less an imperative to live accordingly. We are challenged, however, to cultivate and practice (what Lear calls) a capacity for irony—that is, a readiness to face the uncanny proposals of ironic truth-telling. This means cultivating an openness to the eerie questions posed by ironic figures; becoming keenly self-conscious of the complexities, ambiguities, and strange oppositions lurking in our customary beliefs; gaining a glimpse of how odd and distorted our lives and cultures are when compared with their purported ideals; and, somehow, finding "ways to live well" even with these disruptions.[181] This is not easy, nor is it common. But it is the surest way to avoid falling under the heavy-handed sway of the rigorists or being seduced by the slippery seduction of the sophists. The next meditation illustrates the impact of Erasmian irony on the second question central to the quest for self-knowledge—what ought we to do concerning the conflicts between groups of people, which translates for Erasmus into questions of war and peace, while the third meditation charts the strategies of Erasmian irony with respect to the third question inherent in the search for self-knowledge—what might we hope for, which in Erasmian terms means coming to terms with the place and shape of pleasure in religious life.

181. Lear, *A Case for Irony*, 43.

Second Meditation

War and Sanity

IT SHOULD NOT surprise anyone to find Erasmus donning various costumes, partaking, that is, in a bit of playful, literary dissemblance, in order to speak honestly about war and peace. So he appears, famously, as Peace herself, the gracious benefactor and universal guardian of life, who, sadly, but also perversely, has been shunned and spurned by humankind. As Peace tells us, she has every right to be angry, as people have repelled her love and rejected her benefaction. Given that state of affairs, she might only "lament the wrong" done to her, if it were not for the fact that, in rejecting all she has to offer, people "deny themselves the source of all human happiness," while at the same time bringing on themselves "a sea of disasters." What a strange option this is—what a bizarre choice. Human beings have the chance to prosper and thrive in peace, but instead they trade those "remarkable benefits" for the "foul morass of manifold evils" brought on by warfare. Surely this is the "height of madness," she exclaims. For that self-destructive exchange, she can only "feel pity and sorrow for their plight." What can she do but "shed tears" for the "misery" they willfully but oddly suffer?[1]

Think through exactly what people have done. They could have embraced peace, she tells us, in which case they would have lived and thrived in her bounty, as Peace is in her rather lofty theological self-description, "the fount and source" of all good things, and also the "sustainer, amplifier, and preserver of all the good things of heaven or earth." If a nation opts for peace, its cities could thrive with abundant prosperity, its families can enjoy the confidence of security, its churches might hold fast to the sacred and teach sound morality, and its people would relish pleasures of great variety. In fact, Peace laments, people have, time and time again, rejected her fruits and plunged headlong into the carnage of war. The results of this move, she observes, are disastrous: "prosperity immediately declines, increase dwindles, towers are undermined, sound foundations are destroyed, and sweetness is embittered." In war people find themselves helplessly adrift in, what Erasmus gruesomely calls, an "encircling ocean of all the evils in the world." Might rules, fear devours, cities crumble, disease spreads, blood flows, and death abounds. Given these grim results, Peace wonders if perhaps the creatures who make such a trade have gone completely mad. "Who," she asks, "would believe those beings to be human or possessed of a spark of sanity when they devote so much expenditure and application, such great effort and artifice, amid so many anxieties and dangers, to rid themselves" of peace, while willingly paying "the heavy price" for such a "burden of evils?"[2]

This, in a nutshell, is the complaint of Peace; and these are the questions Erasmus poses to the political leadership of his day and the intellectual and ecclesial culture which supported their san-

1. Erasmus, "A Complaint of Peace Spurned and Rejected by the Whole World," trans. Betty Radice, in *Collected Works of Erasmus: Literary and Educational Writings*, vol. 27, ed. A. H. T. Levi (Toronto: University of Toronto Press), 293.

2. Ibid.

guinary policies; and, too, these are the questions he bequeaths to readers down to our own day, so it is a question we must take up and answer as well.

Unsettling Questions

So, Erasmus asks, are people sane when they trade the benefits of peace for the horrors of war? Is there a spark of sanity in the business of war, or is the whole of it sheer madness? These are familiar questions for Erasmus, reminiscent of the critical treatment of madness in *The Praise of Folly*. Erasmus knows full well, however, that the critique of madness is made in the name of another kind of madness, or at least what will be taken as such by the madmen he has satirized. As we saw in the Introduction, for instance, the fools praised in the closing section of *The Praise of Folly*, the ones who love beyond their own interests, who "ignore injuries, allow themselves to be deceived, [and] make no distinction between friend and foe," these people are guilty of another, perhaps richer and maybe ideal form of madness; and there can be no doubt that the corrupt and vicious fools who succeed so well in the world-as-it-is will think these people are completely out of their minds.[3] Now, Erasmus notes, the same thing happens with respect to war and peace. War has become such an "accepted thing," he observes, that "people are astonished to find anyone who does not like it."[4] Indeed, to question the sanity of warfare, or worse to "dissuade men from war," will be seen by most as simply crazy, or maybe even "heretical," or as many might say today, as "unrealistic."[5] So the critique of the madness of war proceeds with full awareness

3. Erasmus, *The Praise of Folly*, 132.

4. Erasmus, "War is a treat for those who have not tried it," CWE 35:401, adage IV. i. 1.

5. Ibid., 426; see also 35:401. Similarly, Erasmus writes, "it has almost come to the point that it is foolish and irreverent to open one's mouth against war or to speak in favour of what alone found favour on the lips of Christ." Erasmus, "A Complaint of Peace," CWE 27:308.

that both the war-monger and the advocate of peace are "mad," or at least will be seen by each other as such, albeit in significantly different senses.

When he speaks on war and peace, Erasmus develops three lines of argument, each designed to pursue a separate question. Appealing to a Stoic idea of nature, he wonders first whether war is natural; drawing on biblical sources, he asks whether war is Christian; and, finally, observing the sorry state of European towns and fields in times of war, he inquires whether the consequences of warfare are worth the meager political advantages. In each case, however, Erasmus sharpens and reverses the question to serve his argumentative aim. So we find him asking: is war not out of keeping with nature? Does not war utterly contradict the teachings and practices of Christ? And, lastly, does not the carnage of war outweigh any political gains? What makes his reflections so compelling, however, is the manner in which these points are pressed one step further, beyond their expected conclusions, yielding thereby some truly unsettling questions and eerie proposals. These questions and these proposals, which will be laid out briefly in the next few pages, will comprise the focus of this meditation. Their force and their difficulty will become especially clear when put into conversation with other perspectives on war, both classical and contemporary.

In the first place, Erasmus argues, war is "unworthy in every respect" of what a human being is meant to be by nature.[6] Consider, he suggests, how people are gifted by nature with a variety of capacities which can foster concord and overcome conflict, including reason (which is something "common to all" people); speech (the "chief promoter of friendly relationships"); the virtues of "good will and concord" (to cement friendly relations); and a "capacity for tears" (to make reconciliation possible). Addition-

6. Erasmus, "War is a treat," CWE 35:401.

ally, we are told, nature wisely created people "weak and unarmed" (so they would build cities and forge alliances), and she gave them "different and unequal capacities" (to encourage "mutual friendships") and different "products" (to teach "exchange" between them).[7] This language of what nature intended no doubt sounds a bit quaint to modern ears, but it would seem to mean that human beings find themselves to be built in such a manner that would—one would think—lead them proficiently to concord and harmony. But, alas, we well know, this is not what happens. In fact, Erasmus observes, people "fight, brawl, and rage against each other in perpetual discord, strife, and war." Indeed, there does not seem to be any common bond among people sufficient to check the "frenzy for mutual extinction."[8] In all of this, Erasmus concludes, "there is no trace of man in it anywhere."[9] When they hurl themselves ferociously into battle, they no longer seem human; they live (and they fight and die) in conflict with their own natures.

But, of course, this is not quite correct, as there seems to be everything about human nature in war; or rather, warfare has everything to do with being human. Unlike the rest of nature, Erasmus observes, which operates with a "sense of peace and concord," there seems to be an "insatiable lust for fighting in the human heart."[10] A simple review of history and a quick perusal of the world today supplies ample evidence for this dark observation. So how is it, Erasmus asks, that human beings have deviated so far from their natural state. Who, in a word, "first put it into the heart of man to plunge a deadly sword into human vitals?"[11] The reply from Erasmus is a rough sketch of the stages by which warfare emerged and grew in primitive history, starting with the need

7. Erasmus, "A Complaint of Peace," CWE 27:294–95. See also "War is a treat," CWE 35:401–3.

8. Erasmus, "A Complaint of Peace," CWE 27:296.

9. Erasmus, "War is a treat," CWE 35:406.

10. Erasmus, "A Complaint of Peace," CWE 27:294 and 296.

11. Erasmus, "War is a treat," CWE 35:407.

for organized defense from "savage beasts"; moving to the armed assault on harmless animals; developing later with collective assaults by one group on another, initially perhaps for glory but then later for simple gain. As these transitions occurred, he notes, "as savagery increased with habit, as anger rose and ambition became more and more inflamed, ingenuity provided weapons to match their violence." And with that move, people began to "make war everywhere, now in greater numbers, now with weapons," and indeed with ever more potent weapons resulting in ever more deadly effects. Such is the course taken by human nature, Erasmus concludes, as "malice grew gradually side by side with civilization."[12] And such is human nature as it has evolved—aggressive, savage, ingenious, and deadly. Indeed, given how natural it seems for human beings to be at war, Erasmus boldly surmises, "perhaps it is the fatal malady of human nature to be quite unable to carry on without wars."[13] What an eerie proposal, this is, that war is not just an occasional deviation from the natural norm, but that it is inextricably tied into what human existence has come to be.

Erasmus insists, in the second place, that warfare is completely at odds with the life and teachings of Jesus, and consequently, that it has no place in Christian life. "Survey the life of Christ," Erasmus proposes, "from start to finish, and what else is it but a lesson in concord and mutual love?" Indeed, "what else did he teach and expound but peace?" He greets others with an "assurance of peace"; and he exhorts his followers to "love one another" without ceasing. At his death, too, he does not leave his people "horses, bodyguards, empires, or riches"; what he gives them is peace; what he leaves is peace.[14] In a word, peace certainly would seem to define Christian

12. Ibid., 409–10.

13. Erasmus, "A Complaint of Peace," CWE 27:314.

14. Ibid., 299–301. As Erasmus writes elsewhere, "The sum and substance of our religion is peace and concord." Erasmus to Jean De Carondelet, CWE 9:252. For a review of Erasmus's core reading of Jesus as "Prince of Peace," see Hilmar M. Pabel,

life. And yet, we well know, this is not entirely correct, as Christians regularly and enthusiastically engage in war. Warfare seems, in fact, all-too-Christian. So, Erasmus notes, soldiers carry the "cross as their standard," thereby making Christ the "witness" of their crimes. More absurd yet are the occasions where the "cross is displayed in both camps," so the "cross fights the cross and Christ makes war on Christ."[15] In their preaching, meanwhile, priests "fan the flames of bloodshed and carnage" and bishops go to great effort to "aggravate the general fever of the world."[16] Behind the scenes, moreover, theologians craft elaborate justifications of war rooted in slippery scriptural interpretations. In such efforts, Erasmus charges, they "make Christ [the] authority for [war], twisting his words to the point that it seems he commanded ... the practices he had previously forbidden."[17] In sum, though warfare directly contradicts the counsels of Christ, there is no escaping the fact that its practice is thoroughly Christian.

So how did it come to be this way? How did war come to be seen as "just" by Christian pastors and theologians? The reply of Erasmus focuses initially on the political leaders whose interests are being served. Instead of tending to the welfare of the people, Erasmus complains, too many rulers call the world to arms under various "disgraceful and frivolous pretexts," each designed to bolster their power and prestige.[18] To manage such policies, of

"The Prince of Peace: Erasmus' Conception of Jesus," in *The Unbounded Community: Papers in Christian Ecumenism in Honor of Jaroslav Pelikan*, ed. William Cafferro and Duncan G. Fisher (New York: Garland Publishing, 1996), 127–48. As Erasmus usually uses the theological title "Christ," I will follow his usage, unless the context allows a more natural reference to the historical figure of Jesus.

15. Erasmus, "A Complaint of Peace," CWE 27:309.

16. Ibid., 308.

17. Erasmus, "War is a treat," CWE 35:426.

18. Erasmus, "A Complaint of Peace," CWE 27:305–6. Erasmus frequently advised royalty concerning the perils of war and the benefits of peace, most famously in "The Education of a Christian Prince," dedicated to the young Prince Charles, later Charles V, Holy Roman Emperor from 1519 to 1556. See Erasmus, "The Education of

course, it helps to have the seal of legitimation from religion, and it is here that the justification of war in Christian theology comes to the fore. As he tells the story, Christian thought first went awry when it embraced a kind of "erudition" and "eloquence" designed especially for engaging in "controversy" and "overthrowing of heresy." Then, too, "the whole of Aristotle was accepted into the heart of theology"; and where anything said by Jesus conflicted with the "oracles of Aristotle" or contradicted "the way we live," people were "permitted to interpret it differently." The same concessions then were granted to Roman law; and, once again, the teachings of Jesus were "twisted" to accommodate (among other things) the Roman affirmation of war as "praiseworthy" and "just."[19] In response to this adjustment to Christian thinking, Erasmus warns Christian princes of the dangers of "self-deception": is it not the case that everyone thinks their causes are just? Is not self-interest at work in such justifications?[20] Once again, however, Erasmus presses his case one step further, and it is here that his questioning becomes bold and pointed. If, he suggests, someone is so ready to compro-

---

a Christian Prince," trans. Neil M. Cheshire and Michael J. Heath, CWE 27:279–88. As Margaret Mann Phillips notes, however, Erasmus was "not overly-optimistic" that his advice would bear fruit. See Phillips, *The 'Adages' of Erasmus*, 110. Consider Erasmus's satirical adage on the "sheer stupidity" of princes, coupled with his denunciation of the corrupt and careless education that is actually given to royal youth. See Erasmus, "One ought to be born a king or a fool," CWE 31:227–36, adage I. iii. 1. For a more trenchant critique of the self-destructive savagery of tyrants and the ruthless insurrection they arouse, see Erasmus's retelling of "A dung-beetle hunting an eagle," CWE 35:178–214. On this darker side of Erasmus's views of monarchy, see Denis L. Drysdall, "Erasmus on Tyranny and Terrorism: *Scarabaeus aquilam quaerit* and the *Institutio principis christiani*," *Erasmus of Rotterdam Society Yearbook*, vol. 29 (2009): 89–102. Little wonder, therefore, that Erasmus's praise of the contributions to peace from various monarchs, like that at the end of "The Complaint of Peace," must be read carefully. Indeed, as José Chapiro rightly notes, such flattery often is "the trick of a good comedian," as Erasmus makes "them appear even more ridiculous than [if] he had showed them to be evil." Chapiro, *Erasmus and Our Struggle for Peace*, 71.

19. Erasmus, "War is a treat," CWE 35:419–20.

20. Erasmus, "A Complaint of Peace," CWE 27:317.

mise the challenge of peace with legal justifications of warfare, then why not honestly concede the irrelevance of what Jesus has to say. "If Christ is merely a story," he writes, "why do we not frankly spurn it?"[21]

In the third place, Erasmus contends, the consequences of war are so ghastly and so thoroughly inhumane that no rational person and certainly, too, no sane person could suggest that the gains of war outweigh the losses. Consider first the ferocity of the battlefield, "the fearful clash and glitter of arms, the hateful roar of a great multitude, the threatening looks, harsh bugles, the terrifying blare of trumpets, … the mad uproar, [and] the furious clash of battle." Then, Erasmus directs, picture the human fallout, "the monstrous butchery, the merciless fate of the slain and those who kill, the slaughtered lying in heaps, the fields running with gore, [and] the rivers dyed with human blood." But picture, too, the effect on daily life, "crops trampled far and wide, farms burnt out, villages set afire, cattle driven away, virgins raped, old men dragged off in captivity, churches sacked, and robbery, pillaging, violence and confusion everywhere." And consider how the horrors of war fall mercilessly on the weak and unarmed, "peasants plundered, land-owners oppressed, so many old men left desolate, … old women left destitute, … wives left widows, children left orphans, homes filled with mourning, [and] rich folk reduced to poverty."[22] To make matters worse, Erasmus notes, war unleashes a torrent of "mercenaries, robbers, despoilers of churches, and assassins," and in their hands, the "deadly pestilence" spreads beyond control, overtaking even the prince who hired these savage warriors in the first place.[23] In its

21. Erasmus, "War is a treat," CWE 35:438; see also "A Complaint of Peace," CWE 27:304.

22. Erasmus, "War is a treat," CWE 35:404. See also "A Complaint of Peace," CWE 27:316–17. On the direct and indirect impact of warfare on non-combatants, see J. R. Hale, *War and Society in Renaissance Europe, 1450–1620* (Baltimore, Md.: Johns Hopkins University Press, 1985), 179–208.

23. Erasmus, "War is a treat," CWE 35:403–4. See also "A Complaint of Peace,"

wake, human lives, their works, their dreams, their loves, and their homes are disfigured or wiped away.

With these consequences in mind, Erasmus challenges those with power to "calculate whether there is anything to be achieved by exchanging peace for war." Just "do the arithmetic," he suggests, and "weigh up … the cost of war and the cost of peace," and then it will become apparent that peace can be secured for "a tenth part of the worry, effort, distress, risk, expense, and bloodshed that war involves." "Intelligent men" always "weigh up an issue, think it over, and look all round it before they embark on even a private enterprise."[24] So think through the costs before rushing to war, Erasmus says to the princes of Europe, and weigh the price paid against the gains which may or may not be won. In war, he tells them, "you empty your purse, plunder your people, burden the just, and incite the unjust to further crimes, and even when you have ended the war, its legacy remains with you."[25] Indeed, even a war that seems overwhelmingly successful in its purposes carries unthinkable human costs, so that the "sensible victor" surely will "regret having undertaken it."[26] And though peace may at times seem to be a "hard bargain," a thoughtful leader "must work out how much evil you avoid and how much good you can preserve, and [then] … will not regret the cost."[27] What advantages there

CWE 27:316–17. While Erasmus routinely satirizes the base motives of ordinary soldiers, he was especially blunt in criticism of the mercenaries at work in his home country. In "The Education of a Christian Prince," CWE 27:283, Erasmus declares that "there is no class of men more abject and indeed more damnable" than mercenaries. See also Erasmus, "Risk it on a Carian," CWE 32:12–13, adage I, vi. 14; and "War without tears," CWE 33:303, adage II. vi. 23. On the experience of Erasmus with mercenaries, see James D. Tracy, *The Politics of Erasmus: A Pacifist Intellectual and His Political Milieu* (Toronto: University of Toronto Press, 1978), 85–86. On the character and culture of soldiers in this period, see Hale, *War and Society in Renaissance Europe*, 127–52.

24. Erasmus, "A Complaint of Peace," CWE 27:316.

25. Ibid., 317.

26. Erasmus, "War is a treat," CWE 35:415.

27. Erasmus, "A Complaint of Peace," CWE 27:313. Considering the staggering loss

are in war, Erasmus suggests, go "entirely to a small number of utterly criminal bandits, to the mercenary soldiery, to the brazen profiteers, [and] perhaps to the few leaders who connived to stir up war for this very purpose and who are never better off than when the state is on the rocks."[28] For everyone else there is misery, fear, hunger, disease, loss, pain, and death. Given these results, it would seem the "act of a madman" to make such a wager.[29] "How," Erasmus asks, "can we believe that people are in their right mind when they can ensure peace with little trouble yet prefer to resort to war?"[30]

But here, too, Erasmus presses the point one step further. Given the enormous costs of war, he has argued, one would have to be mad to abandon the fruits of peace for the sake of military campaigns. And yet, everyone knows full well, people across the globe regularly and persistently make precisely this choice. So, Erasmus asks us, what would prompt such a decision? Why would human beings throw themselves into warfare given the inevitable destruction that comes with it? His response is blunt and pointed, and it cannot be what anyone wants to hear: in a word, people love war, or at least those do who wield power and who reside at a safe distance from the holocaust they unleash. As Erasmus puts it, "men may suggest what reasons they like for their own malady, but if they did not love war they would not engage in perpetual warfare amongst themselves in the way they do."[31] Once again, what an eerie proposal this is: that people have a "longing for war"[32]—a passion and perhaps even an enthusiasm for the organized and massive use of lethal violence. If they did not love war, in short, they would not so

of life from war, Erasmus insists, "peace will seem cheap at the price, however much you paid for it."

28. Erasmus, "War is a treat," CWE 35:427. See also CWE 35:414.

29. Erasmus, "War is a treat," CWE 35:416.

30. Ibid., 415.

31. Erasmus, "A Complaint of Peace," CWE 27:300.

32. Ibid., 316.

readily ignore all the brutal and deadly consequences of warfare. If they did not have a passion for war, moreover, they would not have such a fancy for romantic tales of battle; they would not be so keen to root their savagery in the meaning of a noble cause; nor would they be so adept at concocting elaborate justifications for their warmongering, unless, of course, they are completely out of their minds. And this, the madness of war and the irrationality of those who ignore the costs, is precisely what Erasmus seeks to expose by magnifying the inhumane consequences of warfare.

So these are the unsettling questions and eerie proposals which Erasmus poses to us. First, while warfare may seem unnatural, in another and more factual sense it is all-too-natural; and, indeed, the malice that animates its practice seems to have grown in passion and cunning with the growth of civilization. And this is the case—to such a degree—that it appears now to be the "fatal malady" of civilized human life to be "quite unable to carry on without wars." Second, though war certainly seems to contradict the words and life of Jesus, in fact, its practice is thoroughly Christian; and, indeed, Christian intellectuals have worked hard to produce intricate justifications of warfare, a service no doubt appreciated by the governing powers of their day. One must wonder, however, whether their efforts to adjust the biblical challenge of peace to the needs of the day are not (at best) self-deceiving or (at worst) simply deceptive. Would it not be more honest to simply admit that everything about "Christ" is nothing more than a "story," and thus to come right out and be done with it for good? Third, given the ghastly and inhumane consequences of warfare, it is hard to see how sane and rational people would so regularly and even eagerly resort to war. Perverse as it may sound, the only thing that could explain this chronic ignorance of the costs of war is that people—at least those untouched by its brutality—have a secret longing and enthusiasm, even a love, for warfare. In keeping with the ironic manner of Erasmus's way of telling the truth, each of these proposals is designed to shake people's comfortably-held self-understanding, startling them with evidence that—when it comes to war and peace—they may not be the kind of creatures they have come to believe they are. The pages that follow will pursue each of these three lines of challenge.

Is War Natural?

Is war natural to human life? Or, is it in some sense an aberration of the norm, or perhaps a malady eliding the healthy state of human existence? But if it is not natural, why in fact is war so common? Given its widespread practice, would it not seem to be entirely natural?

What makes these questions so difficult to answer is that they cut in two directions at once, as "natural" may signify the ideal capacities given at birth to all human beings, or it may indicate the actual practice evident in human life. The ambiguity of the key term, in other words, can cause confusion, as it does classically in Cicero's reflections on natural duties in warfare. To say, for instance, that war is unnatural seems to fly in the face of all too much historical evidence, while to say that war is natural to human existence seems like a cynical denial of our capacity for peaceful resolution of conflict. For someone with a sense of irony, however, this very ambiguity becomes useful fodder for reflecting on the intricate tensions of the ideal and the real in human affairs. Indeed, as we will see presently, both are true—war is both natural and unnatural—albeit in different senses, and the differences make a huge difference.

For his part, Cicero's reflection on war and peace takes place within the broadly Hellenistic but specifically Stoic view that rights and duties can be derived from "Nature and Reason." In this take on the world, human beings are unique among all animals in having a sense of "propriety and order" in "the transactions of daily life," something which gives rise to ideals of "moral rectitude and moral dignity."[33] We have, according to this view, a native capacity for rationally discerning what is right and wrong. It is best, Cicero writes, to "follow Nature as our guide" in discerning the duties incumbent upon the "common bonds" of social life.[34] And the same guidance of reason, he suggests, should govern the resolution of conflicts, including conflicts between people or states. With this in mind, he asserts, it is "characteristic of man" to settle disputes "by discussion," rather than by "physical force," the latter being typical of "the brute"—that is, of animals.[35] On this score, Erasmus generally agrees: when people settle conflicts by negotiating, they are tapping into their natural capacities for reasonable speech. In this sense, peaceful resolution of disputes is natural to the very best of human existence; and warfare would seem to be beneath us.

Cicero is quite right, therefore, to insist that "diplomacy in the friendly settlement of controversies is more desirable than courage in settling them on the battlefield."[36] Contrary to what many people think, "achievements in peace are [often] more important and no less renowned than in war."[37] Many times in Roman history, he observes, "arms [have] yielded to the toga"; and these great moments include his "counsels" and his "vigilance" when serving at the "helm of state," where—as he puts it—he caused the weapons of the "most desperate traitors" to slip suddenly from their hands. "What triumph can be compared to that," he asks rather proudly?[38] Cicero is referring to his efforts as consul to persuade the senate of the gravity of Catiline's conspiracy. As he sees it, his

33. Marcus Tullius Cicero, *De Officiis*, trans. Walter Miller (Cambridge, Mass.: Harvard University Press, 1913) I. v.

34. Ibid., I. vii.

35. Ibid., I. xi.

36. Ibid., I. xxiii. On Cicero's repeated efforts at mediation and diplomacy to settle conflicts internal to Roman governance, see Anthony Everitt, *Cicero: The Life and Times of Rome's Greatest Politician* (New York: Random House, 2003).

37. Cicero, *De Officiis*, I. xxii.

38. Ibid., I. xxii.

efforts illustrate that "civil capacity" in affairs of government relies on rational persuasion rather than armed force to secure the good of the nation.[39] What he values, in short, is civic leadership that lives up to the highest capacities of human nature. On this score, to be sure, it is easy to agree whole-heartedly, though in Cicero's personal example, it should be noted, his civic "courage" led to the execution of five conspirators without trial.[40] In his hands, interestingly, reason drew blood as surely as any weapon.

Despite the primacy given to reason and diplomacy, Cicero contends that there are times when war is simply unavoidable—where discussion appears impossible or futile—and in such situations war may be morally just. We must be careful, he advises, not to take the course of diplomacy "merely for the sake of avoiding war, rather than for the sake of public expediency."[41] In conflicts where it becomes impossible to "avail ourselves of discussion," in other words, warfare is morally justifiable as long as the public good (which in this case means the good of the Roman empire as determined by the ruling elite) is being served. With that goal in mind, as he puts it, "the only excuse … for going to war is that we may live in peace unharmed."[42] Or, as he renders it elsewhere, a war is just only if undertaken for "revenge or defense."[43] Both of these stipulations restrict the use of force, though they also allow a good bit of latitude. To defend the state would seem to exclude the offensive use of force against others; but, as Cicero reasons, since

39. Ibid., I. xxiii. On Cicero's interventions in the Catiline affair, see Everitt, *Cicero*, 91–116.

40. Cicero would later suffer exile when his abrogation of due process was made illegal in February of 58. See Everitt, *Cicero*, 146–49.

41. Cicero, *De Officiis*, I. xxiii.

42. Ibid., I. xi. On Cicero's thinking about just war, and the illustration of how these views find application in selected correspondence, see G. A. Harrer, "Cicero on Peace and War," *The Classical Journal* 14, no. 1 (October, 1918): 26–38.

43. Cicero, *The Republic*, III. xxiv. 35, trans. Clinton Walker Keyes (Cambridge, Mass.: Harvard University Press, 1966), 213. These texts on just war are fragments quoted by Isidore.

there is no such thing as a natural "extinction of a state," to defend its perpetuity could mandate preemptive and aggressive military measures.[44] An auxiliary condition is added, that no war can be considered just unless preceded by "an official demand for satisfaction" and a "formal declaration" to the adversary."[45] Here again Cicero moves to restrict the occasions for the initiation of war, though the latitude for aggression could be as broad as governing officials (and the interests of the far-flung Roman empire) might desire.

That warfare at times may be unavoidable, even necessary, is a common enough sentiment. Even Erasmus grants that war is "permissible sometimes, but [always] with reluctance and sorrow";[46] and he sounds more approving of those who defend their country from attack at their "own peril."[47] But it is precisely this sense of compulsion that fuels the move from diplomacy to warfare, or as Cicero defines things, from what is ideal in human nature to brutish behavior. And it is precisely this "sort of excuse" to justify going to war that Erasmus calls into question. Are you really acting "under compulsion"? Were you truly "dragged unwillingly into war?"[48] Or is it the case—if only those with power to make national decisions were to drop their "pretenses"—that what pulls nations into war with a sense of compulsion and unavoidability is simply "anger, ambition, and folly"? Is there really a need to "fly immediately to arms," one might ask Cicero, in order that a people may "live in peace unharmed"?[49] Or are there other factors at work, perhaps resentment over a national insult, or greed for the resources of others, or just sheer folly? Indeed, Cicero would

44. Ibid., III. xxxiv. 24. This text is a fragment quoted by Augustine.

45. Cicero, *De Officiis*, I. xi; see *The Republic*, III. xxiv. 35. The latter text is a fragment quoted by Isidore.

46. Erasmus, "War is a treat," CWE 35:426.

47. Erasmus, "A Complaint of Peace," CWE 27:314.

48. Ibid., 310.

49. Erasmus, "War is a treat," CWE 35:430.

seem to admit other such motives when he grants the legitimacy of wars fought for "supremacy" or "glory," as long as they serve to allow a people to live in peace unharmed.[50] Allowing these kinds of motives to support the move from diplomacy to warfare, however, signals a fundamental shift in how one looks at human life. No longer can one happily say that it is natural for human beings to settle conflicts through discussion, for now it is conceded that humans regularly—and even justifiably, and now quite naturally—resolve disputes with brute force. In short, in Cicero's concession to the varied motives for engaging in war, it is now more proper to say that war is entirely natural to human life.

It seems, in fact, that in Cicero's hands war has become not only quite natural, but also official and even civilized. This transition appears, initially, when he cautions governing powers to be "careful" not to follow the course of diplomacy "merely for the sake of avoiding war rather than for the sake of public expediency."[51] This would seem to mean that rulers should act primarily for "public expediency," which in Cicero's world means the good of the governing state. With this in mind, he counsels, it may be more advantageous to go to war than to settle for diplomatic solutions, as the latter may prove injurious to the state's interests. On this score Erasmus would be simply incredulous, as the avoidance of war is—in his view—always and everywhere in the "public interest."[52] But

50. Cicero, *De Officiis*, I. xii. Cicero's term as a general of Roman forces in Cilicia (south coastal area of Asia Minor) shows clearly that Roman supremacy and personal glory were not questioned as justifiable motives for warfare. See Everitt, *Cicero*, 195–204. In a letter to Atticus, dated December 51, Cicero describes the victorious siege of the fortified town of Pindenissus, a town that had resisted Roman rule. All the spoils (except the horses), he tells Atticus, were given to his soldiers; and "the captives were sold on the third day of the festival of Saturn," their "auction" netting some twelve million sesterces. Cicero, *Letters to Atticus*, trans. E. O. Winstedt (London: Heinemann, 1912), vol. 1, 391–93. As Everitt notes, Cicero hoped to receive a "Triumph" (or at least an "Ovation") in public honor of his military achievements. See Everitt, *Cicero*, 199 and 130.

51. Cicero, *De Officiis*, I. xxiii.

52. Erasmus, "A Complaint of Peace," CWE 27:312.

now, in the hands of Erasmus, the terms are drawn differently, in a decidedly humanistic manner that puts limits on royal power and restraints on their entry into war. As Erasmus puts it, it is "royalty's duty to know nothing of personal inclinations and to judge everything by the common good."[53] But here the "common good" is defined by the welfare of "peasants and humble citizens," who—Erasmus reminds us—are "also human and free," as much as any king. "Something so highly dangerous," therefore, like taking a people to war, "must not be undertaken except by the consent of the whole people."[54] Unlike Cicero, Erasmus concludes, governing powers should be ever-mindful to follow the course of diplomacy, as "the prevention of war and the establishment of concord" is fundamental to people's lives and well-being.[55] Cicero's problem, it seems, is that he has come to see war as something official, the prerogative of the ruling elite of the empire, and hence a natural feature of civilized existence, something clearly at play in his demand that war be launched only upon an "official demand for satisfaction" and "formal declaration."[56] If that be the case, Erasmus quips, then let "the full force of calamities" fall on the heads of these officials, rather than on the people "who have no interest in war and gave no occasion for it."[57]

Cicero's position becomes more strained when he contemplates the natural duties governing the actual conduct of fighting in a war. To be sure his aim is to civilize the barbarity of armed conflict; he hopes, in a word, to translate what is dictated by Nature through reason into practical duties in the midst of combat. But in doing this, it would seem, there is an unmistakable acquiescence to malice, since it is restrained malice, and not an absence of malice, that Cicero advises. Needless to say, the result is a tenuous

53. Ibid., 313.

54. Ibid., 311–13.

55. Ibid., 312.

56. Cicero, *De Officiis*, I. xi.

57. Erasmus, "A Complaint of Peace," CWE 27:312. See Erasmus, "One pot smashed against another," CWE 35:233, adage III. vii. 29.

and shaky balance of reason and brutishness. Thus, for example, Cicero insists that fighting should be undertaken "in such a way as to make it evident that it has no object than to secure peace," and that is to happen as one is trying to kill an armed adversary. So, he acknowledges, it "takes a brave and resolute spirit not to be disconcerted … or ruffled and thrown off one's feet," so to speak, but actually "to keep one's presence of mind and self-possession and not to swerve from the path of reason."[58] The soldier in battle, therefore, and not simply the general sitting at a safe distance, is to fuse a reasonable and honorable intent with the most violent and brutish of activities. How unthinkably difficult this must be, Cicero concedes. Indeed, how much easier it would be to "mix rashly in the fray," jumping headlong and madly into the most "barbarous and brutish" kind of battle; but it is far nobler and more rational, he counsels, to maintain "prudence and wisdom," even when it is necessary to "gird on the sword" and enter the battle.[59] In each of these comments Cicero works to bring reason into the madness of battle, but by so doing he also acclimates reason to the brutishness of combat. Warfare becomes something that can be lived with, managed, even done nobly and in a rational manner; malice and aggression have become part of civilized life.

The transformation of reason in its alliance with malice is nicely illustrated when Cicero frames specific duties for combat. As an initial example, he tells us, combatants are bound to keep promises to an enemy, even if "under stress of circumstance."[60] What a noble but fragile bit of civility this is, right in the midst of the madness of battle; but when one brings civility together with such madness, civility is accommodated to violence in the process. It now seems that vicious aggression can be tamed, made civil, even while being lethal. But Cicero's examples become more telling when he considers duties regarding the treatment of enemy prisoners and con-

58. Cicero, *De Officiis*, I. xxiii.

59. Ibid., I. xxiii.

60. Ibid., I. xiii.

quered cities. "When victory is won," he advises, "we should spare those who have not been blood-thirsty and barbarous in warfare"; or again, "protection" should be "ensured" to those "who lay down their arms and throw themselves upon the mercy of our generals."[61] To be sure, Cicero hopes to exclude wanton slaughter of captured soldiers; but as reasonable and gracious as this certainly is, he has not ruled out execution of those who have been "blood-thirsty" (or, more likely, who were perceived as being blood-thirsty) or those who (perhaps from pride or courage) do not cower before the victorious generals.[62] In this duty, therefore, aggression and respect are allied; and while aggression is tamed a bit in the process, civility has come to accept aggression.

The same thing is evident when Cicero considers duties pertaining to the destruction and plundering of cities. "Great care should be taken," he counsels, "that nothing be done in reckless cruelty or wantonness." Good soldiers should take "calm and well-considered measures" and follow a "true and honourable course," specifically by singling out "the guilty for punishment" and sparing the rest. But, he quicky adds, as if fearing that he has been too rational, "we must, of course, never be guilty of seeming cowardly and craven in our avoidance of danger."[63] While Cicero certainly wants to limit the rage and fury of conquering troops by bringing a certain rationality and respect into the midst of battle, it remains the case that he has by no means ruled out the triumphant seizure of enemy cities. Plundering cities is no longer purely barbarous because, apparently, it is possible to plunder rationally, with restraint. In saying this, however, one gains civility in warfare, but at the price of accepting savagery within civilized life. It is with this in mind that Erasmus says that "malice grew gradually side by side with civilization."[64]

So, is war natural? Yes, in a manner of speaking, it certainly is. It

61. Ibid., I. xi.

62. Ibid., I. xi.

63. Ibid., I. xxiv.

64. Erasmus, "War is a treat," CWE 35:409–10.

may not be natural if one begins with Cicero's ideal portrait of human nature defined by reason, where conflict is settled by discussion. But it is completely natural if one goes by the evident action and persistent behavior of the species; and this is true to such a degree that the now civilized face of human nature—having incorporated and perfected the arts of malice, including both its weaponry and its rational sense of duty—is, as Erasmus puts it, "quite unable to carry on without wars."[65] To be sure, Cicero aims to bring rational restraint into warfare; but there is in that effort an unmistakable acquiescence to malice and butchery, since restrained malice and rational butchery are quite proper in his view. War and its savagery, in short, have been accepted as serving a greater good; and that good—that "moral purpose," as Stanley Hauerwas puts it—is defined by the interests of the reigning political order.[66] The conditions that Cicero lays down for initiating a war, as well as the stipulations he describes for the conduct for war, therefore, are in the service of what the ruling forces of Rome deem to be their right and just aspirations.[67] In this way, the aggression and butchery of war have been integrated into the heart of what a civilized people can handle rationally and put to good moral use.

Consider, to take just one more example, how easily Cicero contemplates the destruction of a city like Corinth in 146 B.C.E. Recalling that former Roman armies had granted "full rights of citizenship" to some conquered peoples, while razing "Carthage and Numantia to the ground," he writes as follows of Corinth:

65. Erasmus, "A Complaint of Peace," CWE 27:314.

66. Stanley Hauerwas, *Should War Be Eliminated? Philosophical and Theological Investigations* (Milwaukee, Wis.: Marquette University Press, 1984), 3.

67. As Hauerwas puts it, the theory of just war is not a "theory of exceptions" or restraints for engaging in warfare, but "an attempt to limit the destructive potential of war once it is recognized as a moral necessity." It does not "attempt to make war impossible, but rather to make the moral necessity of war serve human purposes." Hauerwas, *Should War Be Eliminated?* 46.

I wish they had not destroyed Corinth; but I believe they had some special reason for what they did—its convenient situation, probably—and fear that its very location might some day furnish a temptation to renew the war.[68]

Though his sentiment shows consideration for a plundered city, Cicero is remarkably composed, even comfortable with the policy and the outcome, even granting and surmising what its rationale must have been. Indeed, he sounds so at peace with war that it would seem quite unnatural not to be engaged in it. In this regard he is a perfect example of the civilized voice of human nature, one that has inculcated both the malice and the restraints of civilization; and he has accommodated himself to the need for war and its violence to such a degree that the ideal of discussion and negotiation are all but forgotten. With this in mind, Erasmus rightly wonders if it is not the fatal malady of human nature to be quite unable to carry on with diplomacy.

Is War Christian?

Is war consistent with the challenges of Christian life, or is it in some manner a degradation of the ideals of love and peace? But if it contradicts these ideals, why is it that Christian history is marked by so much warfare? And, moreover, why is it that Christian theologians have worked so hard to produce moral justifications for war? Perhaps war is part and parcel of Christian life, but can anyone who calls themselves a Christian feel at ease with this statement?

These are sticky questions, no doubt. And they are made sticky—as was the case with the word "natural" in the last section—because the meaning of "Christian" cuts in two directions at once—as the word can signify the ideal virtues of a Christ-like life or it may refer to the actual lives (for better and for worse) of people called

68. Cicero, *De Officiis*, I. xi.

Christian. For Erasmus's part, as we have seen, there is "nothing more wicked" than war; indeed, nothing is "more disastrous, more widely destructive, more persistently ingrained, more unworthy in every respect of a man, not to say a Christian."[69] So hateful and so disastrous, and, too, so completely opposed to Christ's counsel of peace; and yet, Erasmus emphasizes repeatedly, warfare is so "persistently ingrained," and hence, so regularly and artfully practiced by people who think themselves Christian. But Christian scriptures teach one thing, Erasmus insists—"peace with unanimity"—while Christian life, regrettably, is occupied with its very opposite, war.[70] Given this state of affairs, it cannot be too surprising to find a renowned Christian theologian—someone like Thomas Aquinas, for instance—taking upon himself the task of demonstrating that war is not necessarily sinful, but legitimate in Christian life. It would seem, indeed, to be the aim of Aquinas not only to bring the moral wisdom of Christianity to bear on issues of war and peace, but also to accommodate Christian thinking to the warrior culture in which he lives. For Aquinas, most certainly, warfare is a Christian enterprise.

To demonstrate the moral legitimacy of war, Aquinas begins right where Cicero left off, by rooting just war in "the authority of the sovereign by whose command the war is to be waged."[71] His aim in this regard is to defend the sovereign ruler's privileged authority against unjust claims of other individuals or groups. Only the king, Aquinas asserts, who acts "like the soul in the body and God in the world," bears the responsibility to direct a society to its proper (though not its ultimate) end, "to achieve unity in peace."[72]

69. Erasmus, "War is a treat," CWE 35:401.

70. Erasmus, "A Complaint of Peace," CWE 27:303.

71. St. Thomas Aquinas, *Summa Theologiae*, trans. Thomas R. Heath (New York: McGraw-Hill, 1972), II. II, Qu. 40, art. 1; vol. 35, 81.

72. Thomas Aquinas, "On Kingship or the Government of Rulers," in *St. Thomas Aquinas on Politics and Ethics*, trans. Paul E. Sigmund (New York: W. W. Norton, 1988), 26 and 17.

And though he is well aware that the "rule of one man" can easily tilt toward "tyranny"—when the "interest of the ruler is pursued in preference to the common good of the society"[73]—it is, he claims, the sole prerogative of the ruler to "use the sword in lawful defence against domestic disturbances when they punish criminals" and to "use the sword of war to protect the commonweal from foreign attacks."[74] Just war, as Aquinas sees it, requires the official judgment of monarchial power. In saying this, however, a great deal has already been said politically concerning the very specific, and very lethal, power exclusively belonging to kings.

In response, it surely is the case that this condition for just war describes an idealized monarchy where sole power rests in the hands of one individual who is said to care for the "public affairs of the city, kingdom, or province." Such a construct no doubt has been richly appreciated by many supreme rulers who have benefitted from religious legitimation of their policies; and it seems safe to suppose that Louis IX of France and the various kings of Sicily and Naples during Aquinas's life would have expected (and perhaps appreciated) the endorsement coming from the prestigious theologian of the Dominican order.[75] But it must be asked, in this

73. Ibid., 22 and 18.

74. St. Thomas Aquinas, *Summa Theologiae*, II. II, Qu. 40, art. 1; vol. 35, 83.

75. Renowned for his "royal charity and devotion," Louis IX offered considerable financial and legal support to "the two great orders of Friars, the Franciscans and the Dominicans." See William Chester Jordan, *Louis IX and the Challenge of the Crusades: A Study in Rulership* (Princeton, N.J.: Princeton University Press, 1979), 183–84. On a personal level, moreover, there is evidence that Louis's "fondness for the mendicant orders led him to think of himself as something akin to them, [even] as a preacher himself." See William Chester Jordan, "Louis IX: Preaching to Franciscan and Dominican Brothers and Nuns," in *Defenders and Critics of Franciscan Life: Essays in Honor of John V. Fleming*, ed. Michael F. Cusato and G. Geltner (Leiden: E. J. Brill, 2009), 233. During the height of the anti-mendicant movement at the University of Paris in 1255, Louis sent "royal archers" to protect the Dominicans of Paris during the inaugural lecture of a Dominican master. See "Scholars and Friars: A Chapter in the History of Ecclesiastical Strife," *Macmillan's Magazine, Littell's Living Age*, 5th series, vol. 8 (Boston: Littell and Gay, 1874), 304–12. Siding with the mendicant orders,

regard, has the actual conduct of power by the world's assorted supreme rulers ever truly been committed to the interests and welfare of ordinary people? And, for that matter, can any such commitment seriously be said to apply to the monarchies of Aquinas's period? Or has not the common good most often been defined—as Aristotle has it[76]—by the good of the ruler, just as the good of the body is—in the terms of Aquinas—determined by the good of the soul? And, in this light, is not Aquinas's first condition for just war actually designed to protect the sovereign's power, rather than to speak on behalf of the interests or affairs of common people?[77]

Louis finally exiled their chief critic, William of Saint-Amour, from Paris. Upon the return of Aquinas to teach theology at the Priory of San Domenico in Naples, King Charles II also offered legal and monetary support for Aquinas's work. See James A. Weisheipl, *Friar Thomas D'Aquino: His Life, Thought, and Work* (Garden City, N.Y.: Doubleday, 1974), 298–300; and Jean-Pierre Torrell, *Saint Thomas Aquinas: The Person and His Work*, vol. 1, trans. Robert Royal (Washington, D.C.: The Catholic University of America Press, 1996), 249. Though his words giving sole authority for warfare to kings are remarkably free of historical reference, Aquinas cannot have helped but think of the actual kings of his day, especially when they offered so much political and economic support. Minimally one can conclude that Aquinas had no good reason to question and ample reason to support the authority of such kings.

76. As Aristotle writes, the good of the army is "found both in its order and in its leader, and more in the latter; for he does not depend on the order but it depends on him." Aristotle, *Metaphysics*, bk. XII, ch. 10, 1075a, 14–16, in *The Basic Works of Aristotle*, ed. Richard McKeon (New York: Random House, 1941). For Aquinas's exposition of this passage, see Thomas Aquinas, *Commentary on the Metaphysics of Aristotle*, vol. 2, trans. John P. Rowan (Chicago: Henry Regnery, 1961), bk. 12, lesson 12, comments 2630–31, 919.

77. Though the *Commentary on the Metaphysics of Aristotle* is not sufficient evidence that Aquinas agrees with Aristotle's point, it is likely his "personal thought" (as John F. Wippel puts it), where "statements made elsewhere" endorse the point in his own voice. See John F. Wippel, *Metaphysical Themes in Thomas Aquinas*, Studies in Philosophy and the History of Philosophy, vol. 10 (Washington, D.C.: The Catholic University of America Press, 1984), 27. Aquinas uses the image of the army and the general in the same hierarchical sense as Aristotle some fifteen times in the *Summa Theologiae* alone. Such evidence corroborates the argument of Joseph Owens that philosophical ideas such as this are fully in the service of Aquinas's "work of theological wisdom." Joseph Owens, "Aquinas as Aristotelian Commentator," in *St. Thomas Aquinas on the Existence of God: Collected Papers of Joseph Owens, C.Ss.R.*, ed. John R.

It may seem otherwise, inasmuch as Aquinas quotes Psalm 81:4 to suggest that kings should use military force to "rescue the weak and the needy" from "the clutches of the wicked." This biblical allusion, in fact, has little to do with the actual pretexts used by rulers (including those of Aquinas's day) for throwing their countries into war—those "personal grievances between princes," the ethnic or nationalistic hatreds which provide such useful cover for aggression, or even the perceived injustice of a neighboring country's affluence.[78] Contrary to Aquinas, therefore, Erasmus insists that "royalty's duties toward the common good" is defined entirely—and in a strikingly modern and humanistic sense—by the public good; and the latter means nothing but the good of ordinary people, the "peasants and humble citizens, who have no interest in war and gave no occasion for it." No war is just, in the view of Erasmus, if it is launched without the "consent of the whole people."[79] But what merchant, what farmer, what housekeeper will make this choice, unless, that is, they are stirred up by some tyrant of the soul who has been reading the likes of Aquinas?

The second condition for a just war, in Aquinas's view of things, is that there be a "just cause"—"namely that those who are attacked are attacked because they deserve it on account of some wrong they have done."[80] In hearing this, one must grant from the start that, despite the vast range of his thought and despite the intricate detail found in so many sections of his work, the reflections of Aquinas on just war are painfully brief. Indeed, as is the case on many issues in the *Summa Theologiae*, particular "questions"

Catan (Albany, N.Y.: State University of New York, 1980), 1–19. It is precisely this hierarchical notion of authority that undergirds Aquinas's choice of monarchial authority as the first condition for just war.

78. Erasmus, "A Complaint of Peace," CWE 27:314, 314–15, and 306.

79. Ibid., 312 and 313. See also Erasmus, "A Most Useful Discussion Concerning Proposals for War Against the Turks, Including an Exposition of Psalm 28," trans. Michael J. Heath, CWE 64:236.

80. St. Thomas Aquinas, *Summa Theologiae*, II. II, Qu. 40, art. 1; vol. 35, 83.

frequently appear at best to be notes of past debates or blueprints for future disputations. This is understandable, of course, if one keeps Aquinas's own words in mind, where he tells readers that the *Summa Theologiae* is intended for the "training of beginners."[81] This means, therefore, that specific articles in the *Summa Theologiae* cannot fairly be expected to show the kind of precision and thoroughness that one finds in other works of Aquinas.[82] In the present context, consequently, the explanation of what constitutes a just cause for war remains decidedly rudimentary, if not painfully vague. What, we must ask, defines a "wrong" sufficient to justify warfare? For an answer, Aquinas regrettably does not deploy the rich and complex techniques of reasoning found elsewhere in his work; nor, perhaps understandably, does he turn to biblical resources for help. Instead, as is the case often in his statements on war, he merely quotes Augustine to the effect that a cause for war is just if it "avenges wrongs, that is, when a nation or state has to

81. See the Prologue to the *Summa Theologiae*. St. Thomas Aquinas, *Summa Theologiae*, vol. 1, 3. Struck by the range and complexity of Aquinas's work, contemporary readers tend to forget his pedagogical intentions. But, as Leonard E. Boyle has shown, Aquinas began the *Summa Theologiae* at the *studium* at Santa Sabina (something of a "*studium personale*" for Aquinas and select students) as an attempt to "break out of the narrow tradition of practical theology that had hitherto marked the Dominican educational system." See Leonard E. Boyle, "The Setting of the *Summa Theologiae* of Saint Thomas," in *Facing History: A Different Thomas Aquinas,* Textes et études du moyen âge, 13, 65–91, ed. Leonard E. Boyle (Louvain-La-Neuve: Fédération Internationale des Instituts d'Études de Moyen Age, 2000). As Boyle remarks, Aquinas's "summa of general theology" was designed to give "that practical theology a setting which had not been evident in Dominican circles before him."

82. What M.-D. Chenu calls the "stripped-down *Summa*" of Aquinas, while a "masterpiece in the genre characteristic of the School," is not comparable with the more rigorous argumentation of his *Disputed Questions*. M.-D. Chenu, *Toward Understanding Saint Thomas*, trans. A.-M. Landry and D. Hughes (Chicago: Henry Regnery, 1964), 68; see also 298–301. One might think, for instance, of the "relatively brief" space given to the five arguments for the existence of God. See John Wippel, "The Five Ways," in *Aquinas' Summa Theologiae*, ed. Brian Davies (Lanham, Md.: Rowman and Littlefield, 2006), 45. Later reflections on just war in Aquinas often ignore the understandable limitations of the text.

be punished either for refusing to make amends for the outrages done by its subjects, or to restore what it has seized injuriously."[83] While it may be the case that Aquinas intends to restrict the range of legitimate causes for war by citing this passage, it is hard not to be struck by the wide latitude it allows.

It is precisely this moral latitude for aggression that causes the Erasmian concern. For his part, Erasmus is not thinking of the vague generalities of Aquinas, but rather of theologians in his own day who work in the shadow of Aquinas and Augustine, finding in their words the license to fabricate all kinds of flimsy and self-serving excuses for waging war, especially against the Turks.[84] The passage Aquinas quotes from Augustine, after all, gives moral legitimacy to avenging wrongs or inflicting punishment on another nation for failing to make "amends" for "wrongs" committed by its people or for not restoring "what" it has seized. With these conditions in mind, think of all the interminable conflicts that perdure—for generations or even centuries—because of long-held grievances over past wrongs or from age-old and often-told stories of disputed territories; and think, too, of all the malice and savagery issuing from such grievances. In such situations, Erasmus observes, a "whole [list] of wrongs" is vividly recalled and "any benefits received" are quickly forgotten; and as history shows, it only takes a minor event or a cunning manipulator to rekindle these grievances and throw two peoples back into mutual carnage.[85]

83. St. Thomas Aquinas, *Summa Theologiae*, II. II, Qu. 40, art. 1; vol. 35, 83. As Chenu remarks, Aquinas cites Augustine in various ways. Concerning questions of war, clearly, he quotes Augustine for neither "dialectical support" nor as an "ornament," but as an "authority," meaning, as a master whose words sufficiently convey the truth in question. See Chenu, *Toward Understanding Saint Thomas*, 129.

84. See Walter F. Bense, "Paris Theologians on War and Peace, 1521–1529," *Church History: Studies in Christianity and Culture* 41, no. 2 (June 1972): 168–85. On Erasmus's ongoing controversy with the theological faculty of Paris, see James K. Farge, *Orthodoxy and Reform in Early Reformation France: Faculty of Theology of Paris, 1500–1543* (Leiden: E. J. Brill, 1985), 186–196.

85. Erasmus, "A Complaint of Peace," CWE 27:314.

The words of Aquinas on just cause, however, would not inhibit any such conflagration; and, consequently, the door is open wide to both self-deception (a natural enough human vulnerability) and deception (a common political fact). As Erasmus notes, "self-deception" on these matters makes everyone think their cause is just, especially in the "heat of the moment."[86] As for willful deception, what governing power does not think its demands are just? And how many sovereign rulers do not want their subjects to think their cause to be just? Having an Augustine or Aquinas on hand to offer moral legitimacy certainly is in the interests of those who would throw the world into war. Their theories "cloak" the "disease" of war with "respectable names."[87]

For his part, Erasmus seems to concede certain just causes for war, until one notices that the conditions he sets are so impossibly stringent and so unlikely to be fulfilled that no war would ever qualify as just. He says, for instance, that he "would not entirely condemn an expedition against the Turks if they attack us of their own accord"; but then he coyly mentions the unlikely if not impossible condition, as long as "we prosecute the war … in a Christian spirit," which means facing the enemy with a "conduct worthy of the gospel," armed only with the "sword of the gospel word," the "helmet of salvation," and the "shield of faith."[88] A war

86. Ibid., 317.

87. Erasmus, "War is a treat," CWE 35:436.

88. Ibid., 434–35. These points appear again in Erasmus, "A Most Useful Discussion," CWE 64:211–66. Written in 1529 when Vienna was threatened by the troops of Sultan Suleiman, Erasmus suggests that war against the Turks should only be undertaken if it is fought with a "truly Christian spirit." "The best solution of all," he says, "would be to conquer the Turks' empire in the same way that the apostles conquered all the nations of earth for their emperor, Christ." As Michael J. Heath observes, this work is a "parody" of standard pro-crusade literature, as Erasmus's manner of arguing for war is "tantamount to advising against it." See Michael J. Heath, "Erasmus and War against the Turks," *Acta Conventus Neo-Latini Turonensis*, vol. 2 (Paris: J. Vrin, 1980), 991–1001. Insisting that he wants to help Christian culture to fight the Turks "successfully and to win truly splendid triumphs for Christ," Erasmus lays out a series of moral, political, and economic conditions which, if followed, would amount to a

fought with these weapons, Erasmus no doubt chuckles, would not spill a single drop of blood. Elsewhere, too, Erasmus appears to grant certain just causes for war, if—as he says—there is "no way of avoiding it"; but then, once again, he adds that "the full force of the calamities must fall on the heads of those who gave cause for it."[89] Since "princes wage war unscathed," this stipulation surely would dissuade rulers from ever launching wars. Then again, in a similar vein, Erasmus sounds as if he permits warfare where unavoidable, but then quickly demands that the war be conducted in a manner which will "ensure that, being an evil thing, it is the exclusive responsibility of evil people, and is settled with a minimum of bloodshed."[90] Under such a condition, of course, no war would ever be fought, as actual warfare consumes many good people and they are designed for a maximum of bloodshed. With proposals like these, Erasmus will play along with the idea of just causes for war, but only to drive home the senselessness of war.

Aquinas adds, finally, a third condition for warfare to be considered just, to wit, that "those waging war" should be guided by a "right intention"—specifically to "promote the good and to avoid evil." Again recycling words from Augustine, which in turn echo

---

"complete and conspicuous reformation of life ... throughout Christendom." Erasmus, "A Most Useful Discussion," CWE 64:246 and 260. On Erasmus as "the solicitor of a universal and significant moral improvement of Christian life," see A. G. Weiler, "The Turkish Argument and Christian Piety in Desiderius Erasmus' 'Consultatio de Bello Turcis Inferendo' (1530)," in *Erasmus of Rotterdam: The Man and the Scholar*, ed. J. Sperna Weiland and W. Th.M. Frijhoff (Leiden: E. J. Brill, 1988), 37–38. The position of Erasmus quietly dovetails with the stance of Martin Luther that was condemned first by the papal bull *Exsurge Domine* (1520), and then again by the Sorbonne. See Michael J. Heath, "Introductory Note" to Erasmus's "A Most Useful Discussion," CWE 64:205–8.

89. Erasmus, "A Complaint of Peace," CWE 27:312.

90. Erasmus, "War is a treat," CWE 35:438. Erasmus quips that those "who delight in wars, the foulest of men, should have nothing but garlic to eat"—presumably, as Margaret Mann Phillips notes, so as to "make others unmistakably aware of their presence." Erasmus, "Eat neither garlic nor beans," CWE 35:451–52, adage IV. i. 17. See Phillips, *The 'Adages' of Erasmus*, 115.

Cicero, we hear that "the craving to hurt people, the cruel thirst for revenge, the unappeased and unrelenting spirit, the savageness of fighting on, the lust to dominate, and suchlike, all these are rightly condemned in war."[91] Or, additionally, in the reply to the third objection of Qu. 40, art. 1, we find Augustine saying, "we do not seek peace in order to wage war, but we go to war to gain peace. Therefore be peaceful even while you are at war, that you may overcome your enemy and bring him to the prosperity of peace."[92] Here again we find Aquinas, or rather Augustine, echoing Cicero's notion of rational and prudent intention in the midst of battle.

Strangely enough, Erasmus might utter these very words, though he would mean them ironically, knowing that—were they ever to be followed—all warfare would end immediately. In fact, Erasmus observes, actual belligerents are driven by plainer motives and ignoble intentions; "from stupidity or from malice," they are "goaded" by authorities and "rashly" throw themselves into battle, hoping thereby to gain some "small loot" or to achieve some pitiful sense of "nobility."[93] Consider, too, the "loathsome" and "savage" scene of warriors in battle: "their eyes burn, their faces are pale, their step betokens madness, the voice grates, the shouting is mindless, the man is entirely turned to iron; their weapons clang, their cannons spout flashes of lightning."[94] Where in all of this, Erasmus asks, is there any intention to advance the "good" or any sign of being "peaceful … in warring?" Where, indeed, is there anything but a passion to inflict harm, a "cruel thirst for revenge," and an angry spirit? Given the gross opposition between Aquinas's ideal intentions and the actual demeanor of belligerents at war, one might think that this condition for just war might function to challenge military adventures

91. St. Thomas Aquinas, *Summa Theologiae*, II. II, Qu. 40, art. 1; vol. 35, 83.

92. St. Thomas Aquinas, *Summa Theologiae*, II. II, Qu. 40, art. 1; vol. 35, 85.

93. Erasmus, "War is a treat," CWE 35:435 and 422. See, for instance, Erasmus, "Military Affairs," CWE 39:53–63.

94. Erasmus, "War is a treat," CWE 35:406.

or even to condemn warfare. But, Erasmus notes, the power of self-deception turns everything around, so that battles fought in the "spirit of vengeance" come to be understood as expressing a "concern for justice." After all, he asks, "who does not think his own cause just?"[95] Who does not think that they fight to advance some good? And who would not think that way when clergy and theologians insist that all the battle and blood is for the sake of peace. Little wonder that Christian crusaders were able to think of their military mission as sacred expressions of Christian love, as they were told exactly this by popes, canonists, and preachers.[96] Surely they could take solace from Augustine's words, that they were "overcoming" the enemy in order to bring them, dead or alive, into the "prosperity of peace."

In all of this talk of just war, however, there is so much room for evasiveness, deception, and surely also self-deception, as to make one wonder about the sincerity of those who propose such ideas. It seems, sadly enough, that the word "just" has come to refer to "any war declared in any way against anybody by any prince."[97] Such is the extraordinary deference attributed by Aquinas to royal authority. And so, too, it would seem that most any cause for war can be called "just," so long as there is a perception—or even just a memory—of some "wrong" for which amends have not been made. Such is the considerable—and quite deadly, but all-too-common—latitude permitted by Aquinas regarding legitimate causes for warfare. And, finally, it seems that most any warfare can be regarded as "just," as long as the conduct of the war is guided by the intention to "promote the good." But, in all honesty, what people at war does not claim this? Such, therefore, is the vagueness

95. Ibid., 325.

96. Jonathan Riley-Smith, "Crusading as an Act of Love," in *Medieval Religion: New Approaches*, ed. Constance Hoffman Berman (New York: Routledge, 2005), 44–61.

97. Erasmus, "War is a treat," CWE 35:425.

at work in Aquinas's reflections on war. In all of this, however, a Christian ruler who opts for war or a Christian soldier who engages in warfare will find Christian theologians like Aquinas ready at hand with flexible and reassuring moral justifications.

But, additionally, they will find some very carefully crafted readings of biblical passages designed to assuage moral doubts about warfare. How easily, it seems, that biblical texts can be rounded up for support of military policies, or worse yet, "twisted" and bypassed when such texts prove inconvenient.[98] That biblical texts pose a serious challenge, however, is evident from the start of Aquinas's discussion, where the first two objections set forth doubts concerning the morality of warfare. As Chenu points out, such objections invite readers to explore a "question," where some serious conviction is deliberately called into doubt for the sake of a "deeper understanding." In Question 40, therefore, Aquinas begins with a presumption against the morality of war; and, to his credit, he does so because a fuller understanding of these issues requires that one directly face the most difficult opposition possible, which, in this case, is built around some apparently clear-cut biblical sayings of Jesus against warfare. But as Chenu also observes, the boldness with which Aquinas raises doubts does not mean that "there was any real doubt about [the] truths" he hopes to defend, but simply that a fuller understanding demands that the force of such objections be taken seriously.[99]

98. Ibid., 425–26. On Erasmus's critical regard for Aquinas's reading of biblical texts, see Erika Rummel, *Erasmus' Annotations on the New Testament: From Philologist to Theologian* (Toronto: University of Toronto Press, 1986), 77–80. Erasmus was understandably incredulous of the story circulating among Dominicans that St. Paul had appeared during one of Aquinas's lectures on the Pauline epistles in Naples, assuring Aquinas that his account of the epistles was "as adequate as possible in this life." The story comes from the *Historia Ecclesiastica* of Tolomeo of Lucca. See Kenelm Foster, *The Life of Saint Thomas Aquinas: Biographical Documents* (Baltimore, Md.: Helicon, 1959), 135. Those prone to believing such "fairy tales" are prone to believing twisted interpretations to suit the occasion.

99. See M.-D. Chenu, *Toward Understanding Saint Thomas*, 87.

The alternate position announced in the "*Sed contra* [on the contrary]" consists entirely of a quotation from Augustine's "Epistle to Marcellinus." Drawing on Luke 3:14, Augustine notes that when soldiers sought "the salutary advice [in] the Gospel," they were not "told to get rid of their arms and give up soldiering." Rather, Augustine writes, "they were told, do violence to no man, be content with your pay." But as they were ordered to "be satisfied" with their pay, he notes, then "it did not forbid a military career."[100] On this occasion Aquinas lets Augustine do all the talking. No explanation or elaboration is offered, as is not unusual in the "*Sed contra*" passages, the purpose of which is simply to state the alternate position to that taken in the opening "objections."[101] But since the three arguments to follow (Aquinas's "determination" on the question) agree with the *Sed contra*, it is clear that Aquinas is quoting Augustine (who is quoting Luke) as an authority to be heeded. It is, in the end, a biblical passage which is put forth against the biblically-based objections.

What is strange about this text, however, is its passive construction and its opaque reference. In a word, it says "it did not forbid," referring to the "Gospel" itself as the authoritative voice; and yet the passive "they were told" certainly implies a speaker who tells them to "be content with your pay." Augustine and Aquinas certainly knew that the speaker in Luke was John the Baptist, and Aquinas—who, in keeping with medieval Catholic piety, thought John had "a fuller knowledge of the mysteries of faith" because of his proximity to Jesus—certainly would have considered him to be a moral authority worth quoting.[102] And most certainly, in the day of Aquinas, a sovereign keen on military campaigns would be relieved to hear that the Gospel does not forbid military life. But one

100. St. Thomas Aquinas, *Summa Theologiae*, II. II, Qu. 40, art 1; vol. 35, 81.

101. See M.-D. Chenu, *Toward Understanding Saint Thomas*, 44–45.

102. St. Thomas Aquinas, *Summa Theologiae*, vol. 31, trans. T. C. O'Brien (Cambridge: Cambridge University Press, 1974), II. II, Qu. 1, art. 7, reply 4, 39.

has to wonder about Aquinas's move on two counts. First, even in Aquinas's day, is a statement by John the Baptist on a par with one from Jesus? Are the two equivalent moral authorities? Given that the purpose of the *Sed contra* is to announce the position opposing the objections, does this passage hold its own against explicit sayings of Jesus calling warfare into question? Second, why is it that Aquinas and Augustine turn to the John the Baptist of Luke, as opposed to the one portrayed in John? Is it not rather obvious that what they find in Luke (a gospel interested in reconciling Christian faith with life in the Roman empire) is simply what they want to find, whereas John gives them nothing but "the voice of one crying in the wilderness." (John 1:23) Indeed, the context of Augustine's treatment of Luke 3:14 makes clear that his interest is in showing that the "doctrine of Christ" is not in the least "adverse to the State's well-being"; and so, too, Aquinas turns to this passage because he needs an affirmation of military life.[103] If it was really the authority of John the Baptist that determined his selection, then he should have dealt with the varying accounts in the Gospels that do not support his position. In the *Sed Contra*, therefore, it sounds very much like Aquinas (and before him, Augustine) is reaching to find some biblical text to substantiate the position he wishes to defend. "It is ridiculous," Erasmus comments, "when some men seek to prove the validity of warfare on the basis of this passage."[104]

The first two objections constitute a significant obstacle to anyone wanting to make room for warfare in Christian life, and Aquinas surely knows this. In the first case, Aquinas responds to an objection which suggests that "every kind of war is unlawful" on the grounds that the Jesus of Matthew 26:52 says that "all who draw the sword will die by the sword."[105] Aquinas answers,

103. Augustine to Marcellinus, letter 138, in *Writings of Saint Augustine: Letters*, trans. Sister Wilfrid Parsons (New York: Fathers of the Church, 1953), 47–48.

104. See Rummel, *Erasmus' Annotations on the New Testament*, 163.

105. St. Thomas Aquinas, *Summa Theologiae*, II. II, Qu. 40, art. 1; vol. 35, 81.

not surprisingly, with a distinction taken from Augustine—to wit, that "to draw the sword" means to "arm oneself and to spill blood" without the "command" or "permission" of a "superior" or "lawful authority"; whereas, "to use the sword by the authority of the sovereign or judge," or to use it "through zeal for justice, and by the authority, so to speak, of God" is "not to 'draw the sword,'" but to use it as "commissioned by another."[106] How convenient this reading proves to be for the one who wishes to use a lethal weapon in battle, but also wants to sidestep the rather blunt threat from the Jesus of Matthew. All it takes to change the meaning of words, according to Augustine and Aquinas, is a lawful political authority, or even just a "zeal for justice" on the part of a "public person." For them, when a soldier takes up the sword, he is not—apparently—taking up the sword. But who can help but be struck by the willful evasion at work in this bit of exegesis? And who does not notice the defining role played by "rightful authority" in Aquinas's reading of this passage from Matthew? But what, Erasmus asks in another context, "has that to do with the heavenly philosophy of Christ?"[107]

A second example of the twisted arguments in Aquinas comes in the reply to the second objection, where he is confronted with the claim that "war is always a sin" because the Jesus of Matthew 5:39 said not to offer "resistance" to the "wicked man."[108] Here again Aquinas is entirely reliant on Augustine; and, once again, the meaning of the words is diluted and the moral thrust evaded. Paraphrasing Augustine, Aquinas suggests that words like this (from the sermon on the mountain) "must always be borne in readiness of mind, so that a man must always be prepared to refrain from resistance or self-defence if the situation calls for it." And yet, he goes on to say, sometimes it is necessary to set this advice aside and act

106. St. Thomas Aquinas, *Summa Theologiae*, II. II, Qu. 40, art. 1; vol. 35, 83.
107. Rummel, *Erasmus' Annotations on the New Testament*, 164.
108. St. Thomas Aquinas, *Summa Theologiae*, II. II, Qu. 40, art. 1; vol. 35, 81.

otherwise—perhaps to act for the "common good" or "even for the good of his opponents," or as Augustine suggests, to punish someone with a "benign severity."[109] The good Christian, in other words, should keep challenging precepts from the gospel in mind—perhaps as interesting proposals and perhaps at times to be followed—though circumstances likely will warrant policies and actions which are directly opposed to these precepts. Theologians working in the legacy of Augustine and Aquinas, Erasmus observes, habitually regard Christ's counsels of peace as "advice, not instructions."[110] In short, these instructions habitually are ignored.

Put more positively, moral theologians regularly interpret the sayings of Jesus by placing them in a wider framework of competing goods, even if the result dilutes or seems to nullify the original counsel. Such are the "trade-offs" of practical reasoning, as Richard B. Miller rightly calls them, and Erasmus is not immune to making such trades himself when it comes to other stringent counsels from Jesus.[111] Given the structure of Aquinas's "article," it is correct to note that he begins with a presumption against war

109. St. Thomas Aquinas, *Summa Theologiae*, II. II, Qu. 40, art. 1; vol. 35, 85.

110. Erasmus, "War is a treat," CWE 35:425.

111. Richard B. Miller, "Aquinas and the Presumption against Killing and War," *Journal of Religion* 82, no. 2 (April 2002): 186–87. On the question of divorce, for instance, Erasmus readily admits, out of sympathy for ordinary people, but not "as a matter of dogma," to hoping that the church might find a way to interpret "Christ's decrees" as "best may tend to the salvation of men, relaxing here and drawing tighter there, as time and circumstance may require." It is possible, Erasmus observes, that "the spirit of Christ may not have revealed the whole truth to the church all at once," so application and interpretation according to circumstances is only reasonable, something evident in the church's admission of "divorce of a kind." See Erasmus to Jacob Hoogstraten, CWE 7:49–51. It is no surprise, moreover, to find Erasmus interpreting Jesus' injunction to cut off one's hands or feet if they "cause you to sin" (Matthew 5:27–30; 18:8–9) as analogically signifying the "limbs of the mind" or emotions. Such injunctions, in short, are not to be taken literally. And while Erasmus lets stand the injunction against the pursuit of worldly "treasures," he later considered Christian communism of property to be impractical. See Phillips, *The 'Adages' of Erasmus*, 111–12. When it comes to questions of anger, revenge, and hate, however, Erasmus allows the more stringent challenges of Jesus to stand without qualifying

(as Miller argues); but it is stretching things to say (as Chenu does) that Aquinas seeks not to "cast aside" the presumption, but to "underwrite its truthfulness."[112] The aim of the reply is to overcome (or at least to neutralize) the presumption against armed resistance, in deference to another good, one that will be defined by the reigning authority. It is that authority, recall, the authority of the king or prince, who defines the "common good" in his own interests and construes when "punishment" of opponents bears a rightful or "benign" intention. Here again, therefore, as is the case throughout the reflections of Aquinas on just war, we see the central role given to political authority. Such emphasis placed on the sovereign's authority, however, yields dubious readings of biblical texts. "It is with brilliant teachings of this kind," Erasmus remarks sarcastically, "that we feed the greed of princes."[113]

What, in the end, has happened to Christian thinking in Aquinas? Or for that matter, what has happened to war in his hands? A quick answer to both questions: in Aquinas Christianity has accommodated itself to the motivations and passions of a warrior culture; and, through his reflections, war has become a thoroughly respectable and morally legitimate enterprise for Christian life. Aquinas does for Christianity what Cicero did for the classical world's sense of nature: he makes war legitimate and sanctioned, something entirely natural for a civilized people and perfectly proper for a Christian. In this regard it is difficult to see how Aquinas's reasoning has any clear connection to the challenge of peace

application. See Erasmus's paraphrase of these and other injunctions from the "Sermon on the Mount" in *Collected Works of Erasmus: New Testament Scholarship*, vol. 45, trans. Dean Simpson (Toronto: University of Toronto Press, 2008), 98–122. On the efforts of Erasmus to counter the self-serving tendency of "princes and their tame theologians" to palliate the "stringent moral demands of Christ in the Gospel," see James D. Tracy, *Erasmus of the Low Countries*, 108–10.

112. Chenu writes that in Aquinas, "there is an effort to embody the truth that the opposing position contains within a wider framework which, far from casting it aside, underwrites its truthfulness." M.-D. Chenu, *Toward Understanding Saint Thomas*, 96.

113. Erasmus, "War is a treat," CWE 35:425.

that Erasmus sees at the heart of the gospels; or, differently put, it is very difficult to see how warfare has not become an integral focus of this theologian's political task, to construct theories on the basis of which warfare can be considered a righteous Christian enterprise, a service that surely has been appreciated by political authorities over the centuries. No doubt this is why Erasmus has the goddess "Peace" complain that she can find no home among Christians, including—sad to say—among their theologians.[114]

So is war Christian? Yes, in a manner of speaking, it certainly is. It is not Christian if one starts with the gospel of peace which Erasmus finds at the heart of the biblical Christ, and then expects to find something like this in the lives of Christian people. But war is completely Christian if one tends to the evident action and persistent behavior of peoples who call themselves Christian; and this is true to such a degree that Christians engaged in warfare and Christians in the business of justifying its practice should honestly admit that what Christ taught is mostly irrelevant to what they think about war. It is this fact that drives Erasmus so often to issue a blunt challenge to Christian hypocrisy: either cease using the "name of Christian," he says, or "put into practice the teachings of Christ through concord."[115] Though he hopes for the latter, Erasmus is unflinching in pressing the former option. Thus, he asks, "has Christ himself accomplished nothing with his many commandments, mysteries, and parables?" But if, indeed, "Christ achieved nothing, what is the need of so many ceremonies today?" Why the elaborate show if there is nothing to the message of peace? Or again, "if he achieved something that matters, why is he so neglected today, as if all he did was to stage some foolish farce?"[116] But was it, in fact, a foolish farce? If it was a farce, and

114. Erasmus, "A Complaint of Peace," CWE 27:287–99.

115. Ibid., CWE 27:303. Or again, he asks, "how long will their way of life continue to conflict with the name they bear?" Ibid.

116. Ibid., 304.

"Christ is merely a story," integrity would seem to demand that the whole affair be renounced once and for all.[117] If Christ is merely a story, and it would seem that this is the case throughout Christian history and even in the great monuments of Christian theology, then why not just abandon the entire tale as empty myth?

Is War Sane?

Is war sane, or is it entirely mad, beyond the pale of meaning, rationality, and purpose? But if war is beyond meaning (if one can find no sense in it), if in its brutality and carnage it escapes the grasp of reason (if it is impossible to ground it by argument in a manner that justifies and legitimates its pursuit), and if it serves no purpose (if, in the end, its dark savagery leads to no fulfilling end)—if, that is, it fails on each score—then how are sane people (those of us who daily traffic in meaning, who depend on reasons for what we do, and who understand our activities as having one larger purpose or another) to look upon this eerie vacuum? Is it possible to look upon the blood and rage and loss as utterly mad, as a kind of inaccessible darkness, and to leave it at that? Or must war be deemed sane? But if we manage to make it sane, what have we done, and what have we become?

Neither Cicero nor Aquinas would understand these questions. Both have, in their respective manners, come to assume the sanity of war; both certainly find meaning, rationality, and purpose in war. In Cicero's case, war has become entirely natural, something that civilized people can manage in a noble and rational manner. Even plundering cities can be done rationally. For Aquinas, too, war has become morally legitimate as long as its cause and its intention are determined by a sovereign political authority—but those conditions have never been difficult to meet. Erasmus,

117. Erasmus, "War is a treat," CWE 35:438; see also "A Complaint of Peace," CWE 27:304.

however, does feel the force of these questions. So while philosophers and theologians have become accustomed to regarding war as something normal, inevitable, but also manageable and possibly even moral—and, indeed, even an acceptable expression of Christian life—Erasmus works to show one thing: such behavior is simply mad, and those who work to normalize, civilize, and baptize its butchery and carnage are mad in their own right. In fact, he suggests, they may be acting upon a deep-seated passion for war, a kind of exuberance and excitement with the violence, a secret longing and even a love for the meaning and purpose war give to their lives.

Maybe one needs to directly and personally suffer from the effects of war to understand the point of Erasmus. Those of us who live far from war, even from the wars of our own country, are easily seduced through the media's romantic celebration of patriotic heroism or with a fascination with the game-like quality of military technology. Such responses, however, require distance and immunity from the danger, the agony, and the stench of battle, perhaps only sensing widely-scattered personal loss or the indirect impact of war on the economy. No doubt this is why Erasmus gave the words of Pindar to his long adage on war, "War is a treat to those who have not tried it"—though Pindar continues, saying that "anyone who knows what it is, is horrified beyond measure if he meets it in his heart."[118] And Erasmus would agree. War may be filled with meaning and purpose, perhaps even seen as glorious and noble, and certainly, too, regarded as moral and just, for those living and viewing at a distance; but that is not so easy—maybe it is impossible—for those who have seen their towns leveled, markets vacated, homes hollowed, children buried, bodies mutilated, minds terrorized, and futures annulled. For those who have tried it, war is horrifying beyond measure; and its darkness stretches

118. Erasmus, "War is a treat," CWE 35:400.

and strains the narratives of purpose and ideological causes which seek to contain it.

The contemporary French journalist and philosopher Bernard-Henri Lévy is one of the few who has dared to entertain these questions seriously. In the first third of *War, Evil, and the End of History*, Lévy reissues five narratives originally printed in *Le Monde,* which describe his observations and encounters in the "forgotten wars" of Angola, Burundi, Sri Lanka, Sudan, and Colombia.[119] Deliberately avoiding (and, indeed, mocking) the politicized writing of his younger days in Bangladesh,[120] and carefully avoiding the temptation to superimpose one of the "great narratives" of our age on what he encounters, Lévy seeks to say simply and plainly "what really happened down to the smallest detail."[121] As the "engaged traveler" reporting on the "banality of the worst," he focuses on "things and facts"; as journalist, his attention remains on the actual, the local, and the present.[122] What readers receive from this, plainly put, is gruesome and wrenching. The bulk of Lévy's book, however, contains later reflections—his "thoughts [and] images, contemplated with hindsight."[123] Here we find Lévy struggling, sometimes desperately, often with futility, almost always self-critically, to make some kind of sense out of the endless but unseen barbarity of these wars, where people are trapped in "wars without aims."[124] Throughout this process, however, he returns in repeated cycles of self-doubt to concede that there is "something indecent in the act of turning horror into fine phrases."[125] And yet, he insists, it is the

119. Bernard-Henri Lévy, *War, Evil, and the End of History*, trans. Charlotte Mandell (Hoboken, N.J.: Melville, 2004), 4.

120. Lévy, *War, Evil, and the End of History*, 182–98; and then again, 338–44.

121. Ibid., 256–57.

122. Ibid., 6 and 255. Lévy credits Michel Foucault as the "master" of this form of journalism; he calls Foucault the exemplary "diagnostician of the present." Ibid., 257–260.

123. Ibid., 113.

124. Ibid., 4.

125. Ibid., 277.

"role of the intellectual"—or, perhaps he should say, the properly humanistic role of the intellectual—to convey the "faces" of degraded individuals, especially the "victims" and "civilians," though less so the "warriors" and the "strategists."[126] Here, in a word, is Lévy's approach to writing his own "Complaint of Peace."

Lévy's narratives and reflections confront readers with detailed accounts of the desolation and inhumanity of these wars. It is a focus and a concern reminiscent of Erasmus's constant stress on the devastating fallout of warfare on the fields, towns, and peasants of Europe, only now they are named, described in gross detail, and magnified to the point of obscenity. One gets a vivid image, when reading Lévy's accounts, of the desolate landscapes of these countries: the torched fields and coffee groves, abandoned railroads, half-broken bridges, and barely passable roads. But it is the crumbled cities, like those in Angola, which more fully convey the horrifying impact of warfare on people's communal lives. Consider Kuito, having suffered "twenty-one months of siege," its "walls blackened by fire, ... piles of rubble, these sad landscapes, these poor people who have come back home..." to live in "sheet-metal houses or under tarpaulins."[127] Or recall, too, the looted villages of Burundi, "truly looted," Lévy stresses, "when not a tile remains, not a piece of sheet metal or cinder block, ...when an antlike swarm of human activity has scraped off everything, down to the bone and beyond." This is "not a ruin," he remarks, "but a nothingness."[128] It was charred fields and hollowed-out hamlets, recall, which prompted Erasmus to dare the princes of Europe to add up the costs of their wars and weigh them against the relatively small gains to be won. Only now, in the wars reported by Lévy, there is no one to make the calculations.

One meets, too, the fighters of these ghastly wars. They are of-

126. Ibid., 296.

127. Ibid., 15–16.

128. Ibid., 68.

ten thugs wrapped in layers of ideology, like the young Tiger commander who foams "scraps of Maoism, rags of Pol-Potism, a zest of fascist populism," a fascination for the "kamikase," all "marinated" in a "stock of militant and fanatic Hinduism."[129] Or, still in Sri Lanka, they can be children, literally, who are sent "routinely to the front line to spare" the "good regiments."[130] So, too, they can be "honest farmhands," like those Lévy meets in Colombia, these "decent guys" with "childlike and guileless smiles" who welcome Lévy with gracious hospitality; these same fine fellows who perpetrate a massacre at Quebrad Naïn, the peasant woman "crucified in her barn"; "the little girl whose eyes they gouged out before they sent her running, blind, and shot at her like a rabbit"; or "breaking the bones of a man, one by one … before finishing him off with a bullet"; to mention just a few examples.[131] Or, again, surely not a surprise to Erasmus, there are the "genocidal attackers"—the "Hutus of the FNL," the same ones who forced a priest to "eat his own penis before they crucified him … those babies buried alive, those children impaled, sprinkled with gas and burned, in their school, by the principal himself"—who also happen to be "excellent Christians, generally of the Adventist persuasion," and who consequently refrain from spilling blood on their sabbath.[132] More graphic and more perverse, to be sure, but still this is reminiscent of Erasmus's warning that warfare places power in the hands of "blackguards, murderers, [rapists], and thieves"; that it seduces and "inflames" youth; and that—like a "contagious disease"—it sweeps up decent people in its torrent of barbarity.[133] Such a "mass of evils," Erasmus laments, the heart is "loath even to remember it."[134]

One encounters, additionally, the agony of civilian populations, especially on the part of women. Here again we hear Erasmus strik-

129. Ibid., 37.
130. Ibid., 41.
131. Ibid., 299–300.
132. Ibid., 58–59.
133. Erasmus, "War is a treat," CWE 35:437, 435, and 404.
134. Ibid., 404.

ing this same chord, in a way that Cicero and Aquinas never did: what a "pitiable spectacle" it is, he writes, to find "towns in ruins, villages destroyed, churches burnt, and farmland abandoned."[135] But it is Lévy, once again, whose words heighten the agony and despair of the people. We hear, for instance, of civilians in Burundi deliberately placed between the warring parties.[136] And, similarly in Sri Lanka, of common people trapped in a "stranglehold between a fanatical guerilla movement and a barbarous army without principles."[137] The "very image of the desolation of war," however, Lévy finds in the "procession of women" in Sri Lanka," the "villages abandoned by its men where one sees nothing more than abandoned wives and widows."[138] And with that, Lévy observes, there is in these women an eerie "disappearance of laughter, of smiles, of gazes," in a word, the erasure of these centrally human traits which, as much as anything else, give someone their individual personality.[139] Something similar, though more grotesque and more pitiable, appears in Lévy's description of women in Burundi—one woman he observed, "sitting on the ground, almost naked, her breasts dry and flaccid, breast-feeding a child swollen with edema and shivering"; or, too, the "unspeaking, worn-out despair, this end-of-the-world sadness" evident in the "way the women of Bujumbura have of carrying their babies like little corpses."[140] What more indubitable evidence could be found to demonstrate the insanity of the men, the policies, and the strategies of these wars.

And then, finally, there are the dead who fill the pages of Lévy's narratives. There are those dead and buried, of course, in the "huge cemeteries" of Burundi; but, Lévy observes, even the dead are victims of a kind, as their memories too are effaced with the desecration of their grave sites. In the same country, additionally, there

135. Erasmus, "A Complaint of Peace," CWE 27:316.

136. Lévy, *War, Evil, and the End of History*, 54.

137. Ibid., 49.

138. Ibid., 204.

139. Ibid., 207–8.

140. Ibid., 53.

are "mass graves, these ossuaries, these little piles of fresh corpses rotting ... on the edge of a stream, under a vague cover, half devoured by ants and hyenas."[141] Almost at a loss for words, Lévy exclaims, a "desert of bodies, desert of souls."[142] Or, as Erasmus described such deaths in his own day, "the slaughtered lying in heaps, the fields running with gore."[143] Then, too, there are those who are nearly-dead, caught somewhere between life and death, but passing slowly and terribly from the former to the latter. Such is the obscene image Lévy paints of watching three men dying, slowly, absurdly, helplessly, of hunger in Asmara, Eritrea.[144] And, finally, there are the "living-dead of the South Sudan"—"those faces that seemed alive," Lévy writes, "while their eyes were already dead! or those half-dead bodies where it's only the gaze that survived! or those bodies in tatters where you had the feeling that the blood was circulating only in certain zones, the rest already had the blue tint that is a sign that death has begun."[145] Here, in the end, are the consequences of war of which Erasmus complains, only now described in vulgar detail.

Lévy punctuates each of his articles with an eerie suggestion, to wit, that these wars are interminably insane, that they lock their combatants in endless circuits of barbarity, and that they trap their people in a kind of twilight zone framed by misery and death. Angola, Lévy writes, is a "country in tatters, a dismembered, devitalized, lunar space, where everywhere you see traces of war but nowhere its logic, its meaning, or any sign of its end."[146] Similarly with Sri Lanka, where the "insane war" rolls along, with what appears to be a "purely local meaning" of Hindu-Buddhist antipathies, by way of regular massacres of innocent people, all with the "indifference

141. Ibid., 228.
142. Ibid., 229.
143. Erasmus, "War is at treat," 403–4.
144. Lévy, *War, Evil, and the End of History*, 351–52.
145. Ibid., 247; see also 211–12.
146. Ibid., 18.

of the nations and of great international institutions."[147] Burundi, too, with its genocidal convulsions between a Tutsi army and Hutu militia, is something of a "black hole," a "density of infinite suffering for a rarefied place, compacted in on itself, on the way to effacing itself."[148] This war, Lévy comments, is "the most insane of the insane wars."[149] There is also the war in South Sudan, twenty years old with two million dead, and four and a half million displaced, upon Lévy's writing in 2001, where "Sudan's oil" (the ostensible reason for the violence) and "Sudan's dead" (the countless victims) are "mingled" in a deadly cauldron tainted with ideological, ethnic, and religious hatreds. In the midst of this war, Lévy writes, stand the decimated Nuba people, "the great forgotten ones" whose "disappearance wouldn't affect the world's economy in the least."[150] Colombia, lastly, whose war—perhaps more than any other—has been "reduced to [a] clash of criminals and puppets, clones and clowns. Degree zero of politics. Height of buffoonery and depth of naked, unadorned violence, reduced to the bone of its bloody truth."[151] It is here, Lévy notes, where they appear to fight for "no other purpose than the struggle for power, the appropriation of goods and wealth, the triumph of a mafia, traffickers."[152]

Lunar space, insane war, black hole, forgotten ones, and zero degree of politics—who can make sense of these terms? So, Lévy asks, do these wars have meaning? Are they in the service of a cause or purpose? Is there any way to make sense out of what is happening? After all, Lévy notes, there have been times "when people fought for God" (the "traditional wars of religion") and times, too, "where people fought for ersatz Gods" ("wars between nations, races, classes").[153] But in Angola, Colombia, or Burundi, neither rationale seems to fit. So is it possible that there could

147. Ibid., 49 and 156.
148. Ibid., 68.
149. Ibid., 156.
150. Ibid., 97 and 109.
151. Ibid., 89.
152. Ibid., 156.
153. Ibid., 145.

be wars, long wars, immensely lethal ones, savage through and through, that find no culmination, serve no principle, and receive no redemption? If there are such wars, Lévy rightly notes, then we are up against the "very limits of the thinkable," the zenith of madness, Erasmus would suggest, "this idea of a war *for nothing*."[154] And yet, in his typically persistent and honest style, Lévy wonders whether these wars really have so little sense. "The Hindu fanatic who devotes his life to beating up Buddhists ... the South Sudanese Dinka bent on his war against the Nuer," he asks, "is it so completely certain that these viewpoints have no meaning?" Perhaps it is just that their accounts are not "familiar to us."[155] And yet, he counters, even the victims look on these wars as insane, and they are convinced that the outcomes "will change nothing of their fate."[156] Then, again, he wonders whether past wars recorded by history truly had "so much more 'meaning' than those today"; perhaps it just depends on the "point of view"—whether seen from a distance, experienced as a fighter, or suffered as a peasant.[157] Perhaps, as Erasmus suggests, all wars are insane. Is it possible, in the end, that even the wars which purport to be for something, maybe especially those wars, create the greatest lunar space and leave the most forgotten ones in their wake?

At this point Lévy is at his most interesting, precisely where he is most perplexed by the senselessness of the forgotten wars. What is left, he asks, if all this carnage has no meaning? His answer: an "exhausted humanity" resident in black holes; or again, complete "ruins," not like those sites which "testify to the past" (as memorials) and not like those that promise the "Annunciation of some kind of new world order," but "absolute ruins," without memory and without theodicy.[158] We are left with the "extremity of the horror"—"inaccessible to redemption," with "no function"

154. Ibid., 129–31.
155. Ibid., 148.
156. Ibid., 150.
157. Ibid., 147 and 165–66.
158. Ibid., 214, 250, 122, and 120–21.

in the structure of the world, and "incapable of bearing witness."[159] Perhaps, Lévy muses, these wars mark the "end of history," though certainly not in the sense intended by Kojève and Fukuyama.[160] Now, Lévy suggests, as a dark parody of its original meaning, the end of history yields not fullness, but vacuity; not blessed animality, but savage bestiality; "not happiness but horror."[161] The end, moreover, occurs not in Moscow or Berlin, but on the "outskirts of the world," in places like Burundi or Colombia; its scope, additionally, is not universal, but local and "piece-meal"; and, oddly enough, Lévy suggests, these ruins may not be the end at all, but "the place where history can well up and return with a vengeance."[162] However it is expressed, Lévy insists, it is important to try to understand and convey the inaccessible darkness that swallows entire populations.[163]

And yet, despite everything Lévy has said about the insanity of war, he nonetheless admits a certain "nostalgia" for wars with a cause, a purpose, and a clear meaning. While all wars are "atrocious," he writes, he wonders wistfully whether there is not a "dividing line" between wars that "make place for greatness (roughly, the 'just' wars, the 'antifascist' wars)" and those "where not the least move toward greatness is brought about."[164] In the forgotten wars, he suggests, there is no noble service of a transcendent cause; whereas in the other wars, the ones for which he feels nostalgia—"Spain, the Resistance, and even Bosnia"—despite the horror, the

159. Ibid., 248.

160. See Alexandre Kojève, *Introduction to the Reading of Hegel: Lectures on the Phenomenology of Spirit*, trans. James H. Nicols (Ithaca, N.Y.: Cornell University Press, 1980); and Francis Fukuyama, *The End of History and the Last Man* (New York: Macmillan, 1992).

161. Lévy, *War, Evil, and the End of History*, 231–33.

162. Ibid., 229–30, 242, and 239. Thus, Lévy writes, "is it really unimaginable that such unhappiness, humiliation, despair, will one day be converted into resentment, into hatred, and find the technical means to express itself?" Was that Afghanistan? Might it be Somalia or Yemen or Syria? Ibid., 239.

163. Ibid., 290.

164. Ibid., 166.

mud, the waiting, the bestiality that are also their lot, men do in fact sometimes touch on something that surpasses them."[165] Even in saying this, however, Lévy remains keenly suspicious of the urge to romanticize war and its effects;[166] and, too, he is self-conscious of the danger that his own fascination with barbarity might give rise to an "aura of romanticism, a glimmer of lyricism."[167] And yet, one cannot help but detect a certain obsession with warfare, not certainly the kind of "exultation" with evil Lévy enjoyed in his younger days,[168] but a definite longing for the clarity and moral certainty available in those wars that gave rise to "greatness" and which can put us in touch with something transcendent.

In response to this noble euphoria, Erasmus would counsel caution. The attraction of greatness and the lure of transcendence easily lead to self-deception regarding the cause or purpose of warfare; and, too, they surely elide the sacrifices, the dangers, and the disasters incumbent on military campaigns. So, Erasmus suggests, weigh "as in a balance" the military gains against the human costs, remembering the grotesque agony of people trapped in wars, and one might find that "hardly any peace is so unjust that it is not preferable to war, however just that may be."[169] Directly contrary to this, Lévy yearns nostalgically for wars fought with "a necessity, since the alternative to this war would be, not peace, but hell."[170]

165. Ibid., 166.

166. Ibid., 117–19. Consider Lévy's distinction between a romantic grammar of warfare and one that honestly reflects the reality of the experience. Ibid., 157–63.

167. Ibid., 245.

168. Ibid., 197.

169. Erasmus, "A Complaint of Peace," CWE 27:310–11. See also "War is a treat," CWE 35:430, where Erasmus drops the qualification, simply declaring that "an unjust peace is preferable by far to a just war." Interestingly, the dictum comes from Cicero. See the letter where Cicero writes following the outbreak of warfare between Caesar and Pompey: "what opportunity of either warning or remonstrating did I ever let slip, feeling as I did that a peace even on the most unfavourable terms was preferable to the most righteous of wars?" Cicero, *The Letters to His Friends*, vol. 1, trans. W. Glynn Williams (London: William Heinemann, 1927), VI. vi. 6, 457.

170. Lévy, *War, Evil, and the End of History*, 126.

He hopes, in fact, that his "country, Europe" will remember "this nostalgia, if, by chance, a new adversity comes to threaten it."[171]

It is not surprising, therefore, to find Lévy rejecting pacifism, and—in turn—defending the idea of just war in the present age. Indeed, "the failure to make a claim for even the idea of just war," he argues, "was responsible for the non-intervention of the West and, thus, for the prolongation of the siege of Sarajevo, and for its rows of murdered civilians."[172] With this example in mind, therefore, he defends military action for the sake of "freedom" against the "enemies of freedom."[173] It is worth fighting and dying, he insists, when noble ideas—like "liberty or equality"—are at stake; and it is foolish "absurdity"—one that denies that war is a "given of the human condition"—to think that war can be eradicated, or that treacherous adversaries can be dealt with peacefully. With respect to the forgotten wars, Lévy suggests, western governments must act "to defend civilians, first of all … to penalize war crimes, next," but also to "conduct ourselves, in these wars, as warriors of thought, to try to think as war does, that's to say to take the side … not just of the groups alone, but of the ideas that wage war through people." That means, for Lévy, acting in defense of "liberty, right, [and] universality."[174] With respect to "international terrorism and the terrible threat it imposes on democracies," it is the obligation of western powers to "take responsibility of naming the adversary and [to] provide ourselves with the means, at once military, political, and moral, to conquer him."[175] Lévy's nostalgia for clarity of purpose and the greatness of cause find resolute expression in this endorsement of military interventions in regional conflicts worldwide; and it guarantees apparently unlimited support for what is now called the "war on terror."

In response, Erasmus likely would be sympathetic, but he most

171. Ibid., 166.
172. Ibid., 128.
173. Ibid., 176–77.
174. Ibid., 315–16.
175. Ibid., 314.

certainly would be dubious as well. Erasmus himself, after all, was not a dogmatic pacifist. He takes a more approving view, as he puts it, of "men who repel the violent attacks of barbarian invaders by their whole-hearted and loyal determination, and protect the peace and security of their country at their own peril."[176] But Erasmus knows far more than most that even a just war—those fought for "liberty, right, [and] universality"—will not avoid the insanely grotesque and treacherous consequences of the campaign. Indeed, what seems to be truly a war of necessity; what appears to be a war with a truly just cause; and what may even be a victory for that cause; and perhaps, therefore, what is something to be celebrated, still, with all that granted, it remains mad. Why? For all the reasons given by Erasmus and then magnified by Lévy: the savagery, terror, anguish, and death produced by warfare, the very things Erasmus no doubt witnessed in all the inconsequential villages of Europe, the same things again reported by Lévy in his forgotten wars, and, too, the same thing that will result from—what Lévy proposes—the ongoing war on terror and military interventions in countless wars around the world. So it is not the case that just wars are sane wars. And though Lévy seems to understand this, in his nostalgic enthusiasm for wars fought for great causes, he goes silent on the insane consequences incurred even in just wars. But what, one must ask, about the "enormous suffering" of the forgotten ones in our current wars around the globe, the very ones supported by Lévy?[177] And what, too, of the "cruel suffering inflicted on so many thousands of peoples," as western powers (to which Lévy offers his support) "take revenge on a few, or even on one person"?[178]

So is war sane? No, war is not sane—not at all, not in the least, never; though it proves insanely difficult even for serious people not to want to find a way—from a distance, in a theory, far from

176. Erasmus, "A Complaint of Peace," CWE 27:314.

177. Erasmus, "War is a treat," CWE 35:435–36.

178. Ibid., 427.

the actual experience—to rationalize it (ground it in a reason), romanticize it (dressing it up in noble tales), or justify it (rooting it in a grand purpose or higher meaning). From the way it is treated, one would think that people think war is quite sane; or even—odd as it may seem—that they bear a certain love for it. And it is this love—this nostalgia—which ultimately drives Lévy's thinking. What makes Lévy so compelling, in the end, is that he faces the madness of warfare with brutal honesty, but then pulls back to embrace the great cause to legitimate noble wars. To be sure, he is not in a hurry to find reasons for war (as was Cicero); nor will he stand for romantic talk of battle; nor, finally, is he ready to place his trust in some rightful authority (as was Aquinas). And yet he steps back, opting for the perspective yielded by distance, embracing one of those great narratives he earlier rejected for daring to "give a meaning to what had none, namely to the infinite pain of men."[179] What makes Lévy's work so powerful, however, is the vivid immediacy with which he describes the fear, stench, and pain of war. It is the "essence of war," he says, to be trapped in an "absurd hell where one continuously wonders where one is."[180] But this is precisely what is not seen, he insists, by the "omniscient observer, a general for instance, or, what amounts to the same thing, a novelist";[181] or, we might add, by the journalist-philosopher who has shifted ground in order to view human conflicts through a universal lens, that being, "the ideas that wage war through people," and to appraise them according to the "eternal life of [these] ideas."[182] In making this move, Lévy falls in line with the others who would justify war, a stance and an argument that surely are appreciated by the French administration and NATO officials.

179. Lévy, *War, Evil, and the End of History*, 3.

180. Ibid., 294.

181. Ibid., 295.

182. Ibid., 315–16.

Erasmian Proposals

Erasmus poses three chilling questions concerning war; and, though the nature and form of war has changed over the centuries, they are as unsettling in our day as they were in his. Is it the fatal malady of civilization that, in its ever-so-rational environment, we have become comfortable and confident in our ability to manage warfare; so much so, indeed, that we now find ourselves quite unable to carry on without wars? Have people who fancy themselves Christian become so adept at diluting and side-stepping what seem to be the more difficult demands of the biblical Christ that they now feel quite comfortable and amply Christian in embracing the militant policies and legitimations of civic authorities? Are those who have taken the horror of war seriously, who have taken an unflinching look at the brutality and carnage of war, and yet—perhaps from despair, perhaps, too, from nostalgia—stepped back and embraced a noble cause which will make sense of the madness of war, are these people driven by a latent longing—or even a love—for the sense of transcendence yielded by wars dedicated to a great cause? These are truly unsettling questions, because they cut open and expose the possibility that we are not the creatures we thought we were, and perhaps also, that we are not the creatures we might like to be. Have we become people who cannot live without war, who suffer no religious inhibitions about warfare, and who finally love war and the meaning it gives our lives?

The Erasmian questions apply especially to the intellectuals of war, which, in the course of this meditation, means Cicero, Aquinas, and Lévy. The questions just posed, after all, speak not just to the soldiers and generals but to those serious minds who reflect on the rationality and legitimacy of war. In this regard, Cicero is the voice of realism, posing little resistance but plenty of legitimation and good feeling to military campaigns; how commonplace is this realism in our culture, this official self-confidence in managing conflicts with restraint, even cleanly. Aquinas is the voice of assurance that one can still be quite faithful to the ideals of a religious tradition while setting every severe moral challenge aside; how many churches appear quite comfortable with these adjustments to the gospels? Lévy is the voice of hesitant doubt, still clinging to a nostalgia that he also distrusts, insisting that some military campaigns serve a greater good, despite the horror of war that he has witnessed so closely; how many intellectuals make a similar appeal to the transcendent "ideas that work through people" to endorse military actions? Over and against these positions, Erasmus stresses the unmanageable irrationality of warfare, its illegitimate savagery and carnage, and all the atrocities and chaos of war. Why, given these things, is there such a need to rationalize, legitimate, or affirm war? Why not declare that it is thoroughly irrational, illegitimate, and irredeemable? From all the efforts given to defending war, it almost seems that the right to fight had been threatened, and thus needs defense and legitimation; though, curiously, despite the carnage and chaos of war, no such need is felt to defend peace.

Erasmus hopes that it all might be different, and that there might be a different way of thinking about these issues. So the flip side of these questions leads us to ask: might it still be possible for people to live without war? Might people still employ those capacities for rational and civil discussion, enough perhaps to mediate disputes with negotiation? Is it still conceivable that people who would be Christian might take seriously the counsels of peace in their scriptures, enough perhaps to muster the resolve to organize nonviolent responses to injustice? And, finally, is it possible that people might in some manner come to hate war, just enough to cast a shadow of doubt on the apparently great causes which would warrant war? Certainly one will be thought irrational for asking these questions, unrealistic for making these proposals, maybe even inhumane for doubting the legitimacy of war. In the end, as Erasmus acknowledges, his challenges call into question the sanity of others; but this is, of course, purely the complaint of one madman to many others.

In "Charon," one of Erasmus's many charming colloquies, we come upon the ferryman of the underworld "dripping wet." Alastor, who has brought him news of the "hellish dissensions" among the living, wonders if perhaps he was returning from a bath. On the contrary, Charon replies, his boat capsized in the middle of the Stygian swamp, overloaded as it was with the shades of dead warriors. As Charon tells Alastor, he is all too aware of the furious wars and epidemic of hostility which consumes people among the living. Business has been very good in the realm of the dead. In fact, he now is working to get a "good, strong trireme ready," as shades fresh from war are not light, especially as they come loaded with both "debauchery and gluttony" and "bulls, benefices, and many other things," or at least the heavy dreams of such things. At the same time, Charon tells his visitor, he has heard that "there's a certain Polygraphus up there who's incessantly attacking war with his pen and urging men to peace." Alastor tells Charon not to worry: though this man has written a certain "Complaint of Peace," it has had little effect. Indeed, Alastor says, "he's sung to deaf ears this long while"; and, besides, there are more influential preachers in the world who teach that "war is just, holy, and right." On that note Erasmus takes a hearty and healthy laugh at himself and his praise of peace, but also at the business of war and the final destiny of those who would legitimate it.[183]

But, as can be expected from Erasmus, this is a serious laughter, a laughter laced with ironic challenge both for those who persist in trying to legitimate warfare and, too, for the one with the

183. Erasmus, "Charon," CWE 40:818–30. A common lament, Erasmus writes, "not even the misfortunes of so many years have taught us to hate war, nor do we even now at long last begin to think about peace, which ought to be perpetual between Christians." Erasmus, "The Phrygians learn wisdom too late," CWE 31:76–77, adage I. i. 27.

audacity to question both its practice and those who would give it legitimacy. Though lighter and more playful than "A Complaint of Peace," this dialogue of the dead still manages to convey in miniature form the ironic thrust at the heart of Erasmian thinking. It takes its digs, quite naturally, at the violent perpetrators of hell on earth; they may have had their glory in earthly battles, but now they find themselves awash in an underworld swamp. But "Charon" also exposes the madness of the one who questions the sanity of war. In so doing, he shows that he knows full well just how outrageous it is to raise and push this questioning of war to the limit. Are we civilized people really the creatures we think we are, or have we, in fact, in being civilized, become addicted to war? Given the prevalence of war, and, too, the readiness of Christian intellectuals to justify it, would it not be more honest just to come right out and admit that Christ is nothing more than a story? Is anyone, in the end, really serious about a life of peace and an ethic of love? Or again, given the ghastly consequences of war, what would spur supposedly sane and rational people to so regularly and so eagerly resort to war? Do we, in fact, harbor a secret longing, even a perverse love for war? Raising these questions is daring and pressing them to the limit is outrageous, for if anyone were truly to take them to heart, they would prove terribly unsettling and highly disruptive—at least to those able to listen. Knowing, however, that his ironic questioning is no match for those who give legitimacy to war, Erasmus also raises the doubly-eerie specter that not only might we be oblivious to our addiction, contented in our hypocrisy, and ignorant of our perversion, but worse yet, that ironic truth-telling about war and peace ultimately may be futile in the face of both the smooth-talking sophists and the unflinching rigorists of church and court.

Erasmus is not—strictly speaking—a pacifist. It is true, of course, that he certainly sounds like one, with his vehement denunciations of warfare and his endless appeals for peace; and, thus, it is understandable that both supporters and critics would come to call him a pacifist.[184] But, as we have seen repeatedly in these meditations, nothing is ever simple or one-sided for Erasmus. There is always, as Walter Kaiser notes, a "qualifying *but* to any argument," and this capacious and dialectical sensibility is very much at work when Erasmus speaks of war.[185] It is true, of course, as Phillips puts it, that one often finds in Erasmus a "wholesale and wholehearted denunciation of war"; and yet, as she also notes, he draws back from a "complete pacifism" because—perhaps with a "vein of pessimism" or a "sense of helplessness"—he understands that there will be wars.[186] But more than this, Erasmus is keenly aware of the all-too-real pressures and threats which can force a people to war, which is why he shows sympathy for defensive war, why he does not play down the threat posed by Turkish forces, and why—in the end—he never flatly rejects warfare altogether. His manner of thinking, in short, is not intent on shoring up unbending principles, biblical or otherwise, in the face of pressing realities, which is why Erasmus refused to associate himself with the pacifist thinking among the Anabaptists, or for that matter why he seems to distance himself from Luther's early rejection of resistance against the Turks.[187] Nor, in the same vein, is it correct to criticize Erasmus for being naive about politics or overly optimistic regarding the possibility of securing peace.[188] He simply is not the pacifist these critics take him to be.

184. Among sympathetic scholars emphasizing the pacifism of Erasmus, see Olin, *Six Essays on Erasmus*, 17–28. Among those criticizing the pacifism of Erasmus, see José A. Fernández, "Erasmus on Just War," *Journal of the History of Ideas* 34, no. 2 (April–June 1973): 209–26; and Pierre Brachnin, "*Vox Clamantis in Deserto*: Réflexions sur le pacifisme d'Érasme," *Colloquia Erasmia Turonensia*, vol. 1 (Toronto: University of Toronto Press, 1969), 247–76.

185. Kaiser, *Praisers of Folly*, 93.

186. Phillips, *The 'Adages' of Erasmus*, 114.

187. In "A Most Useful Discussion," CWE 64:232–33, Erasmus seeks to distance himself both from warmongers who are "fired up for war on the Turks" and from "those who think that the right to make war is denied totally to Christians."

188. As Tracy shows, Erasmus was "surprisingly well informed" of the politics of his day. See James D. Tracy, *The Politics of Erasmus*, 125.

But it equally is the case that Erasmus is not a proponent of just war. It is true, here again, that he at times sounds like he is making concessions to the reasoning which deems war necessary and just. Indeed, he frequently lists—often in fairly conventional fashion—the criteria for just wars, including last resort, self-defense, protection of civilians, consent of the people, and probability of success.[189] Critics have jumped on these passages, some happy to catch Erasmus in self-contradiction and others to express relief that he finally has accepted the necessity of just wars.[190] Such responses, however, miss the point of Erasmus's thinking on war. Ultimately, as we have seen, Erasmus rejects the notion of just war, or more precisely, he engages the logic of just war only to undermine the entire manner of thinking—first, because (as we have seen) it is impossible to resist the temptation of deception and self-deception when handling the various criteria for just war, especially when the entire discussion (even that of scholars) ultimately serves the purposes of the powerful; second, as the history of wars makes all-too-clear, because it simply is impossible to satisfy the conditions set for justifying warfare, at least if these conditions are taken seriously; and third, because the cataclysmic costs to human beings of all sorts make the gains of most wars seem paltry.[191] Odd as it may seem to his critics, it is the realism of Erasmus which destabilizes and unwinds just war thinking—the knack for reading

189. In addition to "The Complaint of Peace" and "War is a Treat" discussed earlier, see Erasmus, "The Education of a Christian Prince," 27:282–88; "The Soldier and the Carthusian," CWE 39:333; and "A Most Useful Discussion," CWE 64:234–36.

190. Missing the ironic tenor of Erasmus's words, Fernández takes great delight that "in spite of himself Erasmus has joined the ranks of those who defend the theory of just war." See Fernández, "Erasmus on Just War," 209–26. In defense of Erasmus's consistency, see Ross Dealy, "The Dynamics of Erasmus' Thought on War," *Erasmus of Rotterdam Society Yearbook*, vol. 4, 1 (1984): 53–67.

191. As Michael Howard notes, it is "primarily on the grounds of *humanity* that Erasmus condemns war, not those of religion." See Michael Howard, *War and the Liberal Conscience* (New York: Columbia University Press, 2008), 7. This is true with one significant qualification: for Erasmus, humanism is at the heart of authentic religion.

the psychological mechanisms of deceit and self-deceit; the keen percipience of the hidden motivations driving political powers; the blunt insistence to come to terms with the long historical record of unjust wars; and, most importantly, the humane sensitivity to the enormous costs of war for ordinary people. In each of these ways, Erasmus challenges readers to squarely face up to the nonsense, the irrationality, and indeed the madness of just war thinking. To say the least, Erasmus does not fit well in the just war tradition.[192]

In the end, the Erasmian approach to questions of war and peace constitutes an independent line of thinking about war and peace. It is a third track that is reducible to neither pacifism nor the theory of just war; and it gets its independence from the distinctive manner of thinking that—as we have seen throughout these meditations—is capacious and agile, inherently dialectical, and relentlessly ironic. To think in an Erasmian manner about war is not a matter of standing firm in the defense of principle, nor is it concerned with questions of justification; to think along with Erasmus means, rather, to push and prod with relentless questions and proposals, in order to unsettle the common assumptions and disrupt the reigning dogmas current in the cultures of war in which we live. It is a manner of thinking, finally, that is intent on prying open our lives and showing us who we are, and perhaps, too, who we might be. Have we become people who, in being civilized, cannot live without war; who, in professing a Christian faith, suffer no religious inhibitions about warfare; and who finally, despite knowing full well the carnage and sadness involved, actually love war and the meaning it gives our lives? But if this is the case, how sane is that? "How," Erasmus asks, "can we believe that people are

192. Roland Bainton is close to the mark when he notes that, though the thinking of Erasmus "moved within the framework of the traditional just-war theory," he brings this approach to thinking about war "very close to disintegration." Roland H. Bainton, "The *Querela Pacis* of Erasmus: Classical and Christian Sources," *Archiv für Reformationgeschichte* 42 (1951): 45–46.

in their right mind when they can ensure peace with little trouble yet prefer to resort to war?"[193] With this question we come face to face with the ironic upshot of Erasmian thinking on war: though broadly ethical in purpose, the queries of Erasmus shift the focus to—what he calls—our sanity or our madness.

Asked with a kind of stark and even brutal realism, we are left with a truly eerie reflection of ourselves as crazed, deluded, and deadly creatures. We are left, in short, if the force of Erasmian irony has been fully ingested, wondering who we are and what we have become; doubting our own self-understanding and all the comforting rationalizations our culture gives to us and our wars; questioning whether we are seeing things as clearly as we had thought; and perhaps, too, beginning to think that our fascination and addiction to warfare might make us some of the oddest, most bizarre, and lethal creatures ever to walk the earth. Might we be so mad as to actually need and love war, even as we fancy ourselves civilized and Christian? At which point, face to face with the uncanny truth of ourselves, Erasmus would hope that we might begin to ponder whether we can make our way through the world differently, in peace, such that people of all sorts might flourish. But there is no suggestion that there is an easy way out of our madness.[194]

193. Erasmus, "War is a treat," CWE 35:415.

194. Reinhold Niebuhr, a leading Protestant ethicist of the twentieth century, criticizes modern Christian pacifists (calling them "heretical") for absorbing the "Renaissance faith in the goodness of man, having rejected the Christian doctrine of original sin." Their error, and hence, too, the error of Renaissance thinkers, presumably including Erasmus, is to reject the idea "that man remains a tragic creature" who can find "some easy way out of the human situation of 'self-alienation'" without "divine mercy." The mistake, Niebuhr contends, is to believe "that man is essentially good at some level of his being," and thus that it is possible to "eliminate human selfishness and the consequent conflict of life with life." Reinhold Niebuhr, *Reinhold Niebuhr: Theologian of Public Life*, ed. Larry Rasmussen (Minneapolis, Minn.: Fortress, 1991), 240. Given the full force of Erasmian irony, which calls us to face the dark perversity of human existence, it is difficult to see Niebuhr's sweeping indictment of this "Renaissance faith" as anything but a caricature born of archaic reformation hostilities.

Third Meditation

Pleasure and Religion

WERE THERE ever to truly be peace between peoples, were the simmering hatred and sizzling conflicts that embroil human life with incessant violence and terrifying carnage ever to be replaced with peaceful coexistence or even genuine friendship, well then human beings would stand a chance of truly flourishing—that is, of living happy lives filled with abundant pleasures. This is the claim—or perhaps too, the dream—that Erasmus puts forth through the persona of the goddess of Peace; and it is one that finds a central place throughout his reflections on war and peace. It is, moreover, not just that the absence of warfare is itself pleasurable, though a certain line of philosophers will argue just that; but more precisely, for Erasmus, that the abatement of violence clears the way for many good things to follow, the sum of which just might fill life with a host of pleasant things. Peace is, we are told, the "source of all human happiness"; it is the condition for the possibility of all that for which people might rightly hope in a good life—an ample prosperity, stable security, happiness in full, replete with sweetness and pleasures of many kinds.[1]

But how exactly are we to think of these goods? To begin with, what makes for prosperity? Is it solely monetary and material, or might there be other kinds of treasures to be had? What, moreover, constitutes security? And security from what, or from whom? How, too, are we to think of happiness? As a general term for human fulfilment it is overwhelmingly positive, but what does it entail? More specifically, just what sweets might we expect, and for what pleasure might one hope? In sum, what exactly can and should be hoped for, or, as the philosophers of old used to ask, what is the final good of human existence? And, specifically, what kind of goods would peace between armed nations allow? These are truly interesting questions, and certainly, too, they are important for our very existence; and yet, as many have found, they are notoriously difficult. For starters, therefore, let us focus the question a bit by briefly looking at the history of philosophy and religion, taking note therein of the wide gap between those who renounce and those who embrace the life of pleasure.

Focusing the Questions

Plato was right, it seems, when he has Socrates argue that an author can capture the comedy and the tragedy of life in writing.[2] It was after a long night of talk and drink, toward daybreak we are told, when Socrates sought to make this point, all the while sharing a large vessel of wine with Aristophanes and Agathon. The groggy Aristodemus reports that the famous comedian and the celebrity poet were "forced to go along, although they were getting drowsy and hardly following" the argument made by Socrates. But surely the argument must have been good, and in any case the proposal truly is intriguing. Consider, after all, how many different things are

1. Erasmus, "A Complaint of Peace," CWE 27:293.

2. Plato, *Symposium*, 223d.

found to be worthy of a life's love; and recall on how many different levels these characters seek the fulfilment of their lives. One is satisfied with ordinary goods (Phaedrus), while another takes the greatest pleasure from his professional authority (Eryximachus). One of the most thoughtful seeks the joys of drafting clever comedies (Aristophanes), while another revels in popular celebrity of the most shallow sort (Agathon). Then again, one lives in hot pursuit of the bodies of young boys (Pausanias), while another craves intellectual conversation with the same lads (Socrates), one of whom is consumed by the desire for power and fame when he is not dreaming of a night with Socrates (Alcibiades). What a wild display these characters perform! How comical it is to see them going in so many directions at once. But, too, there is tragedy in their loves and the pleasures they pursue—certainly for Socrates and also for Alcibiades, if not for the others. So perhaps Plato has managed to weave the comical and the tragic together in one piece, eliciting from readers both a knowing laughter and an agonized sense of dismay; though admittedly it remains an intriguing challenge to understand how we might think in both manners at once. What an odd juxtaposition, but how thought-provoking as well.

People do, in fact, go crazy over their chosen pleasures. Indeed, they are mad in their loves and demented in their desires. Recall as evidence what Erasmus puts forth in *The Praise of Folly*—truly a teeming collection of loves and an abundant catalogue of madness. One man is brainsick in love with a woman who seems unaware that he exists; an aged woman—so "cadaverous" one would think she was just back from the grave—finds the "utmost pleasure" in wild love for a young man; while a young woman dreams up mad schemes to seduce an octogenarian in order to grab his fortune when he dies.[3] One contented fellow relishes the daily shows in the theater, though the stage in fact is empty, while a self-

3. Erasmus, *The Praise of Folly*, 76–78.

important teacher is possessed with his domineering power, though the classroom is filled entirely with children.[4] Foolish monks go crazy over the special titles reserved for their religious order, while more worldly types "preen themselves on the empty title of nobility."[5] A nobleman is obsessed with hunting wild game and what "exquisite pleasure" he gets when butchering the quarry, while the hearts of gamblers "leap up and throb as soon as they hear the clatter of the dice."[6] One poor idiot fools himself into thinking "he can get rich by refinancing and buying on credit," but no less crazed is the banker who makes the loan, all the while knowing he will never be repaid.[7] Meanwhile, a would-be saint is unhinged with piety, shunning all thoughts of pleasure and giving away all his property, while another impressively adorned with the miter and crosier of a bishop runs amok with love of money.[8] Academics with "beards and robes" are obsessed with the hare-brained dream of concocting an exact system of natural philosophy, while well-churched theologians are inebriated with binding renditions of orthodoxy.[9] What vehemence all this is! In so many, many ways do we lose our minds in the pursuit of pleasure! To be sure, much of this is funny and laughable, and yet many forms of madness are certainly treacherous and some seem downright unhealthy. Our lives, in short, are a comedy of loves, and yet certainly also a tragedy for many. So how are we to think coherently about the divergent loves of human beings? What a demanding coincidence of opposites—at once both comical and tragic.

In one respect, the history of philosophy and religion is an extended effort to bring some sense to all the things people desire. Above all, many have felt the need to bring order to the odd array of human loves; and few have been willing and even fewer have been able to deal with the uncertainty entertained by Plato in

4. Ibid., 58–59 and 79–80.
5. Ibid., 99 and 67.
6. Ibid., 60–62.
7. Ibid., 78.
8. Ibid., 132 and 110.
9. Ibid., 85–86 and 87–97.

the *Symposium* or the zany plurality displayed by Erasmus in *The Praise of Folly*. So much of western philosophy and religion, consequently, becomes a protracted debate over what desires are acceptable and what goods should not be desired; over what goods are superior and which ones are inferior; over what loves should be encouraged and which ones ought to be discouraged; and, I should add, over what pleasures might be permitted and which ones should be prosecuted. The most basic set of conflicts, and hence, too, the most fundamental division, is between those animated by the desire for transcendence from earthly existence and guided by a stern abstinence from bodily pleasures; and those more at ease with worldly life and—within certain limits—happy to embrace its varied pleasures. The former regard the latter as derelict, mired in a prison of false goods, and tragically pursuing pointless lives; while those at ease with what natural life has to offer view the former as deluded, seduced by the promise of empty fantasies, and tragically abstaining from the goods of real life. So who is right? And how might we negotiate their choices?

Christianity, throughout its formative centuries and well into its maturity, has pursued the former path—advising one degree or another of asceticism and fostering an overriding thirst for transcendence. Armed with a fundamental distinction between "things seen" (the "flesh") and "things unseen" (the "spirit") found in the letters of Paul, and inspired by the lure of transcendence widespread in the Platonic culture of Hellenism, early Christian writers typically warn of the grave dangers of bodily pleasures while focusing attention on an eternal home with God.[10] Such a view finds extreme form in the desert fathers—think of Anthony the Great (and all those who would flock to the desert after him) imitating Christ with disciplined austerity and cultivated self-sacrifice; and, too, re-

10. Echoes of Paul's language in I Corinthians 4 and II Corinthians 5 are ubiquitous in early church literature; and recall the influential praise of transcendence in the speech of Diotima in Plato's *Symposium*. See Plato, *The Symposium*, 210a–212d.

call the exhortation to martyrdom coming from someone no less brilliant than Origen of Alexandria.[11] To suffer and even to die, in their view, is a good thing, when it is done with an eye on eternity, in imitation of the savior on the cross. But an ascetic impulse is at work, as well, in the most renowned "fathers" of the church—including, for instance, Ambrose, Gregory of Nyssa, and Tertullian—notably where they struggle mightily to grant some meager legitimacy to sexuality and marriage, even while they regard sexual abstinence (the holy state of "virginity") as the only truly noble lifestyle suited for our eternal destiny.[12] And, indeed, this posture remains in play in the more nuanced work of Augustine, someone who insists that the body is a created good worthy of respect, and yet nonetheless remains terribly uncomfortable with bodily appetites—especially those welling up in the "organs of sex."[13] This displeasure with plea-

11. On the rise and development of ascetic monasticism, see Peter Brown, *The World of Late Antiquity: AD 150–750* (London: Harcourt, Brace, and Jovanovich, 1971), 96–112. Concerning the desert fathers and their ascetic search for "renunciation and detachment," see Douglas Burton-Christie, *The Word in the Desert; Scripture and the Quest for Holiness in Early Christian Monasticism* (Oxford: Oxford University Press, 1993), 192–208 and especially 213–45. For an eloquent eulogy on the "eagerness for martyrdom," see Origen's "An Exhortation to Martyrdom," in *Origen: An Exhortation to Martyrdom, Prayer and Selected Works*, trans. Rowan A. Greer (New York: Paulist Press, 1979), 41–79.

12. On the "practice of permanent sexual renunciation" in early Christianity, see Peter Brown, *The Body and Society: Men, Women and Sexual Renunciation in Early Christianity* (New York: Columbia University Press, 1988). For representative examples, see Ambrose, "Concerning Virgins," trans. H. de Romestin, with E. de Romestin and H. T. F. Duckworth, in *Nicene and Post-Nicene Fathers,* Second Series, vol. 10, ed. Philip Schaff and Henry Wace (Grand Rapids, Mich.: Eerdmans, 1955); Gregory of Nyssa, "On Virginity," trans. William Moore and Henry Austin Wilson, in *Nicene and Post-Nicene Fathers, Second Series*, vol. 5, ed. Philip Schaff and Henry Wace (Grand Rapids, Mich.: Eerdmans, 1955); and Tertullian's address "To His Wife," trans. S. Thelwall, in *Ante-Nicene Fathers*, vol. 4, ed. Alexander Roberts, James Donaldson, and A. Cleveland Coxe (Grand Rapids, Mich.: Eerdmans, 1954), especially book 1.

13. See Augustine, *Concerning the City of God Against the Pagans*, trans. Henry Bettenson (London: Penguin, 1972), book 14, chapters 1–13, for Augustine's argument that the origin of sin rests with the misdirected will and not some innate defect in the body. And yet, too, see book 14, chapters 23 and 26 for Augustine's insistence that

sure, however, becomes a war on pleasure—and, in turn, an actual embrace of pain—in the cult of suffering practiced by Peter Damian (and his followers) in the eleventh century; and it appears again in the heated praise of suffering found in some of the most impressive mystics of late medieval Christianity.[14] In one way or another, there is in all this a surprising, even vehement, discomfort with what the world has to offer. Those of this mind-set appear ill at ease in their own skin, with their bodies, with life itself. They would rather live beside—or perhaps outside—themselves, in something grander and greater than can be conceived. What unimaginably great good they pursue, or so they say; and yet, it must also be said, how much of the natural pleasures of everyday life they forego.

In the ancient world, the alternative view is most clearly heard from Epicurus and his followers. The starting point for Epicurus is the fact that human life is wracked with physical pain (the "cry of the flesh") and stirred by psychological agitation (anxieties and fears of all sorts); and his goal is to convey a way of understanding the world and an ethical prescription that might allow people to live with less pain (and possibly with some pleasure) and with less

---

procreation in paradise would have occurred "without the allurement of passion," but strictly under the will's control; and take note of chapter 24 for Augustine's fascination with rare feats of mental control over the body.

14. Willful infliction of pain on one's own body found a ready home in the Benedictine world of Peter Damian, as well as in the "flagellant brotherhoods" of the late Middle Ages. See Niklaus Largier, *In Praise of the Whip: A Cultural History of Arousal* (New York: Zone Books, 2007), 35–71, for numerous examples of "self-flagellation and other forms of castigation" as "everday ascetic practice" in "late medieval spirituality." On Peter Damian's advocacy and defense of self-flagellation as an ascetic practice, see Largier, *In Praise of the Whip*, 75–100. Examples are to be found in Peter Damian, *Letters*, vol. 2, trans. Owen J. Blum and Irven Michael Resnick (Washington, D.C.: The Catholic University of America Press, 1989), notably letter 44, particularly the section on Dominic; and letter 45, where Damian praises one "who while punishing his flesh with blows, wins back by his suffering the reward he had lost through carnal pleasure." On the more general rendering of suffering, pain, and illness as integral moments in the religious quest of medieval mystics, see Bernard McGinn, *The Flowering of Mysticism: Men and Women in the New Mysticism, 1200–1350* (New York: Crossroad, 1998).

anxiety and fear (and possibly with a sense of calm).[15] The key to the Epicurean system, in a nutshell, is to realize that everything that is, is reducible to atoms and void; and thus that our world and our lives are nothing but atoms running through a never-ending course of configuration, dissolution, and re-ordering. This means, therefore, that there was no original creation (as the conjunction and separation of atoms is infinite and eternal); that the world we know is not alone (since atoms are capable of forming an unlimited number of worlds); that devastating events in the world, like lightning, whirlwinds, earthquakes, and hail, are not the acts of angry gods (such mythic tales are incongruent with the blessedness of the gods, and meteorological phenomena of all sorts are simply the product of natural forces); and that there is no incorporeal and immortal soul which must face the threat of divine judgment (as death is the complete dissolution of body and soul, after which there is nothing left but atoms making their way toward some new configuration).[16] Knowing all this, Epicurus tells us repeatedly, allows people to escape the frightening grip of mythic tales, and instead to live their lives on the basis of a clear and well-founded grasp of the world as it is, expecting nothing less than it has to offer nor fearing anything more than is possible.[17]

The good life for the Epicurean is one shaped by sensible choices between competing desires that are conducive to the "health of the body," while not undercutting the "freedom of the soul from

15. "The Vatican Collection of Epicurean Sayings," 33, in *The Epicurus Reader: Selected Writings and Testimonia*, trans. Brad Inwood and L. P. Gerson (Indianapolis, Ind.: Hackett, 1994), 37. On the therapeutic use of arguments in Epicurus, see Martha C. Nussbaum, *The Therapy of Desire: Theory and Practice in Hellenistic Ethics* (Princeton, N.J.: Princeton University Press, 1994), 102–39.

16. Epicurus, Letter to Herodotus, 34–83, *The Epicurus Reader*, 5–19.

17. See Epicurus, Letter to Pythocles, 120, *The Epicurus Reader*, 28. In the same letter, myth is defined as "irrationality and groundless opinion." Letter to Pythocles, 87, *The Epicurus Reader*, 19. The antidote to myth, for Epicurus, is a firm grasp of the principles of his system verified by one's own immediate experience. See, for instance, Epicurus, Letter to Herodotus, 82, *The Epicurus Reader*, 18.

disturbance." As Epicurus writes to Menoeceus, "we do everything for the sake of being neither in pain nor in terror"; or, put more positively, everything should be done for the sake of pleasure and tranquility.[18] And with that note we come face to face with the resolute hedonism at the heart of this philosophy: bodily and social pleasures are goods to be embraced and relished. At the same time, that does not mean that every pleasure and any extent of pleasure is a wise choice. The "pleasures of the profligate," Epicurus warns, things like "drinking bouts," "continuous parties," and "extravagant table" are self-destructive, bringing on more pain than pleasure and generating ever more tension. The good life, therefore, is one filled with abundant but appropriate pleasures, and the key to realizing this goal is the "sober calculation"—what Epicurus calls "prudence"—which carefully measures out the reasons for "every choice and avoidance."[19] What results is a prescription for living that—more than any other philosophy in the ancient world—counsels people how to live well and at ease with bodily existence in the natural world; and, within certain limits, to embrace life's varied pleasures as fitting goods.

None of this could sit well with early Christian writers. Though it is true that the latter made good use of Epicurean strategies whenever it suited their purposes, there is no shortage of Christian invective aimed at Epicurus and his ideas. In the late second and early third centuries, for instance, when Epicureanism still retained a visible footprint in Roman culture,[20] Clement of Al-

18. Epicurus, Letter to Menoeceus, 128, *The Epicurus Reader*, 30. For a discussion of Epicurean hedonism, see Norman Wentworth DeWitt, *Epicurus and His Philosophy*, (Cleveland, Ohio: Meridian Books, 1967), 216–48.

19. Epicurus, Letter to Menoeceus, 131–32, *The Epicurus Reader*, 30–31.

20. On Epicureanism in the period, see John Ferguson, "Epicureanism under the Roman Empire," revised and supplemented by Jackson P. Hershbell, in *Aufstieg und Niedergang der römischen Welt: Geschichte und Kultur Roms im Spiegel der neuern Forschung*, vol. 2, pt. 36, no. 4, 2286–311. See also Michael Erler, "Epicureanism in the Roman Empire," in *The Cambridge Companion to Epicureanism*, ed. James Warren, 46–64 (Cambridge: Cambridge University Press, 2009).

exandria could appeal positively to Epicurus's well-worded invitation to philosophy, yet complain sharply that the Epicureans were atheists who denied providence while deifying pleasure.[21] With these charges Clement echoes the litany of misgivings widely heard in Christian circles—to wit, that Epicureans reject creation, deny providence, ignore divine judgment, and doubt eternal life; and, worse yet, they willfully embrace natural life and all its pleasures. In their view, therefore, Epicureans are gluttons, perverts, and fools for chasing after the ephemeral pleasures of the world; or worse, as Ambrose would put it, they are purveyors of that very poison which had caused the fall from paradise.[22] For their part, the Epicureans must have been amazed at the Christian discomfort with life itself, and alongside that the strange obsession with tran-

21. See Clement of Alexandria, "The Stromata, or Miscellanies," in *The Ante-Nicene Fathers*, vol. 2, ed. Alexander Roberts and James Donaldson (Grand Rapids, Mich.: Eerdmans, 1951), book 4, chapter 8 on the exhortation to philosophy; book 1, chapter 1 on Epicurus as the leader of atheism; and book 1, chapter 11 on Epicurus as the one who abolishes providence and deifies pleasure. In Clement's view, God gave philosophy to the Greeks "as a covenant peculiar to them," though the "impiety and voluptuousness of Epicurus" are weeds in the divine garden. See Clement, "The Stromata," book 6, chapter 8. Alternatively, in "Against Jovinanus," Jerome could brand Epicurus as the "patron of pleasure" (book 1, chapter 48) and yet note with respect his restrained and simple way of living (book 2, chapter 11). See Jerome, "Against Jovinianum," in *Nicene and Post-Nicene Fathers of the Christian Church*, Second Series, vol. 6, ed. Philip Schaff and Henry Wace (Grand Rapids, Mich.: Eerdmans, 1954), 385 and 396. For an overview of the often surprisingly positive uses of Epicurean ideas, both acknowledged and unacknowledged, in the largely anti-Epicurean thinking of early Christian literature, see Richard P. Jungkuntz, "Christian Approval of Epicureanism," *Church History* 31(1962): 279–93.

22. For Ambrose, the Epicurean view of pleasure is refuted by Holy Scripture, for the latter teaches us "that pleasure was suggested to Adam and Eve by the crafty enticements of the serpent. If the serpent itself is pleasure, then the passions of pleasure are changeable and slippery, and are infected, as it were, with the poison of corruption. It is certain, then, that Adam, deceived by the desire of pleasure, fell away from the command of God and from the enjoyment of grace. How, then, can pleasure call us back to paradise, when by itself it deprived us of paradise?" Ambrose to the church at Vercelli, letter 59, in *Saint Ambrose: Letters 1–91*, trans. Mary Melchior Beyenka (New York: Fathers of the Church, 1954), 326.

scending worldly life altogether. Perhaps, in response, they would repeat what Epicurus said to the person who wishes to escape life as quickly as possible. "If he really believes what he says," Epicurus wryly suggests, "why doesn't he leave life? For it is easy for him to do, if he has firmly decided on it."[23] Surely many church fathers would deserve such a riposte, with all their negativity toward life. But what, too, could a late-surviving Epicurean say when hearing someone no less esteemed than Augustine praise the value of fear, while dismissing the most ordinary of pleasures as sordid?[24] What a strange cult, the Epicurean surely would think, that insists upon fear and renunciation as a prescription for human life.

To say the least, we have a serious clash of perspectives on our hands. How strange these two parties find each other! What disparate worlds they seem to inhabit, and what antithetical prescriptions they offer humanity. Though a religious huckster such as Lucian of Samasota's "Alexander" might lump Christians and Epicureans together as allied foes of his bogus cult and fake prophecies—"out with the Christians," Alexander would shout; and "out with the Epicureans" the deluded people would reply—their differences override any strategic similarities.[25] Indeed, the early fathers of the church were correct—oddly enough—in their antipathy to-

23. Epicurus, Letter to Menoeceus, 126–27, *The Epicurus Reader*, 29.

24. See Augustine, "On the Fear of God (Sermon 348)," in *Saint Augustine, Sermons 341–400* (III/10), vol. 1, ed. John E. Rotelle (New York: New City, 1995), 91–94. Working from Romans 11:20, Augustine writes, "Because he thinks highly of himself, you see, and for that reason does not fear, his never being afraid is of course something dangerously destructive, since it means he is not set on a solid foundation, but being blown by puffs of pride." In fact, Augustine suggests, lacking fear leads to criminal behavior. For Augustine, additionally, the Epicureans' lack of fear is based on "the love of the most sordid pleasure." Far better, Augustine argues with reference to Psalm 19:9, is a "fear of the Lord, which is chaste, abiding forever and ever."

25. Lucian, "Alexander the False Prophet," *Lucian*, vol. 4, 225. On Lucian's sympathies toward Epicureanism, capped off with a Cynic dig at the false prophet, see R. Bracht Branham, *Unruly Eloquence: Lucian and the Comedy of Traditions* (Cambridge, Mass.: Harvard University Press, 1989), 181–215.

ward the Epicurean, at least insofar as they rightly perceived that Epicurean physics and ethics represented the antithesis of what Christianity had become. Other forms of Hellenistic philosophy could be integrated into the fabric of Christian thinking, but—as we have seen above—Epicureanism represented a uniquely dangerous foe to its ascetic vision of human life. So what are we to make of this impasse? Each finds the other laughable, and each regards the other's loves as tragically defective. But is not their impasse itself rather laughable? And, too, is not their opposition yet another expression of the tragic fragmentation of human desires? Is this impasse so fundamental as to be definitive of human life? Or is there, indeed, a way to think about the rival loves of humanity cohesively?

It is against this backdrop—the deep and wide rift between Christian asceticism and Epicurean hedonism—that Erasmus works to answer the fundamental questions concerning the quest for happiness. What can human beings hope for? What good should they desire as the proper goal of their existence? Without doubt the replies of Erasmus proceed within a Christian framework shaped by close familiarity with Pauline and Augustinian theology.[26] It is not surprising, therefore, to find Erasmus using the term "Epicurean" in the standard, negative fashion; though before too much is made of that, it should not be forgotten that he could also speak of Christians in a decidedly negative manner when faced with corruption

26. See, for instance, Erasmus, "The Handbook of the Christian Soldier," especially CWE 66:65–67, where he lays out a strict division between the "intelligible" and the "visible" worlds. As he puts it, "perfect piety is the attempt to progress always away from visible things, which are usually imperfect or indifferent, to invisible." Or as he writes earlier, in stock Platonic language, the soul is to turn inward away from the body, and "remembering its heavenly origin," it "strives upwards with all its might and struggles against its earthly burden." Erasmus, "The Handbook of the Christian Soldier," CWE 66:41. For a basic survey of these standard divisions of existence inherited by Erasmus, see David Marsh, "Erasmus and the Antithesis of Body and Soul," *Journal of the History of Ideas* 37, no. 4 (October–December, 1976): 673–88.

in the church.[27] Elsewhere, however, Erasmus strangely breaks with the anti-Epicurean mold so common in Christian tradition. In "The Epicurean," for instance, the last of his many *Colloquies*, he has "Hedonius" claim that "there are no people more Epicurean than godly Christians." Spudaeus is shocked at such a proposal, as he thinks of Christians as people who "wear themselves out by fasting and bewailing their sins." Indeed, he claims, Christian life is "as far as possible from pleasure."[28] And he is right, of course, if one thinks in the terms set by the fathers of the early church and developed within the monastic and mystical traditions of medieval Christianity. So the claim of Erasmus is startling, to say the least.

Oddly enough, however, Erasmus made roughly the same claim in "On Disdaining the World," a text written when he was only twenty years old and residing in the monastery he soon would find to be suffocating. A stock form of monastic writing, it repeats the familiar warnings about life in the world and the deadly pleasures of the flesh, only to turn abruptly to claim that monastic life is a "paradise of delights." Indeed, he writes, Christian monks "live wholly by the rule of Epicurus."[29] But how odd and unexpected is this, and what a wild suggestion. But what exactly does it mean? It would seem, on the face of it, to undermine the very theological heritage within which Erasmus works. Or has he seen a way beyond the impasse of Christian asceticism and Epicurean hedonism? Something new is afoot. To get a sense of what Erasmus has in mind, consider next the shape and merit of this strange propos-

27. For negative uses of the word "Epicurean," see Erasmus, "The Antibarbarians," trans. Margaret Mann Phillips, in *CWE* 23:75; and Erasmus, "The Handbook of the Christian Soldier," CWE 66:89.

28. Erasmus, "The Epicurean," CWE 40:1075.

29. Erasmus, "On Disdaining the World," trans. Erika Rummel, CWE 66:165. In speaking of the monastery as a tranquil garden and paradise, R. Bultot observes, the young Erasmus taps into a "traditional theme of monastic spirituality." See R. Bultot, "Érasme, Épicure et le 'De Contemptu Mundi,'" *Scrinium Erasmianum*, vol. 2, ed. J. Coppens (Leiden: E. J. Brill, 1969), 221–26.

al, now listening more intently to what he has to say in "On Disdaining the World" and "The Epicurean," set against the backdrop of various other options for handling the same impasse.

Variations and Options

When it comes to Epicurus and his philosophy, there are two constants in the ancient sources—the first is Epicurus's dogmatic self-certainty, and the second is his opponents' dogmatic disdain for Epicurus. The first makes it rather difficult for the modern reader to warm up to this ancient philosopher, whose followers regarded him as something of a savior; the second makes it hard to separate out his true views from the generally misleading (if not slanderous) accounts passed down by his critics. But, read carefully, Epicurus appears to be saying something eminently sane. His is a philosophy designed to equip people with intellectual tools for sorting through difficult questions in life on their own. Again and again he encourages his followers to memorize the basic principles of his system, and in light of these principles to judge all questions with recourse to the direct evidence of personal experience.[30] Doing so, this philosophy promises, allows people to be on guard against all notions of religious transcendence that threaten or degrade human life in the natural world; and hence to escape (what Lucretius calls) the clutches of the "priests and all their dark religion"—meaning, that way of living based on fear and trembling before ominous powers and rooted in repression of the body and denigration of the mind.[31] Put positively, Epicureanism is a philosophy designed for the "health of the soul."[32] It hopes, in a word, to promote a way of living and thinking which is stable and free, on the basis of which people might flourish as happy creatures within the limits of natural existence.

30. See, for instance, Epicurus's Letter to Herodotus, 35–38, *The Epicurus Reader*, 5.

31. Lucretius, *On the Nature of the Universe*, trans. Ronald Melville (Oxford: Oxford University Press, 1997), book 1, 6.

32. Epicurus, Letter to Menoeceus, 122, *The Epicurean Reader*, 28.

An Epicurean life remained a viable option in the world of ancient Rome, something clearly at play in the free and eclectic poetry of Horace. Calling himself a "pig from Epicurus' herd," Horace gives voice to a happy and balanced hedonism.[33] "Different things and crazes grip mankind," he observes, but whatever the chosen pleasure—whether it be food, money, sex, or fame—people have a terrible time finding a "mean in living," thereby generating a good deal more pain than pleasure.[34] Echoing Epicurus, therefore, Horace counsels a life of abundant yet balanced pleasure. Such a view, of course, found plenty of opposition from other schools of philosophy. In one of several dialogues of Diogenes, for instance, Stoic-Cynic philosopher Dio Chrysostom counsels ascetic renunciation when faced with the seductive lure of pleasure, a formidable adversary he says, who "deceives and casts a spell with baneful drugs."[35] And no doubt the Platonist philosopher Plotinus is thinking of Epicureans when he describes those philosophers who give so much priority to the world of the senses that they become "like the heavy sort of birds who have taken much from the earth and are weighed down by it and so are unable to fly high although

33. *Horace's Satires and Epistles*, Ep. I. 4. 16. Horace cites the Epicurean Philodemus explicitly in *Satires* I. 2. 120–22 and obliquely in *Satires* I. 2. 92. As part of the circle of friends, including Virgil, Plotius Tucca, and Varius Rufus (*Satires* 1. 5. 40 and 1. 10. 81), Horace may have had contact with Philodemus and the Epicureans near Naples, though there is insufficient evidence to think that Horace studied with Philodemus. See Robert Cowan, "Introduction" to *Horace's Satires and Epistles*, (Oxford: Oxford University Press, 2011), xii–xiii; and A. Tsakiropoulos-Summers, "Horace, Philodemus and the Epicureans at Herculaneum," *Mnemosyne*, 4th series, vol. 51, fasc. 1 (February 1998): 20–29.

34. *Horace's Satires and Epistles*, Ep. I. 1. 81 and Sat. I. 1. 106.

35. Dio Chrysostom, "The Eighth Discourse: Diogenes or On Virtue," in *Dio Chrysostom*, vol. 1, trans. J. W. Cohoon (London: William Heinemann, 1932), 389. Described as a feminine force, pleasure is said to "undo men through sight, sound, smell, taste, and touch, with food too, and drink and carnal lust, tempting the waking and the sleeping alike." Dio's Diogenes counsels listeners to give pleasure the "widest berth possible," for it is "impossible to dwell with her for any length of time without being completely enslaved." *Dio Chrysostom*, 389–91.

nature has given them wings."[36] As mentioned above, exactly the same notes—at once ascetic and bent on transcendence—are heard from Christian sources in their dissent from the Epicurean worldview. In all of this, there would seem to be no middle ground between the hedonist and the ascetic.

However, a third option does appear, quite surprisingly, from the hand of Augustine, and then again from those who work under his influence in later centuries. Despite his deep-seated anxieties regarding the appetites of the body, Augustine makes a crucial distinction which allows him to grant a relative value to worldly appetites. As he puts it, only the supreme good (eternal life with God) should be truly "enjoyed," as this is the one place where one can truly rest one's heart and find lasting peace.[37] Everything else in life—all the goods and pleasures that human existence has to offer—may be "used" but not (strictly speaking) "enjoyed." This means that natural goods might be embraced as yielding a relative pleasure, but only insofar as they are taken so as to refer beyond themselves to that one peace which "shall be so perfect and so great as to admit of neither improvement nor increase."[38] Natural goods (and the pleasures they yield), therefore, need not be shunned, as would be advised by a strict asceticism; rather, Augustine suggests, they should be used in a limited but significant manner—partly as "supports" to help with the "burdens" of bodily life, but more importantly as pointers or steps oriented to that one transcendent Good that is to be "desired for its own sake."[39] What we receive from Augustine, therefore, is a kind of mitigated asceticism, one that makes it possible to affirm the value of worldly goods (and the pleasures they yield), but only if that value is made to point beyond the good in question. True felicity, even in this

36. Plotinus, *Enneads*, V. 9. 1, in *Plotinus*, vol. 7, trans. A. H. Armstrong (Cambridge, Mass.: Harvard University Press, 1984), 287.

37. See Augustine, *Concerning the City of God Against the Pagans*, 864 and 871.

38. Ibid., 865.

39. Ibid., 877 and 843.

option, ultimately requires transcendence of natural existence, the very thing to which the Epicurean stands opposed. So the impasse between the Epicurean and the Christian perdures despite Augustine's moves to order lesser goods toward the highest one.

A similar approach is taken by Anselm of Canterbury in a rarely noticed set of chapters toward the end of the "Proslogion." Anselm's work is dedicated to lifting the mind above the limits of human finitude to conceive the infinite greatness of God's being. The most well-known effort in this regard is the so-called ontological proof of God's existence in chapters two and three, though the entire text is comprised of apophatic exercises in the service of mystical contemplation. In the closing chapters, however, we find a series of exercises—clearly inspired by Augustine—where Anselm imagines and accentuates the immense contrast between the pleasure taken from worldly goods and the enjoyment received from the divine creator. As he puts it, "if there are many great joys in enjoyable things," and the suggestion is that in fact there are a great many such joys, then "how rich and how great must be the joy [to be found] in Him who made these enjoyable things."[40] Natural goods, in other words, provide a stepping off point for imagining that Good than which no greater good can be imagined. Take any good, he suggests, whether it be beauty, strength, longevity, melody, intoxication, friendship, power, honor, security, and even pleasure; and then, with an imaginative leap to the transcendent, consider how much greater each of these goods would be in the God who is the origin and fullness of these things.[41] Since Anselm's focus rests

40. Anselm of Canterbury, "Proslogion," in *Anselm of Canterbury*, vol. 1, ed. and trans. Jasper Hopkins and Herbert Richardson (Toronto: Edwin Mellen, 1974), 109. On Anselm's "Proslogion" as a "piece of mystical theology" culminating in the joy of contemplating the divine, see Anselm Stolz, "Anselm's Theology in the Proslogion," in *Many-Faced Argument: Recent Studies on the Ontological Argument for the Existence of God*, ed. John Hick and Arthur C. McGill (New York: Macmillan, 1967), 183–206, especially 190–91.

41. Anselm, "Proslogion," 109–111.

squarely on the transcendent, he spends little time disparaging the value of natural goods, though—as with Augustine—all such goods have worth only insofar as they prove useful in pointing beyond themselves toward mystical felicity. Here again, therefore, we find a Christian position—more mystical in its aim but still in line with the Augustinian approach—that remains fundamentally at odds with an Epicurean perspective.

Less than a hundred years after Anselm, however, a novel proposal appears from the hand of John of Salisbury, a secretary to successive archbishops of Canterbury and one of the most creative philosophical figures of the Renaissance of the twelfth century. Typically stressing the practical and political side of philosophical questions, John's works are saturated with references to classical literature and philosophy;[42] and that includes—for the purposes of this meditation—a fresh and rather daring approach to the challenge of Epicurus. On the one hand, John endorses Jerome's negative branding of Epicurus as the "exponent of pleasure," and yet he also applauds the restraint in diet attributed to Epicurus; and, for his part, he thinks Epicurus suffered the "stigma of infamy" largely because of the "foul herd that followed him."[43] Despite this concession to the personal character of Epicurus, John persists in arguing that "the garden of the Epicureans" has its source in "lust"—for wealth, for personal gratification, for self-sufficiency, and for emi-

42. On the "extent and depth of classical reading" in John of Salisbury, see Charles Homer Haskins, *The Renaissance of the Twelfth Century* (Cambridge, Mass.: Harvard University Press, 1933), 100–126. Haskins acknowledges John's reliance on collections and anthologies.

43. *Frivolities of Courtiers and Footprints of Philosophers: Translated Selections of the Policraticus of John of Salisbury*, trans. Joseph B. Pike (New York: Octagon, 1972), 337–38. A similar ambivalence appears in the *Entheticus*, where John seems to approve of Epicurus's location of the "supreme good" in the "joys of the mind," as long as "the pleasure is pure" and the goal is "true joys." See John of Salisbury, *Entheticus Major and Minor*, vol. 1, ed. Jan van Laarhoven (Leiden: E. J. Brill, 1987), 140, lines 527–37. Comments on the physics and the hedonism of Epicurus, however, do not clearly distinguish Epicurus from his followers.

nence—and, moreover, that a life driven by these kind of desires leads inevitably to misery, sorrow, and death.[44] On the other hand, John readily acknowledges that Epicurus's rendering of the final goal of human life—one that is "always filled with such joy that there is no place for even the slightest suggestion of sadness or even perturbation"—is "a true and excellently turned definition."[45] Indeed, as a Christian philosopher John seems quite content with this account of the final good, only insisting that the Epicurean means (as he construes them) do not yield the intended goal. Far better, he contends, is the way built up from humble fear and love of God, and, too, by doing good and cultivating justice. Such, he concludes, is the "true dependable road" for attaining "the good and happy life" desired by Epicurus.[46]

What we receive from this Christian philosopher, quite clearly, is something truly remarkable given the standard antipathies directed toward Epicureanism from the Christian world. With a tremendously open and genial frame of mind, in fact, he allows Epicurus to define the ultimate felicity, the ideal of which is then integrated into Christian thinking on the good life. In essence, therefore, the practical life lived by Christian standards yields the ultimate of Epicurean pleasure. This is not to say that John wants people to become explicitly Epicurean—far from it, as he remains keenly vigilant as to all those vices typically credited to an Epicurean life. Those who live Epicurean lives, according to John—and there are a great many in the "court and beyond," even though they

44. John of Salisbury, *Policraticus*, 397–405. In the *Entheticus*, the payback of Epicurean living amounts to "flames, dung, [and] worms." "These are joys of stupid lust," John writes, "the ultimate end is woe, the utmost glory is shame." John of Salisbury, *Entheticus*, 142–43, lines 588–92.

45. John of Salisbury, *Policraticus*, 273. Indeed, John approves wholeheartedly of the Epicurean understanding of the final good of human existence as "the ever joyful and quiet condition of a tranquil life." See 405.

46. John of Salisbury, *Policraticus*, 405–11. See R. Bultot, "Érasme, Épicure et le 'De Contemptu Mundi,'" 230–34.

do not claim the title—are slaves to their own lusts.[47] At the same time, however—and what makes John so striking as a writer—is that he is ever ready to embrace truth wherever he finds it, which is why one is as likely to find in his works references to Horace, Cicero, or Petronius as to the Psalms, Gospels, or Paul. And, too, this is why he has invited Epicurus into the world of Christian thought, in a way that was unthinkable for Augustine and Anselm, as Epicurus speaks the truth about the highest and final felicity for human existence. Added to that, John was far too tactful when offering practical advice to bishops, popes, and kings to resort to the negative strictures of ascetic religion;[48] his interest rests, rather, in the cultivation of Christian philosophy, the graced quest for individual and collective happiness in this life, and the sure route to eternal rest with God.[49] What a free, gracious, and practical mind, this is, and what a rare move and what a rare moment in Christian history.[50] It is almost as if John wants to say that the good Christian becomes the good Epicurean, but being so frank about such a fusion will have to wait for the intellectual freedom of a later Renaissance.

Some intriguing steps in this very direction appear in a dialogue by Lorenzo Valla, the fifteenth century Christian humanist most famous for exposing the "Donation of Constantine" as a fraudulent justification of the church's rule over the western Roman empire.[51] Called *On Pleasure; De voluptate*, Valla's dialogue features

47. See Cary J. Nederman, *John of Salisbury*, Medieval and Renaissance Texts and Studies, vol. 288 (Tempe, Ariz.: Arizona Center for Medieval and Renaissance Studies, 2005), 52.

48. See, for instance, John of Salisbury, *Policraticus*, 177–80.

49. See John of Salisbury, *Entheticus*, 222, lines 1809–41 and 140, lines 540–54.

50. On the intellectual vitality of the cultural world in which John of Salisbury lived, see R. W. Southern, *Medieval Humanism, and Other Studies* (Oxford: Blackwell, 1970).

51. See Lorenzo Valla, *On the Donation of Constantine*, trans. G. W. Bowersock (Cambridge, Mass.: Harvard University Press, 2007). For a brief account of Valla's life and work, see Charles Trinkaus's entry on Valla in *Contemporaries of Erasmus: A*

three main speakers—a Stoic, an Epicurean, and a Christian—who debate what is the highest good of human existence. The Stoic speaks briefly in praise of virtue but is rapidly dismissed by both of his interlocutors. It is the Epicurean, however, who speaks at greatest length, arguing—as we would expect—that "nothing is more amiable and good than pleasure."[52] This includes goods of the body—things such as "health, beauty, [and] strength"—but special praise is reserved for wine ("for the praise of which all speech is inadequate") and sexual pleasures (a set of goods so vital for human life as to make the very idea of "virginity" an "intolerable torment").[53] And it includes goods of the soul (virtues such as courage and justice) and human skills (the liberal arts, crafts, and oratory), all of which receive their value, the Epicurean argues, from the "advantage" (that is to say, the pleasure) they provide to the living person.[54] Once the individual dies, moreover, "nothing remains" whatsoever, as "all goods belong to the living" and "those buried have no pleasure just as they have no trouble."[55] How startling it is to hear such a passionate and protracted defense of Epicurean ideas, all of which had been presumed dead and buried since the fourth century. Not surprisingly, therefore, the fact that the Epicurean plays such a prominent role in the dialogue gave rise to the suspicion that Valla's text is a "subversive assault on Christian doctrine."[56]

Biographical Register of the Renaissance and Reformation, vol. 3, ed. Peter G. Bietenholz (Toronto: University of Toronto Press, 1987), 372–75.

52. Lorenzo Valla, *On Pleasure; De voluptate*, trans. A. Kent Hieatt and Maristella Lorch (New York: Abaris Books, 1977), 91. On Valla's creative use of the dialogue form, see David Marsh, *The Quattrocento Dialogue: Classical Tradition and Humanist Innovation* (Cambridge, Mass.: Harvard University Press, 1980).

53. Valla, *On Pleasure; De voluptate*, 93, 105–9, and 123–29.

54. See Valla, *On Pleasure; De voluptate*, 137–225.

55. Valla, *On Pleasure; De voluptate*, 219, 155, and 159.

56. See Stephen Greenblatt, *The Swerve: How the World Became Modern* (New York: W. W. Norton, 2012), 223. As Greenblatt notes, "the dialogue's Epicurean speaks in defense of pleasure with an energy, subtlety, and persuasiveness that had not been

The final book of Valla's dialogue, however, is given over to the Christian speaker, and it is with this section that we begin to glean something of Valla's real agenda. Though he tips his hat to the Epicurean in preference to the Stoic, Valla's Christian is focused entirely on a heavenly felicity which—he insists—will outstrip anything earthly life may offer. Staunchly opposed to the Epicurean emphasis on the pleasures of natural life, he insists that one "must abstain from the pleasure here below if we want to enjoy the one above."[57] A life of virtue, therefore, becomes "a step toward that perfect happiness" which the soul (and apparently the body, too) will receive in full at death.[58] In reading the gospels, similarly, the good Christian is "transported in mind into I know not what loftier place, and we feel ourselves filled with ineffable sweetness."[59] It is only with death, however, that the soul truly will be "drawn upward ... with an incredibly pleasing movement" to a heavenly realm of "eternal felicity."[60] Sounding a great deal like Anselm, Valla's Christian repeatedly accentuates the incomparably great contrast of natural and heavenly joy: for every conceivable delight experienced in this world, he insists, "how much more shall we esteem the joys of this world as slight when we have known the joys of Paradise."[61] "So much more," he exclaims, "and indeed more than more, you will experience joy in nearing the very font of felicity."[62] With these kinds of statements, Valla's Christian repeats the mitigated asceticism of Augustine (where temporal goods are used as stepping-stones and left behind for the sake of realizing

heard for more than a millennium" (Greenblatt, *The Swerve*, 225–26). On the retrieval of Epicurus in the Renaissance, see Don Cameron Allen, "The Rehabilitation of Epicurus and His Theory of Pleasure in the Early Renaissance," *Studies in Philology* 41, no. 1 (January 1944): 1–15.

57. Valla, *On Pleasure; De voluptate*, 267. "Remember," the Christian speaker says, "that you must abstain from the love of earthly beauty if you wish to possess the heavenly kind." Ibid., 295.

58. Ibid., 267.

59. Ibid., 289.

60. Ibid., 287, 291, and 301.

61. Ibid., 301–3 and 305.

62. Ibid., 311.

eternal life with God); and, too, he echoes the mystical language for transcendence so evident in Anselm. Following as it does the Epicurean's speech, Valla would seem to be offering a traditional "containment" of the Epicurean position.[63] What is novel in Valla, however, beyond the already significant willingness to engage Epicureanism in dialogue, is the sensuous, almost rapturous manner in which the Christian speaker describes heavenly felicity. In this regard, it would seem, Valla boldly—though quietly, and perhaps also cleverly, and just possibly ironically—integrates an Epicurean emphasis on pleasure into the Christian take on transcendent felicity, even as the latter serves to contain and correct the errors of the Epicurean philosophy.[64] The most attractive feature of Epicureanism, therefore, finds new life within a mystical focus on transcendent felicity.

It is only with Erasmus that we find a more audacious proposal for dealing with the impasse of the Christian drive for transcendence and the Epicurean comfort with natural existence. Reflecting his Augustinian heritage, entertaining a Horatian zest for life, having read Valla, and keenly aware of the slur of Epicureanism hurled at him repeatedly by Martin Luther, Erasmus drafts "The

63. See Greenblatt, *The Swerve*, 228.

64. Valla's dialogue has proven notoriously difficult to interpret. For a brief sketch of the rival readings, see Maristella de Panizza Lorch, "Introduction" to Valla, *On Pleasure, De voluptate*, 44–46, footnote 8. One of Valla's achievements may have been to keep readers wondering what he had in mind, though such a strategy naturally invites ironic readings of the dialogue. See, for instance, Peter G. Bietenholz, "Erasmus, His Mistress Folly, and the Garden of Epicurus," 122–23. A fuller view, though still ironic, is found in Charles Trinkaus, *In Our Image and Likeness: Humanity and Divinity in Italian Humanist Thought*, vol. 1 (Chicago: University of Chicago Press, 1970), 148–50. As Trinkaus puts it, Christianity offered Valla a "genuine and not a pseudo alternative to man's universal hedonism" espoused by the Epicurean speaker, thereby lifting mankind to "an Epicureanism of the passions and the spirit" where "pleasure is sublimated" into the "joy of loving." From this angle, the best of Epicureanism (its affirmation of sensuous pleasure) is sublated into the higher Christian truth, but now stripped of the harsher notes (the comments on the rape of Lucretia, for instance) given by the Epicurean speaker. See Trinkaus, *In Our Image and Likeness*, 149.

Epicurean" in 1533 for the express purpose of advancing a startling claim—to wit, that "there are no people more Epicurean than godly Christians."[65] As mentioned earlier, this claim stuns Spudaeus, the character Erasmus creates to represent the point of view of a traditional Christian. As Spudaeus sees things, Christian life is severe and ascetic; indeed, he insists, their "sort of life seems as far as possible from pleasure." Not true, says the Erasmian Hedonius. While they may appear to mourn, they actually are "joyful and live agreeably"; indeed, he counters wryly, even the most famous of classical voluptuaries live "sad and miserable" lives compared to good Christians.[66] In this regard, Hedonius adds later, Christians emulate the "revered founder and head of the Christian philosophy" who was anything but "sad and gloomy in character." Christ did not call people to lead a "dismal mode of life," he argues, but in fact led "the most enjoyable life of all and the one most full of true pleasure."[67] Amazingly, much the same claim appears forty some years earlier in "On Disdaining the World," a work where the young Erasmus practices the well-worn genre of praising monastic life. After the standard denunciations of worldly honor and the pleasures of the flesh, Erasmus allows that in fact monastic life is a "paradise of delights." "Pleasure in monasteries," one has

65. Erasmus, "The Epicurean," CWE 40:1075. On the likelihood that Erasmus would have read Valla's dialogue, see Bietenholz, "Erasmus, His Mistress Folly, and the Garden of Epicurus," 118–25. In any case, Erasmus shows his familiarity with the dialogue in Erasmus, "Refutation of the Accusations of Josse Clichtove against the *Suasoria* of Desiderius Erasmus of Rotterdam in Praise of Marriage," trans. Charles Fantazzi, in *Collected Works of Erasmus: Controversies*, vol. 83, ed. Guy Bedouelle (Toronto: University of Toronto Press, 1998), 143–44. On Erasmus's familiarity with and borrowing from Valla's dialogue, see Letizia Panizza, "Valla's *De voluptate ac de vero bono* and Erasmus' *Stultitiae Laus*: Renewing Christian Ethics," *Erasmus of Rotterdam Society Yearbook* 15 (1995): 1–25. For a more general review of the developing connection between Valla and Erasmus, see R. J. Schoeck, "Erasmus and Valla: The Dynamics of a Relationship," *Erasmus of Rotterdam Society Yearbook* 12 (1992): 45–63.

66. Erasmus, "The Epicurean," CWE 40:1076.

67. Ibid., 1086.

to wonder? But yes, Erasmus responds, as monks "live wholly by the rule of Epicurus."[68] They do? What could this mean? Epicurean monks? And Christian Epicureans?

Quite clearly Erasmus is aware of how odd, startling, maybe even scandalous these claims must sound. Certainly he would have known that appeals to "our wise Epicurus" in the midst of monastic life would—if nothing else—have turned a few heads.[69] And, most assuredly, he knew full well that "The Epicurean" would be taken as a direct, though tacit, response to Luther's repeated charge that Erasmus is drunk with the "folly of Epicurus," a phrase Luther used for those who did not believe in the word of God, at least as he preached it.[70] In fact, "The Epicurean" is very much a "conversation with Luther," and, as Boyle puts it, it is one in which Erasmus could "honey the lesson with pleasure" by writing in a dialogue form that is calm, moderate, and lightly ironic—in short, precisely the kind of writing so evident throughout the *Colloquies*.[71] But like the eleventh chapter of "On Disdaining the

68. Erasmus, "On Disdaining the World," CWE 66:165.

69. Ibid., 166.

70. See Boyle, *Christening Pagan Mysteries*, 67–95. As Boyle observes, Luther consolidated a great deal of what he scorned into the term "Epicurean"—godlessness, denial of providence, fearlessness before death, indifference to divine judgment, carnal and dissolute living, and a theology which stresses God's "glorious manifestation" in nature and culture at the expense of a "theology of the cross" and a "discipleship in suffering." In Luther's view, Erasmus was a godless scholar of "heathen business" and defender of Epicurus. See *Luther's Works: Table Talk*, vol. 54, ed. and trans. Theodore G. Tappert (Philadelphia, Pa.: Fortress, 1967), 77–78. Luther refers to Erasmus as an "epicurean" in "Table Talk," 50. With seething hostility toward Erasmus, Luther charges, "you reek of nothing but Lucian, and you breathe out on me the vast drunken folly of Epicurus." Martin Luther, *Bondage of the Will*, trans. Philip S. Watson, in *Luther's Works: Career of the Reformer*, vol. 33 (Philadelphia, Pa.: Fortress, 1972), 29.

71. Boyle, *Christening Pagan Mysteries*, 75 and 72. On Erasmus's use of the genre of dialogue, see Martin, *Living Words*, 249–316. Indeed, as a dialogue, "The Epicurean" manifests a "playful lightness," as Marie Delcourt and Marcelle Derwa put it in "Trois Aspect Humanistes de L'Épicurisme Chrétien," in *Colloquium Erasmianum: Actes du Colloque International réuni à Mons du 26 au 29 octobre 1967* (Mons: Centre Universitaire de L'État, 1968), 130.

World," "The Epicurean" makes an audacious claim, one that is unexpected and startling, if not (as it was for Luther) infuriating and scandalous. It is interesting to see in these two texts, therefore, just how committed Erasmus was—from his youth to old age—to getting at the truth of things by playfully yet seriously confronting readers with such jarring and incongruous juxtapositions.[72] It is the Erasmian manner of thinking at work, once again, yet now proceeding by means of an odd juxtaposition of opposites designed to break open a space for reconsidering fixed assumptions about the very nature of religious life. What could it possibly mean to call Christians Epicurean? Is Christianity Christian if it is filled with pleasure? And what pleasures? And what Christianity?

For starters it must be stressed again that—no matter how novel the ironic agenda of Erasmus may be—he still proceeds in a framework that is quite traditional. This should not be surprising, as he surely cannot escape his own theological heritage, even if he wished to do so, which he surely has no desire of doing. "On Disdaining the World," for instance, repeats the long familiar counsel to reject the world's "vulgar physical pleasures" for the sake of "obtaining the preferable and sweeter pleasures of the spirit"; and "The Epicurean"—with less severity but the same dualistic terms—urges people to shun all those "empty shadows of goods" for the

72. We have here yet another instance of Erasmus being playful in order to make a serious point. As Gordon notes, Erasmus applies the adage of Anacharsis ("Play in order to be serious") to the "joke" ("there are no people more Epicurean than the godly, mournful Christian") in search of "serious validation." Gordon, *Humanist Play and Belief*, 122. See the adage IV. viii. 39 in *Collected Works of Erasmus: Adages*, vol. 36, trans. John N. Grant and Betty I. Knott (Toronto: University of Toronto Press, 2006), 381. Though Erasmus takes the saying from Aristotle's *Nicomachean Ethics* 10. 5 (1176b, 32–36), play and amusement for Aristotle are treated merely as a temporary form of "relaxation." In the same vein, Aristotle goes on to say that "serious things are better than laughable things" (1177a, 3). As Gordon shows, however, Erasmus has far more invested in juxtaposing the playful and the serious. Indeed, as we have seen throughout these meditations, play and belief are woven together in the service of dialectically getting at the truth.

sake of the "real pleasures of the mind."[73] In the midst of all this, however, Erasmus interjects the startling appeal to Epicurus, and his reasoning is remarkably consistent across both texts. He begins by noting—very much as Epicurus did—how "much bitterness" accompanies "shameless love, unlawful passion, excessive wining and dining." Indeed, he has Hedonius say, "when fever, headache, colic, fuzzy mindedness, disgrace, loss of memory, vomiting, ruined digestion, and palsy follow too much drinking, would even Epicurus think that a pleasure worthy seeking?" Certainly not, as no pleasure is worth that much pain, as Epicurus plainly says. The worst pain of all, however, is the "torment of conscience"—that gnawing sense of regret or guilt, mixed with "enmity with God [and] expectation of eternal punishment." What a "strange bargain" that is, as Epicurus surely agrees, to bring on such psychological agony for the sake of fleeting pleasures.[74] Conversely, we are told, the greatest pleasure is a "good conscience"—which for Erasmus entails both "righteousness" (an ethical life unburdened of remorse) and "godliness" (a sense of reconciliation with God).[75] In keeping with Epicurus, therefore, Erasmus concentrates attention on the psychological dimensions of pleasure and pain. For Erasmus, however, it is precisely this—the pleasure of a godly and righteous conscience—that defines the ideal Christian life. Relieved by Christ of the torment of bad conscience, the true Christian possesses "the most enjoyable life of all and the one most full of true pleasure."[76] How far this is from the asceticism of so much

73. Erasmus, "On Disdaining the World," CWE 66:166; and Erasmus, "The Epicurean," CWE 40:1078–79.

74. Erasmus, "The Epicurean," CWE 40:1080.

75. Ibid., 1082.

76. Ibid., 1086. Elsewhere Erasmus writes, "Even Epicurus concedes that nothing in man's life can be pleasurable unless he possesses a mind conscious of no wrongs in itself—from which alone, as from a fountain, true delight gushes." Erasmus, "Paraclesis: or, An Exhortation," in *The Praise of Folly and Other Writings*, trans. Robert M. Adams (New York: Norton, 1989), 124. See also Erasmus, "The Handbook of

Christian thinking, and how Epicurean this Christian has come to sound!

In "On Disdaining the World," the young Erasmus conceives of the pleasures of being relieved of a bad conscience in decidedly heavenly and mystical terms. What a pleasure it is, he writes, "to contemplate the heavenly, the eternal delights we hope for." Though such delights cannot be fully perceived until the soul is freed from "its bleak prison to fly back whence it came," Erasmus assures us that "pious minds" are "able to catch a certain glimpse of that eternal light." What rare and precious moments these truly are, to get a "sort of foretaste or presentiment" of heavenly felicity. Sounding a great deal like Anselm and yet echoing the sensuous language evident in the Christian speaker in Valla's dialogue, Erasmus invites us to think just "how bountiful such pleasures must be when even the slightest taste provides such delight, such refreshment, such emotion."[77] Indeed he claims with an ascetic flourish, one can only "disdain [the] false pleasures" savored by the "champions of the world," when one considers in contrast—as Christian mystics contemplating the *Song of Songs* so often do—"that sweet, sweet pleasure" when the "bridegroom embraces the bride languishing with desire for his love."[78] Quite clearly the youthful Erasmus is fully at home with the ascetic and mystical line of thinking

---

the Christian Soldier," CWE 66:89. On these points, Erasmus has a rare precedent in Christian literature, where Peter Abelard has a "philosopher" in dialogue with a "Christian" argue that "what Epicurus calls pleasure" (freedom from the "consciousness of sin") is the same as what "Christ calls the kingdom of heaven." Peter Abelard, *A Dialogue of a Philosopher with a Jew, and a Christian*, trans. Pierre J. Payer (Toronto: Pontifical Institute of Mediaeval Studies, 1979), 94 and 97.

77. Erasmus, "On Disdaining the World," CWE 66:167.

78. Ibid., 167–68. See, for instance, Bernard of Clairvaux, *On the Song of Songs*, 2 vols., trans. Kilian J. Walsh (Kalamazoo, Mich.: Cistercian Publications, 1976), material with which Erasmus was familiar. Consider also the highly sensuous language in Teresa of Avila, "Meditations on the Song of Songs," in *The Collected Works of St. Teresa of Avila*, trans. Kieran Kavanaugh and Otilio Rodriguez (Washington, D.C.: ICS Publications, 1980), 207–60.

in Christian tradition, only taking the liberty of calling these mystical delights "Epicurean."

Even in this text, however, there are a few counter-currents—places where the pleasures of the pious life are to be enjoyed in this world, without renunciation and without a mystical flare. It is no small matter, for instance, when Erasmus praises the freedom and leisure to be found in enjoying all the books—including even the "philosophers and poets"—held in the monastic library. With such pleasures at hand, he asks, "can there be room for boredom in such variety?"[79] But that means, I take it, that there are pleasures at hand, indeed wonderful pleasures which keep life interesting and intellectually alive. With comments such as this, however, it is hard to see Erasmus in any great hurry to escape the confines of natural life. The library, in short, is not a bleak prison. A more significant counter to the ascetic and otherworldly option appears in the twelfth chapter, where Erasmus warns his readers against monastic life. Appended to this text some years later, the mature Erasmus now observes that "most monasteries"—far from renouncing the body and far from transcending the world—revel in "worldly affairs," are driven by the "interests of the stomach," and commit "all kinds of fornication freely and without constraints."[80] Monasteries, in other words, are not very good places for a righteous and godly life. Far better, he counsels, to "leave the world in another sense," simply by keeping company with "men of integrity" and virtue.[81] But that means, of course, that it is not necessary (nor is it advisable) to leave the world in the sense intended by the monastic tradition. Instead, Erasmus argues, the pleasures of the righteous and godly conscience can be enjoyed in the midst of the social worlds in which we live and breathe.

79. Erasmus, "On Disdaining the World," CWE 66:170–71.

80. Ibid., 173. On the purpose and likely dating of chapter 12, see Erika Rummel, introductory note to ibid., 130–33.

81. Ibid., 174–75. See Erasmus, "The Handbook of the Christian Soldier," CWE 66:127.

"The Epicurean" is devoted to this same line of thinking. "If people who live agreeably are Epicureans," Hedonius argues, then "none are more truly Epicureans than the righteous and godly."[82] But that must mean that the pious enjoy "no less delight" than the impious or the worldly, even while they experience such delight "in a different fashion," but still—it must be stressed—they experience such delight "in this life."[83] "Wherever is a pure heart," Hedonius explains, "there God is. Wherever God is, there is paradise, heaven, happiness. Where happiness is, there is true gladness and unfeigned cheerfulness."[84] All the gladness of heaven resides, therefore, in the actual life of the godly and righteous person. This is evident in the first place, Hedonius suggests, in the way the godly handle misfortunes in life, knowing as they do that all the afflictions of worldly life are "lighter and briefer, in comparison with eternal sufferings."[85] They still suffer, to be sure, but—according to Epicurean principle—the milder pain is actually pleasant compared to a stronger pain; so the pious may be said to enjoy a kind of paradise in contrast to the prospect of eternal torment.

On a brighter note, but certainly one with which Epicurus would not agree, the godly person is said to enjoy "far more pleasure" than the ungodly when looking at the splendor of the natural world, since only the believer can find "inward delight" in the world as a well-crafted gift of creation.[86] It is more stunning, however, when Erasmus has Hedonius argue that the godly person finds great pleasure in banquets and in sexual love, certainly very down-to-earth sources of pleasure, and ones usually shunned by the religiously austere. But Erasmus will have none of that, insisting that godly people enjoy fine banquets far more than the "vulgar gourmand," as they feast on modest food and rich conversation seasoned with thanksgiving; and, too, that they savor "sexual

82. Erasmus, "The Epicurean," CWE 40:1086.

83. Ibid., 1084.

84. Ibid., 1083.

85. Ibid., 1083.

86. Ibid., 1084.

love" with great intensity, as their "pleasure [is] derived from [the] unbroken intimacy" between two people "who love each other equally and sincerely."[87] With these stunning examples, it becomes clear what Erasmus is after—to restore pleasures of the earthly sort to the heart of religious life, though now imbued with religious depth.

We have in "The Epicurean," therefore, the makings of a distinctively Erasmian option—one that continues to operate within the framework of traditional dualities, even while it juxtaposes an Epicurean viewpoint to stand over and against the asceticism and otherworldliness of traditional theology. It is—as we have seen so often in these meditations—an ironic point that Erasmus makes. Here again, however, irony does not mean simply being clever (though Erasmus's point is that), nor does it suggest that he does not mean what he is saying (as he very much means what he is proposing). To get the gist of his irony in this case requires mental agility in holding together imbalanced opposites, even as their mutual recalcitrance undercuts the possibility of lasting synthesis. Concerning the impasse of Christian asceticism and the Epicurean comfort with natural life, therefore, Erasmus is not proposing a balanced compromise; and neither is he endorsing an Augustinian ordering of natural goods—in a kind of graduated progression—to one transcendental good. Erasmus is, rather, bringing Epicurean delight back into religious life, but not with any simple reconciliation, as the long-standing opposition of the ascetic and the hedonist will not allow that. For Erasmus, finally, the good Christian is neither other-worldly nor ascetic, and also neither impious nor hedonistic, but rather ironically Epicurean. And the irony lies in the unfinished and unrelenting equipoise of both poles, startling though that may be for both the traditional Christian and the unabashed hedonist.

87. Ibid., 1085.

It is a daring proposal, to be sure, that Christians are Epicurean. But, of course, it cannot be overlooked that Erasmus has a highly selective understanding of Epicureanism. He starts with a strong sympathy with Epicurus's concern with the debilitating effects of fear and remorse, a psychological focus which feeds Erasmus's own thinking on good and bad conscience.[88] He is attracted as well to the Epicurean emphasis on prudent choices of pleasure, along with the warning to be mindful of the painful fallout stemming from bad choices. But there is not a word about the atoms of Epicurus, nor anything concerning the complete transcendence of Epicurean gods, as Erasmus happily remains in a theistic world with a God who creates, guides, and redeems the world. So Erasmus is quietly selective in what he takes in and leaves out from Epicurus. But if this is the case, and it is, then it is equally true that Erasmus is quietly selective about Christianity. Indeed, as we have seen from "The Epicurean," Erasmus sets aside certain things written into some of the earliest traditions in Christian history—namely, a rigorous and joyless asceticism and a world-despising urge for transcendence. In their place comes the strangest things—a kind of Christian hedonism, modest and measured to be sure, but still not afraid to praise the joy of sexuality in a tradition given over to honoring celibacy; and, too, something of a Christian naturalism, where the natural world is measured by and imbued with a transcendent goodness, not degraded as a bleak prison worthy only of escape. While hardly anyone would care that Erasmus was selec-

88. The idea of good versus bad conscience has roots in Seneca and Paul. For Pauline sources, see 1 Timothy 1:5, 1:18–19, and 3:9; as well as the reports of Acts 23:1. From Seneca, see letters 43, 105.8, 122.14; and, too, see letter 97.12–15, where Seneca credits Epicurus for the point. *Seneca ad Lucilium Epistulae Morales*, 3 vols., trans. Richard M. Gummere (Cambridge, Mass.: Harvard University Press, 1934). But certainly Epicurus's concern with fear of disclosure as a disturbance in moral life also fits what Erasmus has in mind by a bad conscience. Thus Epicurus writes, "Let nothing be done in your life which will cause you to fear if it is discovered by your neighbour." Epicurus, "The Vatican Collection of Epicurean Sayings," 70, *The Epicurus Reader*, 39.

tive in his Epicureanism, defenders of orthodoxy could be alarmed at this kind of theological freedom with Christian doctrine. Of course, if they were honest they would admit that this is not so unusual, as theologies vary as they do precisely because authors select and stress certain strands of tradition more than others. It has always been this way. What is startling from Erasmus, however, is that he seeks to integrate notes from a philosophy that had largely been vanquished since the fourth century and despised for even longer.[89]

The ironic juxtaposition of Christianity and Epicureanism generates deeply unsettling questions striking at the very core of life in the Christian world. What would you have Christianity be, the reader of Erasmus might ask? But of course that is precisely the question with which Erasmus confronts his readers. But is Christianity actually Christianity if it is Epicurean, the reader might protest? Or, equally jarring, as Erasmus would respond, can Christianity be Christian if it is not Epicurean? These are not questions designed to challenge specific doctrines or to criticize particular theologies; rather, they call into question the very viability of Christianity itself. For those who would be Christian, of course, this can be nothing but an eerie line of inquiry. Has Christian thinking, in fact, been wrong about itself in excluding the Epicurean element? But where does that leave the long centuries of Christian tradition, the reader might worry? And where, Erasmus would retort, does that leave the truth? But what, finally, is the truth of Christianity? "The Epicurean" suggests a distinctive kind of theology, one that is neither ascetic nor hedonistic, but rather keeps transcendence and eternal felicity in view, while yet remaining joyful and delighted in everyday life; or, alternatively put, one that affirms transcendent goodness without denigration of the human, while affirming hu-

89. On the evidence for the last days of active Epicureanism in the fourth century, see Ferguson, "Epicureanism under the Roman Empire," 2311–27.

manity without alienation from the transcendent. But what exactly does this mean, and how is it managed? What are its implications, and can Christians handle this?

Neither "On Disdaining the World" nor "The Epicurean" go very far in developing these proposals. "The Epicurean" poses the startling question and gives us some leads, but Erasmus goes much further elsewhere—first, in *The Praise of Folly*, as we saw in the Introduction; and then, second, in a number of *Colloquies* where he offers a better idea of the kind of ironic equipoise he has in mind for thinking about the place of pleasure in religious life. Let us turn now to these writings, therefore, in pursuit of a better grasp of this odd but intriguing Erasmian option.

An Erasmian Counterpoint

Nothing is more basic to Erasmian thinking than to acknowledge that absolutely everyone is full of folly; and, too, that people go mad in many different ways. It is precisely these differences, as we saw earlier when discussing *The Praise of Folly*, that make life what it is—wonderfully odd, truly interesting, and downright confusing. What we find in this work, recall, are three distinct forms of folly: the first is natural and innocent enough, and it is handled comically; the second is cultivated and decidedly treacherous, and it is treated satirically; while the third is mystical and apparently noble, and it is dealt with in what seems to be unmitigated praise. The problem for readers, once again, is to figure out how all this fits together. Folly keeps praising things, but the sum of what she says cannot be true, as the forms of life she praises are irreconcilable, or so it would seem. The question, therefore, is how each form of madness—the innocent, the vicious, and the saintly—can each be praised. They seem so different, at odds with each other, even grossly contradictory, so readers have every right to wonder whether Folly's self-praise is at all coherent. And along the same lines, they have every right to question whether Erasmus's book itself has any coherence.

Where is the unity of the work? What, in short, is Erasmus's point? Or, in the terms of this meditation, how can human life be both fully natural and yet called to mystical ends? Can the two be reconciled with any coherence, or does one nullify the other?

Though readers in Erasmus's own day—both adversaries and allies—might reasonably regard the satirical section as the clear voice of Erasmus, since in those passages one could make direct connections to current events, the reigning view in recent scholarship has focused instead on the work's mystical finale. It is M. A. Screech, more than anyone else, who has made the case so extensively that the heart of Erasmian theology is to be found in the "truly astonishing end" of *The Praise of Folly*. The "religious ecstasy" praised in this final section is, according to Screech, "the highest form of Christian folly."[90] In his words, at once serious and striking,

> The divine, erotic *mania* leads the Christian who is seized by it to love God *vehementer*, so that he lives not in himself but in him whom he loves. Ecstatic joy of this intensity is reserved for only the few; it is a priceless foretaste of the durable, ineffable rapture which awaits all pious Christian souls in death.[91]

To make his case, Screech marshals abundant evidence to show that the concern of Erasmus with "Christian ecstasy" has deep roots throughout his writings. It reflects, Screech insists, Erasmus's "constant concern with the spiritual as against the carnal, the invisible as against the visible," something already evident in the early "Handbook of the Christian Soldier"; and it is—he insists—especially prominent in "later writings," notably the commentaries on various Psalms.[92] What is most impressive in Screech's work, and certainly what has persuaded many a reader, is the sheer volume of

90. Screech, *Erasmus: Ecstasy and the Praise of Folly*, 9.

91. Ibid., 141–42.

92. Ibid., 8 and 172. Screech argues that the mystical notes struck by Folly are "part of the permanent preoccupations and beliefs of Erasmus as expressed in his later writings."

references showing Erasmus's mention of mystical issues of ecstasy, visions, and rapture. Screech rightly claims, therefore, that such evidence reveals a "very different Erasmus" from the common portrait.[93] But, at the same time, one might also wonder whether so much else in Erasmus is not elided by Screech's exclusive focus on raptures, visions, and ecstasy. It is true, in short, that Erasmus is more than a satirist or a moralist, but is it not equally clear that he is much more than a mystic? Or again, in the terms of this meditation, is it not true that he is interested in much more than heavenly felicity? And, too, that he is very much concerned with the course and quality of natural and social life as we know it?

Wayne Rebhorn and Walter Gordon agree with Screech that the serious point of Erasmus in *The Praise of Folly* rests in the mystical section, though unlike Screech both do so in a manner which seeks to better integrate the comical and the satirical sections into the work's mystical point. For Rebhorn, Erasmus's work "embodies a strategy of conversion." Therefore,

> The meaning of the *Praise* … does not reside in the complex irony of the first part or the straight invective of the middle or even the Christian transvaluation at the end. The meaning is the total structure, the process of movement itself, which leads from comedy to tragedy and then beyond.[94]

And yet, though Rebhorn rightly stresses the "dialectical and dynamic unity" at work in *The Praise of Folly*, it is for him the culmination of the process that constitutes the work's ultimate purpose; it is there, Rebhorn notes, that one discovers that life has "transcendent meaning and, what is just as important, sure direction."[95] And it is there, consequently, that one finds the unity of Erasmus's project. For Gordon as well, as we saw in the introduction, *The Praise*

93. Ibid., xviii.

94. Wayne E. Rebhorn, "The Metamorphoses of *Moria*: Structure and Meaning in *The Praise of Folly*," 472.

95. Ibid., 464 and 473.

of Folly "celebrates a festive madness of intemperate and mindless enjoyment [in the first section] only to have this image serve as an analogue for and introduction to the final vision of celestial ecstasy."[96] While Gordon admits that Folly herself does not resolve the indiscriminate praise of three very different forms of madness, he insists nonetheless that Erasmus most definitely resolves the life of folly in its ultimate, mystical form. Natural madness, therefore, serves as an analogue or pointer—but nothing more than that—for the unifying goal of "celestial madness."[97] Both of these studies have an advantage over Screech, at least as far as a sound reading of *The Praise of Folly* goes, but the question remains whether the mystical finale deserves such prominence. Is the whole point of Erasmian thinking really to encourage mystical madness? Or, once more in the terms of this meditation, is natural life and its pleasures really nothing more than a passing means to the end of heavenly felicity?

Without doubt mystical readings of *The Praise of Folly* make a valid point, or so it would seem. For one thing, the work does indeed end with a blazing tribute to mystical madness. But, additionally, it is not uncommon to find Erasmus giving voice to an otherworldly or transcendental view of things with deep roots in Paul and Augustine. In "An Exposition of Psalm 38," for instance, Erasmus insists—in quite traditional language—that it is necessary to

> break free from all restraints and ties of the flesh. How can we leap up when we are weighed down by the lead of our sins? How can we fly up when we are entangled by pleasure, trapped by the thorns of wealth, enveloped by luxury, intoxicated by the sweetness of worldly fame, and stuck deep in the mud of earthly care which makes it almost impossible to lift one's head up into the purer air?[98]

96. Gordon, *Humanist Play and Belief*, 210.

97. Ibid., 217.

98. Erasmus, "An Exposition of Psalm 38," trans. Caroline White, in *Collected Works of Erasmus: Expositions of the Psalms*, vol. 65, ed. Dominic Baker-Smith (Toronto: University of Toronto Press, 2010), 26.

And in the same commentary we hear Erasmus showing his lively sense for the dazzling language of mystical life, where he calls David a "true Idythun"—"one who has already become a spiritual being and has *leaped over* all human passions." In this, Erasmus comments, David prefigures Jesus Christ, truly "the foremost and greatest of leapers."[99] What a wild image, and one that Erasmus would naturally enjoy. Moreover, as Screech rightly observes, Erasmus plays up the crazier mystical passages in Christian scriptures—Paul's "rapture" to the third heaven (2 Corinthians 12:1–4), Peter's "trance" and vision of the "great linen sheet" filled with every beast, fowl, and creeping thing that lives on the earth (Acts 10:9–16), the three disciples' vision of the transfiguration of Jesus (Matthew 17:1–8; Mark 9:2–8; and Luke 9:28–36), and the glorious intoxication on the day of Pentecost (Acts 2)—repeatedly using the language of rapture and ecstasy that resonates with his description of the holy fools in *The Praise of Folly*.[100] So there certainly is no reason to deny that Erasmus was keenly sensitive to this form of madness; and thus, too, there is good reason to seriously attend to its place in the structure and purpose of *The Praise of Folly*. But whether it is the dominant concern which appears to exclude all others (Screech), or whether it is the ultimate end which orders while transcending the other forms of folly (Gordon and Rebhorn)

99. Ibid., 13.

100. For examples of Erasmus's paraphrase of Peter, James, and John's vision of the transfiguration, see Erasmus "Paraphrase on Matthew," trans. Dean Simpson, in *Collected Works of Erasmus: New Testament Scholarship*, vol. 45, ed. Robert D. Sider (Toronto: University of Toronto Press, 2008), 251–53; and Erasmus, "Paraphrase on Mark," trans. Erika Rummel, in *Collected Works of Erasmus: New Testament Scholarship*, vol. 49, ed. Robert D. Sider (Toronto: University of Toronto Press, 1988), 109–10. Referring to the ecstasy of Peter, James, and John, Screech comments that "it is so central to Erasmus' doctrine of ecstasy—and ecstasy is so central to his religion—that ideally every subsequent allusion to it should be noted and analyzed." Indeed, he writes, "the whole end of the Moria is seen as an allusion to the events portrayed in Matthew 17:1–8; Mark 9:2–8; Luke 9:33–end." Screech, *Erasmus: Ecstasy and the Praise of Folly*, 200.

is another question altogether. Is there not more at stake and more in life—certainly for Erasmus, but also for us—than transcending everything we know and feel? Are not the joys of natural life—at once bodily, mental, emotional, and social—truly good things worthy of desire?

The Erasmian manner of thinking, after all, is nothing if not capacious. Indeed, as we have seen throughout these meditations, there are always other sides to be considered and rival angles to be heard; and failing to tend to them is to miss out on something vital to the larger truth in question. So as we are considering in this meditation the classical question of the goods or ends of human existence—what may we hope for and for what should we desire and strive?—it is unthinkable that Erasmus would not urge us on to consider and to appreciate the other side of the issue. The temptation—here as in *The Praise of Folly*—is to structure the relation of the natural to the transcendent in an Augustinian manner, and by that means to find a resting place in the mystical finale that affirms while overcoming everything that usefully led up to that point. Doing so, however, freezes thought; and, as we saw earlier, Erasmus insists upon a manner of thinking that is too capacious and too dynamic to settle exclusively with any one form of life.

The alternative approach to the mystical readings, as Clarence Miller observes, is to see how Erasmus has Folly lead us "to find opposite positions equally plausible," without compromise to either option. Thus, for example, "only the worldly fool is happy, only the otherworldly fool is happy"—both make sense "while Folly concentrates on it, but how can we believe both?"[101] How, in fact, can we entertain both at once, as the happiness each promises—one natural and worldly, the other mystical and transcendent—would seem to point in opposite directions? But that is precisely the Erasmian gambit—to insist that natural and mystical felicity be held in

101. Miller, "The Logic and Rhetoric of Proverbs in Erasmus's *Praise of Folly*," 93.

an enduring equipoise, where the heavenly might well signal the fulfilment of the worldly, while the natural offers a lasting counterpoint to the madness of the mystical. In this reading of *The Praise of Folly*, therefore, we are led to a kind of ironic coinciding of opposites, where the tension between the poles remains unresolved, and the mind-spinning challenge is to accommodate their difference without reduction and without conflation.

There is a good deal of evidence for this understanding of Erasmus both within *The Praise of Folly* and from other Erasmian sources. Recall, for instance, that from the very beginning Folly declares her intention to "play the sophist"; and remember too that there is no good reason to think that she has dropped this role as we move into the closing section on mystical madness.[102] As I argued earlier, for instance, Folly brags that her random and twisted arguments from biblical authority are modeled on the style of "picayune lawyers" and "great masters of divinity," but the sophistry of each of these professions becomes the target of Erasmian satire in the second section.[103] So this hardly gives confidence that the praise of mystical ecstasy should be taken at face-value. Then again, as we saw earlier, Folly defends her authority with appeal to some classical proverbs, but her reasoning is slippery at best. The first two, in fact, combine to advise deception by pretense, arguing that where one lacks the reality of something, one should capitalize on how things appear. But this—quite clearly—is a recipe for sophistry, as we heard from a master like Gorgias in the first meditation. Then again Folly argues for the excellence of folly based on its ubiquity. After all, she asks with appeal to another proverb, "who does not know that the more widespread any good thing is,

102. Erasmus, *The Praise of Folly*, 9–17. As Miller aptly puts it, Folly is a "consummate sophist." Miller, "Introduction" to *The Praise of Folly*, xx. For his part, understandably, Gordon asserts that Folly has "long ago abandoned the role of the Sophist." Gordon, *Humanist Play and Belief*, 195.

103. Erasmus, *The Praise of Folly*, 177 and 127.

the more excellent it is."[104] But this, too, is a standard designed for sophistry, as all good sophists—being performers skilled in manipulating an audience—measure their excellence by popularity. As we saw in the first meditation, however, for Erasmus it is the worst of things that are the most showy, and for that very reason the most popular, whereas "what is excellent in any way is always the least showy."[105] So clearly we have every reason to be on guard when this goddess praises mystical ecstasy, as Erasmus gives us very definite warning signals that she still is playing the sophist.

A fuller and more dialectical reading of *The Praise of Folly* comes into sharper focus when closer attention is paid to the many natural forms of folly in the book's first section. By far the most delightful part of the book, Folly takes us on an extended romp through the fields of ordinary pleasures. "Is there any part of life," she asks, "that is not sad, cheerless, dull, insipid, and wearisome unless you season it with pleasure, that is, with the spice of folly?"[106] Clearly not, we are shown, as absolutely everyone—including even the self-serious Stoics who "scorn pleasure" in public while enjoying it in private—gets through life with "the balm of manifold pleasures."[107] In all this, as Peter G. Bietenholz nicely argues, Folly shows herself to be a "worthy disciple of Epicurus," celebrating the common pleasures of ordinary life, a great many of which are "wholesome and innocent."[108] Among the many happy fools, there are men and women in love—women with their "cosmetics, baths, [and] coiffures" to make themselves "attractive to men," and men talking "childishly" to

104. Ibid., 117–18.

105. Erasmus, "The Sileni of Alcibiades," 274.

106. Erasmus, *The Praise of Folly*, 19.

107. Ibid., 19 and 58.

108. Bietenholz, "Erasmus, His Mistress Folly, and the Garden of Epicurus," 129 and 127. Though Erasmus refrains from calling this form of folly "Epicurean," Folly herself draws explicitly from Lucretius and Horace; and the entire tenor of the section magnifies the value of Epicurean pleasure at the expense of Stoic reserve. For this reason, Kaiser notes a "revival of Epicureanism—or pseudo-Epicureanism" in this part of *The Praise of Folly*. See Kaiser, *Praisers of Folly*, 53.

gain the favor of women.[109] There is a good bit of drinking, too, and hence a lot of drunks—some tipplers seeking relief from life's burdens, some finding a "surging hope" to face the future, and others simply enjoying the revelry of wild parties.[110] And there are Christians as well, a great many happily entranced—innocently enough—with miracles, magic, and other "soothing self-delusions.[111] In all of these cases and many more, Bietenholz observes, the "true originality of Erasmus" lies in Folly's "compassionate approach to the common—and pleasurable—follies of human existence."[112] Indeed, as we have seen, Erasmus embraces the "fairly innocent follies" of everyday life; he relishes the ordinary "foibles" which make life pleasant; and, indeed, he even appreciates the role of "weakness" and delusion as a "source of pleasure"—all of which, quite rightly, elicits a "sympathetic smile" from the reader.[113] Unlike "The Epicurean," moreover, in *The Praise of Folly* Erasmus shows no desire to give these worldly pleasures an ethical richness or to consecrate them with a "religious value."[114] Rather, they are relished in their own right, in all their wonderful oddity, an ungraced nature held over and against mystical transcendence, one form of folly standing over and against another. In this move, therefore, Erasmus celebrates the Epicurean quality of natural madness; and thereby creates a delicate and ironic suspense of opposition with the mystical.

A great deal more evidence to offset the mystical reading of *The Praise of Folly* is at hand in other writings of Erasmus. Without gainsaying the place reserved for mystical transcendence in *The Praise of Folly* and other works cited by Screech, there is no

109. Erasmus, *The Praise of Folly*, 29.

110. Ibid., 21, 73, and 30. On Folly's "jocular praise" of wine and drink, see Kaiser, *Praisers of Folly*, 65–68.

111. Erasmus, *The Praise of Folly*, 62–66.

112. Bietenholz, "Erasmus, His Mistress Folly, and the Garden of Epicurus," 133.

113. Ibid. Kaiser also notes the "sympathy for human frailty" in this section of *The Praise of Folly*. See Kaiser, *Praisers of Folly*, 61.

114. Bietenholz, "Erasmus, His Mistress Folly, and the Garden of Epicurus," 138.

shortage of texts which point in a far more worldly, natural, and practical direction. We have seen in the first two meditations, certainly, an Erasmus deeply concerned with ethical questions that are crucial to the character and quality of human existence. In the first meditation, recall, Erasmus is concerned with the viability of truth-telling in a world split between sophists and dogmatists. And in the second meditation, we find Erasmus devoted to what is most certainly his most enduring preoccupation—the cause of peace between nations in a world given over to the carnage of warfare. In both contexts Erasmus concentrates on ethical and practical issues, and within that focus shows a deep and abiding commitment to human flourishing. When Erasmus comes to praise the folly of human existence, therefore, his focus is by no means centered exclusively on rapture and ecstasy. Far more often, in fact, he dwells on the utterly mundane ways of everyday life, including those odd and frequently charming forms of folly rehearsed in the first section of *The Praise of Folly*. In so many other works of Erasmus, additionally—those, in particular, dealing with life and death, marriage and sexuality, and the pleasure of conversation at banquets—we discover a very different portrait of the ideal human life, one that is simple and unpretentious, intelligent with a zest for conversation, and, too, humane to others and committed to the cause of peace. On each of these topics, as we presently will see, there is far too much evidence of this understanding of human life to be swept away in deference to mystical felicity.

(a) *On Lives and Deaths*

Consider, in the first place, the Erasmian colloquies on lives and deaths. It is worth remembering, in this regard, the hope expressed by Epicurus that people might enjoy—above all—"a good life and a good death."[115] And it is precisely this hope—focused so well on

115. Epicurus, Letter to Menoeceus, 126, *The Epicurus Reader*, 29.

the living and how they manage their lives and their deaths—that Erasmus entertains in two of his many charming colloquies. The first brings together four old friends who have not seen each other since their days in Paris, some forty-two years ago. Agreeing to share a carriage, they also share their stories of life, both to pass the time of travel and to determine why some have aged so much more quickly than others. Called "Old Men's Chat, or the Carriage," we meet the dissolute but not unlikeable Polygamus, who has managed to marry eight times and have children from each. Recalling that he never had much "aversion to Epicurus," he has aged a great deal, as "nothing brings on old age so much as hard drinking, … endless amours, and unrestrained sexuality."[116] We find an opposite though unimpressive character in Eusebius, who has lived correctly and comfortably on the "prebend" he received from a "cathedral chapter." Content with his "honourable office, … well-appointed house, sufficient annual revenues, respectable society, and a church besides," he has lived "quietly," he confesses, "not eager for anything more."[117] If Polygamous has spent his life in debauchery, however, it seems that Eusebius has mortgaged his for propriety and privilege. But how different altogether is the life of Pampirus! Having squandered opportunities in his youth, he has bounced from one religious order to another, changing "costumes" as needed, making his way through life in a free but careless manner.[118] None of these characters has lived very well, though it certainly is true, as Craig R. Thompson notes, that Pampirus is the "most interesting" of the three, and "well worth knowing."[119]

116. Erasmus, "The Old Men's Chat, or The Carriage," CWE 39:454–55. Here, the reference to Epicurus carries the common negative meaning. On the role of this colloquy in the cultivation of happiness, see Brenda Dunn-Lardeau, "Érasme, pédagogue du bonheur, dans les *Colloques*," *Renaissance and Reformation/Renaissance et Réforme* 30, no. 1 (Winter 2006): 103–18.

117. Erasmus, "The Old Men's Chat," CWE 39:460.

118. Ibid., 459.

119. See ibid., 448

But, as these three comment, it is Glycion who has aged the least; and for good reason, it turns out, as he has lived the best. Happily married with children, he was widowed after eight years ("the bitterest blow of my life") and did not remarry ("for the sake of the children").[120] Though "studies" are his "main pleasure of life," he held a modest public office for a spell, but never sought a higher position, as "exceptional good fortune" invites "envy," and in any case—echoing Horace—the "middle state is safer."[121] In life with others, he has been helpful to friends in need; he has shunned quarrels and mitigated conflicts where possible; and he has been pleasant and courteous to all, avoiding gossip and "reckless talk."[122] Above all, Glycion has sought to avoid all "wrongdoings," as "nothing is more disquieting than a bad conscience"; and conversely, nothing is more desirable than the "true serenity" or "tranquility" that comes from being at peace with God and others.[123] With those notes, quite clearly, we discover that Glycion's life has followed Erasmus's version of the Epicurean rule. To be sure his life is both more pious and virtuous than we find among Folly's cast of natural fools. And yet, as an Erasmian ideal of a life well-lived, he is not given to ecstasy and rapture like the mystical fools at the end of *The Praise of Folly*. He is detached only from the excesses of life, not from life itself. Glycion, in fact, has lived his life with remarkable ethical richness—with family, in public, among friends—and for that very reason, with great pleasure. For Erasmus this is truly an Epicurean life—an old man among friends, not worrying about death, but relishing the joy of "living honourably and agreeably."[124]

120. Ibid., 451–52.

121. Ibid., 453 and 451. In "Odes" 2. 10. 5, Horace writes, "Who values most the middle way avoids discreetly both the squalor of the slum and a palace liable to excite envy." See Horace, *The Complete Odes and Epodes*, trans. W. G. Shepherd (London: Penguin, 1983), 114.

122. Erasmus, "The Old Men's Chat," CWE 39:52.

123. Ibid., 453.

124. Ibid. 453. As Thompson notes in the introduction, "nowhere do we find a

From a colloquy on how lives are lived, Erasmus turns to consider contrasting manners of dealing with impending death. It is so very tempting to die badly, apparently, as the example of George in "The Funeral" makes vividly clear. A general in the army, rich from "ill-gotten gains from robberies, sacrileges, and extortions," he spares no cost in securing his passage to heaven with the purchase of a papal brief "promising forgiveness of all sins" and marked by an elaborate (and "ostentatious") funeral; and "to have God further in his debt," he pledges his wife and children to mendicant orders, despite their protests.[125] How different are the last days of Cornelius, who approaches his death with calm and quiet confidence. He see no reason to buy extra merits for salvation, as "there is sufficient abundance of merits in Christ," and he has faith in God's "boundless and inexpressible" mercy. In fact, he feels no need to be attended by "holy men," only receiving "extreme unction" and communion; and he declines a final confession, as he has "no lingering anxieties on his mind."[126] In this, it is clear, Cornelius is very much an Epicurean in the Erasmian sense, as he faces his own death with a good conscience. Though he appears "eager and joyous" when listening to biblical passages on the "rewards of immortality," there is nothing from him resembling mystical rapture. Unlike the mad fools we meet at the end of *The Praise of Folly*, Cornelius dies the way he lived, "without being burdensome to anyone" and without fear of death.[127] The most striking feature of his preparations for death, in fact, are the warm words of comfort he gives to his wife and children. For Erasmus this is truly an Epicurean death—an honest and decent man with family and friends, not worrying about death, but confidently anticipating the joys of heaven.

---

better illustration of the Erasmian prescription for a good life." Ibid., 448. On this colloquy, see Brenda Dunn-Lardeau, "Érasme, pédagogue du bonheur, dans les *Colloques*," 103–18.

125. Erasmus, "The Funeral," CWE 40, 770–71.

126. Ibid., 777.

127. Ibid., 776.

(b) *Marriage and Sexuality*

Erasmus was not a mystic, nor was he married. But he wrote about both subjects, and he did so with imagination and passion. Though he could write with fervor about the rapturous love of ecstatic mystics (as Screech and others show us), he also could write with clarity and warmth about the down-to-earth joys and troubles of courtship and marriage. Here again, therefore, we find a set of writings focused on the utterly natural lives of ordinary people, not as something to be shunned or overcome, as the ascetic streak in so much of traditional Christianity would have it; but as something worthy of respect, certainly as an equal way of life and possibility as a superior one to the virginity and celibacy long commended in clerical and monastic worlds. As he did so—one should by now not be surprised—Erasmus frequently sounds very conventional, indeed, painfully so for modern sensibilities; and yet quite often, as we also have come to expect, he stretches the boundaries of Christian thinking on many of these topics. And doing so spawned a great deal of controversy, to which Erasmus repeatedly felt obliged to engage. In his responses, he sometimes excuses what he had written as a youthful exercise in "declamation," though he would make exactly the same claim in other places.[128] Or, alternatively, and often with

128. Erasmus claims, for instance, that "The Praise of Marriage" (written in 1498–1499, but only published in 1518) is a "declamation"—a work dealing with "imaginary subjects for the purpose of exercising one's ingenuity." So he insists that he "wished to provide young men with a sample of [his] youthful writing so that in treating similar arguments they might exercise their writing ability and their inventiveness." The author of a declamation, therefore, "disclaims all responsibility for the opinions stated." Erasmus, "The Defense of the Declamation on Marriage," trans. Charles Fantazzi, in *Collected Works of Erasmus: Controversies*, vol. 71, ed. J. K. Sowards (Toronto: University of Toronto Press, 1993), 91. Consistent with this explanation is the fact that "The Praise of Marriage" came to appear in a larger work devoted to explaining and illustrating the art of writing letters. See Erasmus, "The Praise of Marriage," as part of "A Formula for the Composition of Letters," trans. Charles Fantazzi, CWE 25:10–267. What Erasmus says about the placement of "The Praise of Marriage" is true, though the fact remains that Erasmus makes very much the same points in other writings,

dazzling dexterity, he will invert the standard order of things and combine things normally thought to be irreconcilable, thereby generating proposals whose irony cannot help but be—and probably was meant to be—deeply disturbing to those holding conventional views. In a word, we find Erasmus bent on stirring up reflection in a manner designed to unsettle ascetic doctrine while prompting a more humane take on marital relationships.

As Erasmus defines it, marriage is "the complete and perpetual intermingling of two destinies," establishing thereby "a tranquil and blessed partnership" for the "purposes of begetting offspring."[129] What could be greater folly, he wonders, than for someone to "shun what has been instituted by God, sanctioned by nature, prompted by reason, praised in divine and human writings alike, laid down by the law, ratified by the consensus of all peoples, and encouraged by the example of all good men?"[130] Only a madman, perhaps a misanthrope such as Timon of Athens, lives for himself alone, loving no one and loved by no one in return.[131] But, in fact, Erasmus is not thinking of Timon but of the orthodox champions of religious celibacy when he asks, "what pleasure can there be for a man who is alone?"[132] Indeed, a man who castrates himself is terribly mad, the charming and clever Maria in "Courtship" declares; and her suitor

so that readers can have confidence (as Thompson notes) that the point in the declamation "may be taken seriously." See Craig R. Thompson's introduction to Erasmus, "The Girl with No Interest in Marriage," CWE 39:280. But that is, oddly enough, precisely what the critics of Erasmus claimed—that the views found in "The Praise of Marriage" are the serious views of Erasmus. What we have here, interestingly, is a good example of Erasmus playfully dissembling to make a serious claim to truth—exactly the kind of ironic truth-telling defended in the material treated in the first meditation. The same thing may be said, not surprisingly, of *The Praise of Folly*, which also is called a "declamation." See Erasmus, *The Praise of Folly*, 9.

129. "The Institution of Christian Matrimony," trans. Michael J. Heath, in *Collected Works of Erasmus: Spiritualia and Pastoralia*, vol. 69, ed. John W. O'Malley and Louis A. Perraud (Toronto: University of Toronto Press, 1999), 346 and 219.

130. Erasmus, "The Praise of Marriage," CWE 25:139.

131. Ibid., 140. See Lucian's "Timon, or the Misanthrope," *Lucian*, vol. 2, 325–93.

132. Erasmus, "The Praise of Marriage," CWE 25:142.

Pamphilus makes the intended connection explicit when he adds, "those who renounce marriage by a strict vow castrate themselves, in a sense."[133] The problem, Erasmus observes, is the inordinate exaltation of virginity and purity at the expense of marriage found in early church literature.[134] For his part, Erasmus dismisses this "immodest enthusiasm" with a few minor concessions. Perhaps these unnatural rigors were an "appropriate emotion for that period," he suggests, but that is no reason to apply the identical standard to later times.[135] Perhaps celibacy is fitting for select individuals, he concedes elsewhere, but that does not mean it is the right choice for others, as "not all modes of life are equally suitable to all persons."[136] Or again, perhaps celibacy has its merits, though if it were extended too far, he notes with a smile, "all of mankind must perish utterly" within a few years. And besides, Erasmus adds with a satirical bite, "not everything's virginal among those virgins."[137]

These quips and questions about celibacy, however, are just the prelude for a more daring and paradoxical set of suggestions. In "The Defense of the Declamation on Marriage," Erasmus tells us that he extols "marriage so greatly in order to extol virginity even more," which he then adds is something that he "attributes

133. Erasmus, "Courtship," CWE 39:265.

134. See Erasmus, "The Institution of Christian Matrimony," CWE 69:243–44.

135. Ibid. See also Erasmus, "The Praise of Marriage," CWE 25:137 and 138.

136. Erasmus, "The Girl with No Interest in Marriage," CWE 39:288. Besides, Erasmus warns, one should not enter "rashly into something there's no escape from afterwards." See CWE 39:288 and 293. "The Repentant Girl" is offered as evidence of such regret. Erasmus, "The Repentant Girl," CWE 39:302–5.

137. Erasmus, "The Girl with No Interest in Marriage," CWE 39:290. A common barb from Erasmus, and often with savage wit: "'Fathers,' they're called, and this name they often take care to deserve." See ibid., 288. Or again, Erasmus wryly says he will refrain from being "too eloquent" about the "hideous and widespread lusts" found among those claiming to live holy and celibate lives. Erasmus, "The Defense of the Declamation on Marriage," CWE 71:94. At times, however, he could not restrain himself, writing that he only wished "that those who conceal their vices behind the high-sounding name of castration, and under the pretense of chastity gratify worse lusts, were truly castrated." Erasmus, "The Praise of Marriage," CWE 25:137.

to angels, apostles, and apostolic men." A very well-crafted point, indeed, and one about which we are left wondering whether or not virginity actually has been praised, as few (if any) living men would seem to fit the bill of angels or apostles. But then, Erasmus adds that the marriage he praises "is very similar to virginity, a marriage in which one has a wife for the production of offspring, not the satisfaction of lust."[138] Indeed, he writes later, the marriage he extols is "a marriage that is restrained, modest and chaste, and, as far as possible, like the state of virginity."[139] But what is that supposed to mean? The terms seem twisted, or rather reversed, or somehow turned inside-out. Chastity, we are told, is more likely to be practiced in marriage than in the monastery, where in fact celibate monks too often are not in the least bit chaste. But how, a sane reader will be wondering, is virginity to be practiced in marriage? It is exactly that, in fact, that Maria asks of her suitor after he promises that their marriage will not fall much short of virginity. In his words, "perhaps some day we'll live as Joseph and Mary did. But meantime we'll learn virginity; for one does not reach the summit all at once."[140] What are you suggesting, she asks, that "virginity be violated in order to be learned?"[141] And she is right, of course, as these are paradoxical points that Erasmus has his characters make. However, "the paradox is effective," as Thompson notes, "because it forces the reader to think more sharply about the nature of virginity," or for that matter, to think about the nature of marriage and its "comparative value" in religious life.[142] The ironic equipoise of virginity and marriage, in short, is designed to unsettle and disturb orthodox assumptions. It is, as we have seen so often from Erasmus, a playful maneuver tending toward a serious point.

138. Erasmus, "The Defense of the Declamation on Marriage," CWE 71:92–93.

139. Erasmus, "The Institution of Christian Matrimony," CWE 69:387.

140. Erasmus, "Courtship," CWE 39:265. For similar claims, see Erasmus, "The Praise of Marriage," CWE 25:131.

141. Erasmus, "Courtship," CWE 39:265.

142. See ibid., 272–73, footnote 53. Others, in fact, have resolved the paradox by

The serious point would seem to be this—that it is not a question of which lifestyle one chooses, for that is simply a matter of changing one costume for another, as Erasmus often says.[143] What matters, in the end, is how one lives and handles natural sexual desires in a world that is still religious. To make that point, not surprisingly, Erasmus brings together what are frequently thought to be incompatible features of life—sex and religion—and he holds them in a suggestive but unnerving balance. At times, it is true, Erasmus can sound more than a little prudish, as when he counsels infrequent intercourse, which he does frequently. What he seems to be looking for, however, is a way of handling sexuality that neither denies its natural value nor concedes too much to raw and aggressive hedonism. The natural value of sexuality, for Erasmus, clearly includes the good of procreation. But there is more to it than that, as the good of sexual union is a "bodily pleasure" enhanced by the affection and sharing which comprise the "happiness" of husband and wife.[144] In defiance of the ascetic tradition,

---

taking the proposal of Pamphilus at face value, thereby attributing to Erasmus an "ascetical ideal of Christian marriage." See, for instance, Alan W. Reese, "Learning Virginity: Erasmus' Ideal of Christian Marriage," *Bibiothèque d'Humanisme et Renaissance* 57, no. 3 (1995): 551–67. Taking this route, however, reduces marriage to a pathway to spiritual purity, while dismissing the proper role of intimacy and affection; and, consequently, it misses the ironic tension at play on these matters. For Erasmus, "virginity" is a "flower of the soul"—the purity and faithfulness of a soul to Christ—that is "reflected" in "the countenance, in the eyes, and in the whole disposition of the body." It is, in short, an interior disposition, and not something reducible to abstinence from sexual intercourse. See Erasmus, "A Comparison of the Virgin and the Martyr," CWE 69:168, 175, and 181.

143. See Erasmus, "The Girl with No Interest in Marriage," CWE 39:291–92. For a dialogue on the conventions of dress, see Erasmus, "The Well-To-Do Beggars," CWE 39:476–82.

144. Erasmus, "The Praise of Marriage," CWE 25:139–40. Erasmus's well-wishes to Pieter Gillis on the occasion of his marriage corroborates the idea that the happiness of marriage very much includes intimacy and tenderness. Hoping that "no anger or boredom may ever come between them," Erasmus has the Muses sing, "For the rest of her days she'll hear nothing but 'my darling'; he in turn nothing but 'sweetheart.' And not even old age will diminish this joy but rather enhance it." See "The Epithalamium of Pieter Gillis," CWE 39:524. Recall, too, the praise of sexual love, and "the pleasure

therefore, Erasmus insists that the desires and the pleasures of sexual life arise from nature, not from some sinful condition.[145] Sex is not inherently sinful, and abstinence "from sexual intercourse isn't a virtue."[146] In fact, for Erasmus sexual life may well be "downright virtuous," as Gordon puts it.[147]

At the same time, however, and in the same writings, without contradicting this affirmation of natural sexuality, Erasmus entertains some theological comparisons. To be sure, the introduction of doctrinal reflections right alongside these down-to-earth considerations of the natural good of sexuality is a jarring juxtaposition; and we can only surmise that the effect on readers was premeditated by Erasmus. As he puts it, marriage recalls the Incarnation of Christ—"when in an expressible way he joined our nature to himself, as if in a marriage; then again when he chose the congregation of saints as his bride."[148] So marriage reflects a sacred mystery of divinely initiated union—the Incarnation. But, of course, that means that this glorious mystery partakes of something very much like sexual intercourse.[149] Indeed, with tantalizing irony, Erasmus suggests that "it would not be irreverent to

derived from unbroken intimacy" between people "who love each other equally and sincerely." Erasmus, "The Epicurean," CWE 40:1085.

145. Erasmus, "The Praise of Marriage," CWE 25:136. See Erasmus, "The Defense of the Declamation on Marriage," CWE 71:93. As Michael J. Heath notes, "in regarding sexual activity as a natural necessity rather than a mere concession to human weakness," Erasmus instigates "a breach with an ascetic tradition dating back essentially to St. Paul." See Michael J. Heath's introduction to Erasmus, "The Institution of Christian Matrimony," CWE 69:205. For a more complicated explanation, though arriving at the same conclusion, see Erasmus, "Refutation of the Accusations of Josse Clichtove," CWE 83:139–43. On the manner in which Erasmus's "rhetoric of intimacy"—especially when writing in the form of a dialogue—works to bolster his "humanizing turn" regarding sexuality, see Reinier Leushuis, "Dialogue and Intimacy in Erasmus's Matrimonial Writings," *Renaissance Quarterly* 57, no. 4 (Winter 2004): 1287–1307.

146. Erasmus, "Courtship," CWE 39:265.

147. Gordon, *Humanist Play and Belief*, 228.

148. Erasmus, "The Institution of Christian Matrimony," CWE 69:345.

149. See ibid., 226–32.

picture God the Father as the bridegroom, the holy Virgin as the bride, the angel as the intermediary, the Holy Ghost as the agent of conception, the newborn child as both God and man, the offspring of God and man."[150] Perhaps it was not irreverent, though it did not prove reverent enough for many, as it seems to suggest something truly outrageous—namely, a sexual coupling of the divine and the human. In response, Erasmus insists that his language is not obscene in the least; and, in any case, he notes plenty of precedents from scripture and church fathers for using "words such as *coitus* and *coire* metaphorically." He then proceeds to repeat—in much the same language—that "the power of the Most High overshadowed the Virgin as if in a mystic embrace, and, by the action of the Holy Spirit in the place of a seed, made her pregnant with the heavenly issue, who would take the nature of both parents: the divine nature of the Father, the human nature of his mother."[151] But what a delicious piece of irony this is, as the natural and the heavenly are brought together not by mystically transcending natural functions, but by integrating the divine into the intimacy and delights of sexual existence. Though bound to disturb and shake those harboring ascetic prejudices against bodily existence, it is a strong counterpoint to asceticism for anyone wishing to uphold the integrity of natural life.

With each of these points, it seems clear, Erasmus is less inter-

150. Ibid., 230. Erasmus had paraphrased the angel's words to Mary in the beginning of Luke in much the same language—at once graphic ("the Holy Spirit will descend into you from on high") and sensuous ("a holy embrace" adapted to "the workings of human nature so that it will be able to sustain this intercourse"). For a translation of this passage, see Gordon, *Humanist Play and Belief*, 244. Erasmus also replaced "full of grace" in the angel's greeting to Mary with "graceful," a term some found to be too intimate. See Rummel, *Erasmus' Annotations on the New Testament*, 167–69.

151. Erasmus, "Desiderius Erasmus of Rotterdam against a Most Slanderous Letter of Martin Luther," trans. Peter Macardle, in *Collected Works of Erasmus: Controversies*, vol. 78 (Toronto: University of Toronto Press, 2011), 439–44. See also Erasmus, "Paraphrase on Matthew," CWE 45:41–43 for equally bold language.

ested in defending a position on marriage than he is to hold alternative truths in ironic juxtaposition, and thus to make his points by disturbing people's certainties and prompting new reflection. He hopes, in the end, to jostle loose ascetic and celibate strictures, allowing for more humane responses to the "many unhappy and burdensome marriages."[152] It is undeniable, of course, that Erasmus remains sadly conventional regarding the husband's authority and the wife's duty of obedience and submission, even while he emphasizes "mutual respect" in other places.[153] Think, for instance, of the colloquy called "Marriage," where Eulalia reminds the angry Xanthippe that she "must put up with [her] husband, whatever he's like"; though, once again, Erasmus surely gives the best lines to Xanthippe, who ably protests the injustice of her situation.[154] At his best, however, Erasmus's ironic reflections on marriage free him to vent his moral outrage at the abuse of young women—certainly in arranged marriages of children; but more strikingly where a "very young girl is married to a septuagenarian;" or worse yet, in those ghastly cases where parents "hand over a pure and healthy virgin to a husband riddled with the new leprosy."[155] And with that moral fury, Erasmus seizes the freedom to propose a number of changes

152. Erasmus, "The Institution of Christian Matrimony," CWE 69:334.

153. See, for instance, ibid., 336–37, 363–68, and 398–99, on the husband's authority and the wife's duty of obedience; but see also 340–45 for more humane advice.

154. Erasmus, "Marriage," CWE 39:314. Complaining that her husband spends everything on "wine—whores—dice," Xanthippe laments that "wives have an unhappy lot for sure if they must simply put up with husbands who are angry, drunk, and whatever else they please." Erasmus, "Marriage," CWE 39:310 and 313. When Eulalia reminds her that she best adapt and try to reform her husband, as Christ abolished divorce, it is easy to sympathize with her incredulous, "I can scarcely believe it." Erasmus, "Marriage," CWE 39:311. It is impossible to imagine what Erasmus was thinking, however, when he says that some women "find themselves married, by God's will, to husbands who are drunkards, spendthrifts, plunderers of the poor, adulterers, gamblers, so that they may win their husbands for God." Erasmus, "The Institution of Christian Matrimony," CWE 69:401.

155. For examples where Erasmus shows his moral outrage, see Erasmus, "The Institution of Christian Matrimony," CWE 69:241–42, 325–26, and 327–28. See also Erasmus, "A Marriage in Name Only, or The Unequal Match," CWE 40:842–59.

to church laws on marriage and divorce, almost all of them aiming to "help [the] many thousands now struggling in the toils of disastrous marriages."[156] That, in a nutshell, is the point of Erasmus's reflections on marriage and sexuality—to carve out the possibility for a kind of Epicurean marriage—where, freed from oppressive marriages and rigid church laws, men and women find "pure and gentle" lives together, filled with "mutual affection," friendly conversation, and "modest and virtuous" lovemaking, for the sake of building and enjoying new families together.[157]

(c) *Banquet Colloquies*

Again and again, it is clear, Erasmus turns his focus to people's lives with the hope that they might be filled with many delights—at once physical, intellectual, ethical, and religious. It is an Epicurean hope, in the Erasmian sense of the term, and one that vividly reappears in the handful of *Colloquies* staged as banquets.[158] Only one of these *Colloquies* appeals to Epicurus by name, very much in the manner of the goddess Folly, to praise the value of pleasure (and especially wine) at the expense of "Stoic sternness."[159] But a number take place in gardens, always an Epicurean signal; and all are devoted to the pleasure of the participants—treating their bodies to a variety of dishes and their minds to "conversation as pleasant as it is profitable."[160] So there is most definitely an Epicurean quality to these banquets, at least in the Erasmian sense of the term, as the participants gather in friendship, to savor varied dishes, while feasting on some fine intellectual conversation. It hardly seems to be a coinci-

156. Erasmus, "The Institution of Christian Matrimony," CWE 69:301. See also 278–79, where Erasmus calls upon the church to "alter the laws it has made" for "the benefit of the flock."

157. Ibid., 347, 343, and 345.

158. See Lawrence V. Ryan, "*Erasmi Conviva*: The Banquet Colloquies of Erasmus," *Acta Conventus Neo-Latini Turonesis*, vol. 1 (Paris: J. Vrin, 1980), 303–14.

159. Erasmus, "The Profane Feast," CWE 39, 134–139 and 146–147.

160. Erasmus, "The Sober Feast," CWE 40:928.

dence, in fact, that the character named Augustine sounds so much like Folly, when he closes out the evening with a salubrious "drink briskly and live merrily!"[161]

Nowhere does this Epicurean hope appear more vibrantly, however, than in "The Godly Feast," truly a utopian banquet where Erasmus dreams of a little community of friends where all things are reconciled in balance and fruitful harmony.[162] It presents, as Boyle nicely puts it, a "microcosm of the Christian commonwealth," and it does so in "the Epicurean gardens" of a "country villa," far removed from the "smoky cities," where a small circle of friends gather to enjoy a meal and some fine conversation.[163] It is, to be sure, a natural community—in a home not a church, among laymen not priests, for a meal not a liturgy—but it is one that is enriched and graced by the abundant variety of goods which are brought together in harmony. So, for instance, the natural beauty of the gardens is completed by the "inventiveness of the painter," the beauty of both reflecting the "goodness of God."[164] At lunch they "eat with pleasure but listen with even more pleasure" to readings from scripture, as both the body and the mind deserve "refreshment."[165] And to complement the passages from scripture, they share reflections on philosophical classics as well, as these, too, surely reflect wise counsel on how to live a good life.[166] What a sumptuous feast, the host exclaims, "at once equally learned and devout."[167] Indeed, one of the guests responds, "who could be bored in this house?"[168] And the Erasmian answer, quite clearly,

161. Erasmus, "The Profane Feast," CWE 39:147.

162. Erasmus, "The Godly Feast," CWE 39:171–243. See Martin, *Living Words*, 291–98.

163. Marjorie O'Rourke Boyle, *Erasmus on Language and Method in Theology*, 140. See Erasmus, "The Godly Feast," CWE 39:175–78.

164. Erasmus, "The Godly Feast," CWE 39:179.

165. Ibid., 183 and 189.

166. Ibid., 192–94.

167. Ibid., 204.

168. Ibid., 206. Roughly the same sentiment is made earlier in the dialogue, where

is that no one possibly can be bored in such a paradise—a natural one to be sure, but one enriched with amiable conversation and blessed with intelligent piety, a fitting home for the Christian who also is an Epicurean in the Erasmian sense.

What we glean from these assorted texts—those on life and death, marriage and virginity, and intellectual banquets—is how intensely Erasmus strives to affirm the pleasures and richness of natural human life. At times Erasmus shows remarkable generosity, as he genuinely appreciates the lives of very ordinary characters, even if they are not shining examples of piety and morality. Think, for instance of Pampirus—the jack-of-all-trades from "Old Men's Chat"—who bounces aimlessly from one religious order to another; or perhaps also Augustine from "The Profane Feast," who happily sings the praise of wine and food.[169] Both are presented as thoroughly likeable characters, much as the goddess Folly did with her happy fools in the first section of *The Praise of Folly*. But Erasmus knows, of course, how badly things can turn in human life. The mockery of George's self-serving extravagance and heartless treachery in "The Funeral," or the outrage hurled at the insane parents who give their young daughter in marriage to a syphilitic nobleman, vividly recall the satirical criticism at work in the second section of *The Praise of Folly*.[170] None of this, however, is sufficient reason to shun the world, to debase bodily existence, and to denigrate human capacities. Indeed, as we have seen in the preceding pages, it is possible to live well (as the steady life of Glycion illus-

---

one character exclaims when seeing the great variety of beautiful things in the gardens, "good heavens, who could possibly become bored in this changing scene?" See ibid., 181. Here, interestingly, Erasmus repeats the same enjoyment of life that he earlier found—at least for a time—in monastic life. See Erasmus, "On Disdaining the World," CWE 66:170–71.

169. Erasmus, "The Old Men's Chat," CWE 39:455–59; and Erasmus, "The Profane Feast," CWE 39:135–39.

170. Erasmus, "The Funeral," CWE 40:767–75; and Erasmus, "A Marriage in Name Only," CWE 40:845–54.

trates); it is possible to marry well (as Maria and Pamphilus seem likely to do); and, too, it is possible to die well (as the last few days of Cornelius give evidence).[171] But it is precisely these things—the hope for a good life and a good death—that animated the philosophy of Epicurus; and they are, in turn, as we have seen, the ideals that define what might be called the "Christian Epicurean" in the work of Erasmus. It is a vision of natural existence enriched with ethical and religious value, a graced nature as it were, which stands as a lasting counterpoint to the mystical fervor evident in other texts of Erasmus.

In the final section of this meditation, finally, it is worth pausing to dig a bit more into the point and purpose of this striking notion of the "Christian Epicurean." We should ask, as well, just what is accomplished by entertaining such an unusual juxtaposition of opposites. What, in a word, is the point of thinking about life in such a manner? And what does this Erasmian option tell us about that good—or goods—which will offer fulfilment to human aspirations? What, in the end, is worthy of a life's love for the Christian Epicurean?

The Christian Epicurean

At the start of "The Epicurean" we find Spudaeus—true to his name—diligently studying a classical text in moral theory—specifically, the book titled *On Moral Ends,* written by Cicero in 45 B.C.E.[172] Like many of Cicero's works on philosophical topics, this piece gathers together fictional representatives of the different schools of Greek philosophy and puts them in dialogue with each other. In this case they address and debate the question of what constitutes the final aim of human aspiration—that good, in other

171. Erasmus, "The Old Men's Chat," CWE 39:451–54; Erasmus, "Courtship," CWE 39:256–78; and Erasmus, "The Funeral," CWE 40:776–79.

172. Cicero, *On Moral Ends*, ed. Julia Annas and trans. Raphael Woolf (Cambridge: Cambridge University Press, 2001).

words, that will complete human life and offer it fulfilment; and, too, that good which orders and makes sense of all the other things people love and desire. In the colloquy of Erasmus, Spudaeus is understandably confused. He cannot "get over the fact that on so important a subject there was so much conflicting opinion among such eminent men."[173] It is no accident, however, that Erasmus launches his colloquy with reference to this work, in part because for centuries it was one of the major sources of information concerning the views of Epicurus; but also, and more importantly, because it framed the way later centuries of writers—from Augustine to Valla—went about reflecting upon this central philosophical issue.[174] Quite rightly, therefore, it provides the key question that has guided this meditation—in sum, what is worthy of a life's love? What can and should be hoped for in human life? And, additionally, it does so in a way that makes it clear from the start that there are a number of contending answers at hand.

What is so interesting about Erasmus, in this regard, is how much intellectual enjoyment he finds in the sheer variety of human loves; and, with that, too, how persistently he faces up to the complexity at play in each and every question. Everything, it seems, is interesting, or at least potentially so. And nothing is simple or one-dimensional, so every question naturally allows for rival angles and every answer demands qualifications. As a Christian by faith, of course, Erasmus willingly concedes to the authority of the church, at least in principle; and as a Christian scholar shaped in the Augustinian tradition, moreover, it is not unusual to find him making some very strong claims regarding one or another theological issue. But neither fact nullifies his fundamentally capacious regard for the

173. Erasmus, "The Epicurean," CWE 40:1075.

174. See Augustine, *Concerning the City of God against the Pagans*, book 19, on the ordering of goods to the final Good; and note that Valla's *On Pleasure; De voluptate* (originally titled *De vero bono*) is structured in the manner of a Ciceronian dialogue on the same issue.

variety of life, nor is he thereby driven to make definitive claims that would close off other important possibilities. Indeed, as he famously says, he prefers to be an "inquirer" than a "dogmatist."[175] And what makes that stance possible is not so much a streak of skepticism, though there is plenty to doubt in most everything, but rather a capacious manner of thinking and a generosity of spirit. There are, as we have seen, so many different ways of going mad in one's loves—mostly natural, many vicious, and a few mystical—but no one of them is explained away by another. The great variety of life persists—sometimes comically, at other times tragically—but all of it is a marvel to behold. As Erasmus surely would ask of us, who can possibility be bored in such a theater? Given that capacious enthusiasm with the forms of life, therefore, it is understandable that narrow views and exclusive claims prove insufficient.

The problem with so much religion, in fact, including to be sure a great deal of the Christian tradition, is that the urge to transcend the world comes at the expense of natural life. Indeed, as we have seen in this meditation, whether in the classics of Christian theology or in the great mystics of the Middle Ages, the location of the final good with eternal peace in God often is supported by especially strong forms of asceticism—ones that consistently bear hostility to the world, loathing of the body, suspicion of the passions, abasement of the will, and denigration of the mind. There are variations, to be sure, and occasionally an exception; but the tradition is loaded—it must be said—with negativity toward life itself. It often seems, in fact, that those of this ilk will only be content when they escape the world altogether; and it seems, indeed, that they share the view of those ancient writers, who once said "that it is best not to be born at all."[176] In the same adage in which Erasmus collects a number of these life-weary pronouncements, he offers a classi-

175. Erasmus, "A Discussion of Free Will," trans. Peter Macardle, in *Collected Works of Erasmus: Controversies*, vol. 76 (Toronto: University of Toronto Press, 1999), 8.

176. See Erasmus, "Not to be born is best," CWE 33:160–62, adage II. iii. 49.

cal counterpoint from Metrodorus of Lampsacus, a close friend and avid disciple of Epicurus. In the passage provided by Erasmus, Metrodorus recounts the many pleasures life offers, whichever path one may have chosen and whatever life has thrown one's way; and then he concludes by saying that "life is good every way."[177] What a bright take on life, that is; and one that surely fits the Epicurean commitment to help people enjoy full, pleasant, and stable lives.

Not surprisingly it is this very sentiment that we hear from Glycion in "The Old Men's Chat." "Attracted by Metrodorus," he tells the others, he "takes whatever good he can find from whatever source." That way, he notes, life is made "sweeter" and more tranquil.[178] But, of course, this could be said by any of the Erasmian characters who approach life in what Erasmus calls an Epicurean manner—all those, in short, who are not afraid of life and do not tremble at death, who embrace the goods of natural and social existence with a steady resolve and a good conscience, and who are keen on living well and eventually dying well. It is this, however, that is missing in the ascetic line that has dominated Christian thinking for so long. And that is why, again echoing both Epicurus and Metrodorus, Erasmus dares those who would be Christian "to run the risk of human life," even with all of its uncertainties and troubles. "All of us," the character Pamphilus says in "Courtship," "kings and commoners alike," are "equally liable" to encounter difficulty and to suffer pain.[179] But that is no reason to turn against life, to despise the body, to denigrate the mind, or to hate the world. Is this really what religion is all about—to scorn pleasure and, ultimately, to fear life? If this is really what people think, Epicurus would say again, then they should get down to business

177. Erasmus, "Not to be born is best," CWE 33:161. See *The Greek Anthology*, vol. 3, book 9, epigram 359, ed. E. Capps, T. E. Page, and W. H. D. Rouse (London: William Heinemann, 1915), 193–95.

178. Erasmus, "The Old Men's Chat," CWE 39:452.

179. Erasmus, "Courtship," CWE 39:266.

and leave life now. The means are at hand, if they are serious.[180] Interestingly, Erasmus makes the same quip through Pamphilus, when he suggests that those who refuse to run the risk of living life—even for deeply religious reasons, Erasmus might add—simply "ought to give up life."[181] And that, I take it, is his parting shot at ascetic Christianity.

It is equally true, we should not forget, that Erasmus also levels some very harsh criticisms of unbridled hedonism. Those who so fear the world that they yearn to escape it may be mad; but those who take the opposite course, who hurl themselves with abandon into the many pleasures the world offers are also quite crazy. We met some of these characters in *The Praise of Folly*, some of whom receive a genial embrace, but many of whom are the butt of Erasmian satire. Though it is true that Erasmus can be gentle with individuals who have lived a hedonistic life (Cannius the "Gospel-bearer" comes to mind),[182] he also can be quite stern in warning against the dangers of false and excessive pleasures. Those enthralled with what the masses of people call pleasure are deceived, Erasmus writes, for "the sole true pleasure is the joy of a

180. Epicurus, Letter to Menoeceus, 126–27, *Epicurus Reader*, 29.

181. Erasmus, "Courtship," CWE 39:266. Similar advice is given to Catherine in "The Girl with No Interest in Marriage," when she wishes to escape the talk of married people which she finds too embarrassing. See Erasmus, "The Girl with No Interest in Marriage," CWE 39:289. And see also Erasmus, "The Praise of Marriage," CWE: 25:142.

182. Erasmus, "Cyclops, or the Gospel-Bearer," CWE 40:863–76. Though Cannius carries the Gospels under his arm, he has led an "Epicurean life" (in the negative sense), not an "evangelical one." Indeed, he brags, his like pursue "full bellies; plenty of work for the organs below the belly; a livelihood from somewhere or other; [and] finally, freedom to do as we like." Though Polyphemus explains how such a life is hypocritical for one who carries the Gospels, Cannius remains a likeable character, perhaps because he gave a "hell of a beating" to a Franciscan who "kept babbling from the pulpit against Erasmus' [translation of the] New Testament." Surely that is "promoting the gospel," Polyphemus insists; and besides, he recalls, he gave the Franciscan absolution "by banging him on the head three times with this very same book, raising three lumps, in the name of the Father, Son, and Holy Ghost." Cannius concedes that this truly is the "evangelical spirit!" Clearly, in the eyes of Erasmus, there are things to be admired in this hedonist.

pure conscience." What all the "devisers of pleasures" have to offer, he adds, are nothing in comparison with the love of Christ.[183] On Epicurean terms alone, Erasmus notes, the unrestrained pursuit of sensual pleasure—excessive drinking, for instance—yields far more discomfort (if not misery) than the fleeting pleasure it promises.[184] Or ponder, too, he warns, the "long train of evils" that follow from the "seductive pestilence" of sexual lust—a ruined reputation, loss of health, "loathsome diseases," ever more vices, and even the forfeiture of reason. Indeed, Erasmus says in some of his fiercest language, the allurement of lust "calls us away irrevocably from all honourable pursuits and immerses man from head to foot in the muck, with the result that he likes to think of nothing but what is sordid, lowly, and filthy."[185] So, quite clearly, Erasmus is as critical of hedonism as he is of asceticism, often using the tropes common in ascetic literature to take his stab at the dangers of raw hedonism. In the end, if asceticism is life-denying renunciation, then hedonism is life-destroying indulgence, and Erasmus rejects both. In their place, as we have seen, he puts forward the ideal of what might be called a Christian Epicurean.

But what exactly is a Christian Epicurean? This is, to say the least, a remarkably odd and striking term, as Christianity so often is ascetic and Epicureanism commonly is known for its hedonism. So how could anyone be both? How are we to make sense of this hybrid combination? To think along with Erasmus on this question requires, I suggest, a very specific form of dialectical thinking. The first step, as we have just seen, involves a double negation. The life well-lived is *neither* ascetic *nor* hedonistic. Asserting this, however, divorces Christianity from asceticism and Epicureanism from raw hedonism, so something new is afoot on both sides. But now taking the opposite tack, the second step involves an encom-

183. Erasmus, "The Handbook of the Christian Soldier," CWE: 66:89–90.

184. Erasmus, "The Epicurean," CWE 40:1080.

185. Erasmus, "The Handbook of the Christian Soldier," CWE 66:114–16.

passing affirmation. In some sense the heroes of life for Erasmus are both Christian *and* Epicurean. What that means is that they bring together in their lives and deaths both transcendent goods and pleasures of earthly life. As Kaiser puts it, it is "not a matter of bifurcation but of intertwining" what are too often thought to be incompatible—joys of godly piety *and* physical, intellectual, and social pleasures.[186] Though opposites in the good to which they point, they are not so discrepant once stripped of their links to asceticism and hedonism. We find them combined, after all, in those remarkable characters from the *Colloquies* who manage to live and die so well. And yet now, as a third step, though these figures seem to embody something of a living balance, it is by no means a completely settled combination. Enough of a tension between the godly and the worldly persists, in other words, to make them rather odd—interesting and impressive to be sure—but curious nonetheless. The Christian Epicurean, in short, is an ironic figure, albeit in a fairly mild sense—one who combines opposites in a relatively balanced way, but still with sufficient tension so as to grab our attention, stimulate a bit of surprise, and gently stir reflection.

So what are we to make of these ideal and yet ironic figures? And how are we to think of them in connection with those wild mystics from the end of *The Praise of Folly*, the ones so emphasized by Screech and others, who soar beyond their bodies and their world for the love of what is ultimate? It is true, after all, that Erasmus can speak of very worldly things—like love and marriage, for instance—in decidedly mystical terms. In one spot, for instance, he suggests in strongly Platonic terms that the "loving and chaste fire of mutual affection" in marriages among the virtuous reflect their source in God, "the source of all true beauty." In "Christian piety," we are told, the lover is pulled away from "physical preliminaries," and "led by the hand" toward "inward beauty, inward

186. Kaiser, *Praisers of Folly*, 82.

riches, [and] inward nobility." Thus, Erasmus says, when someone is "enraptured" by someone physically beautiful, the lover is "being made aware, as if in a dream, of that other, truly supreme beauty" which is God. With a "glimpse" of the "Supreme Beauty," finally, "the lover is transported by love for it," and from there "it creates and fosters those faultless relationships that grow ever deeper and better."[187] Though this Platonic riff appears to spiritualize natural relationships, its agenda is purely mystical. Its designs, in fact, are beyond anything like human marriage—as lovers are "pulled away" from natural life—"as if in a dream" where they are "transported" beyond the world.

Such language recalls the ecstasy and raptures of the mystical fools at the end of *The Praise of Folly*, though the characters encountered in this meditation, those Christians who live Epicurean lives in the Erasmian sense, are not nearly so demented. In "Courtship," however, it is true that Pamphilus adopts mystical language—albeit playfully—to convey his love for Maria. His soul has left his body, he complains, like one slain (and so dead) or like one "seized by divine inspiration" (and so "possessed by what it ardently loves").[188] But Maria is too well-grounded and too sensible to take this romantic hyperbole seriously, as she has seen him talk, walk, and eat; and in any case, she knows full well that her suitor is fully and wonderfully natural. Their marriage may well involve, as Erasmus casts it, a startling juxtaposition of the transcendent and the natural, yielding something odd and ironic—virginity in marriage—but it will not be mystical, and there will be no dream-like ascent to the "Supreme Beauty" on high. Like the other Christian Epicureans we have met, their lives are tempered and far more balanced than the zany madness of Folly's mystics.

What we receive from Erasmus, therefore, is an invitation to

187. Erasmus, "The Institution of Christian Matrimony," CWE 69:356–57.
188. Erasmus, "Courtship," CWE 39:258–59.

take another look at our lives; specifically to think again about what can be hoped for in life, about the final good of human aspiration. In doing that, we have seen, he challenges those who would be Christians to rethink their religion in a way that goes beyond the impasse of Christianity and Epicureanism. In searching for the truth of these matters, however, Erasmus encourages us to inquire rather than dogmatize. He is committed to finding the truth, as we saw at the end of the first meditation, but doing so requires a kind of dialectical agility, indeed a juggling of opposites, and a readiness to absorb the unsettling irony that is discovered. Are Christians to be ascetic or hedonistic? Should they be oriented to the heavens or at home with natural existence? As Kaiser rightly asks, "how can we tell which he means?" The only answer—confusing and dialectical though it might be—is "that he means neither one nor the other, but both, and more than both."[189] Christian life, in other words, should be neither ascetic nor hedonistic, while nonetheless combining both a pious sense of the transcendent with enjoyment of the pleasures of natural life; but doing that yields something more than the sum of the opposites. It yields, as we have seen, an unsettled and unsettling juxtaposition of opposites which pull and tug our lives in finally irreconcilable directions.

Such are the lives and the deaths of the Christian Epicureans we have met in the *Colloquies* of Erasmus—those odd but still balanced figures wherein transcendent and natural goods are ironically held in suggestive equipoise. And what odd and fascinating characters they are—the old man who has not aged (Glycion); a dying man tranquil in the face of death (Cornelius); a marriage which will aspire to virginity (Pamphilus and Maria); and a godly feast of ordinary lay men ("The Godly Feast"). As we saw in the Introduction to these meditations, *The Praise of Folly* confronts readers with an especially intense and disturbing case of Erasmian

189. Kaiser, *Praisers of Folly*, 37–38.

irony—when the zany madness of the mystic is juxtaposed without settlement with the utterly natural and convivial richness of human existence. If in that classic Erasmus dramatically leaves readers in the lurch, challenging us to grapple with the ironic equipoise of antithetical forms of madness, his experiments with the Christian Epicurean offer a more tempered though still ironic resolution. These remarkable and yet completely human figures, as we have seen, manage to embody a taste of the ultimate and final good, even as they remain well-grounded in their natural and social worlds; and, thus, while the ironic tension between that ultimate good and everyday life persists, it is entertained in a way that is fully conceivable as a way of living a human life. As with all things Erasmian, however, this is a temporary resting place, as there is always another side and more complications to consider.

But what, in the end, is the purpose of thinking about life in this manner? Why rethink religious life in a way that disturbs settled convictions and confuses long-held distinctions? Or, for that matter, why open up oneself to the turbulence of Erasmian irony? Why not make do with the simpler and more definitive answers of tradition? There has never been a shortage, after all, of people or institutions offering what purport to be final truths, so why deliberately engage the disturbing prospects of irony? In general terms, I suggest, it is good to follow along with Erasmian thinking on these questions because human life is diminished when it abandons the experience of irony; or, turned around, it is enhanced when it stands open to the startling and unsettling prospects of irony. As Lear often notes, this means more than a willingness to engage criticism. It means, far more profoundly, "cultivating an experience of oneself" (or of one's world) as "uncanny" or "out of joint," not what we had thought at all.[190] In the present context one might wonder, for instance, whether Christianity is still Christian

190. Lear, *A Case for Irony*, 37.

if it is Epicurean? But then, in a more disturbing vein, one might ask if Christianity is Christian if it is not Epicurean? But what then is Christianity? For the one who cares about things Christian, these doubts must be unsettling; and, for Erasmus, that is a very good thing. When Erasmus injects Epicurean sentiments into the heart of Christian life, therefore, he pushes people to ponder the sanity of all those Christian positions which in some manner denigrate and degrade natural human existence; and so many of them have done precisely that. In Tracy's language, is not "a Christianity predicated on humiliating the human spirit," in fact, a "false Christianity" altogether?[191] Or, to borrow Kaiser's more positive language, can Christianity be Christian if it does not become a "joyous humanism," one that rejoices in the pleasures of the world, even as it insists that "the only true pleasures are those of the mind, that the pleasures most people seek are more painful than pleasurable, [and] that God is the fountain of joy?"[192] However the points are posed, such questions open us to deeply ironic experiences—in this case, to tremble with great distress over the tragic fallout of ascetic Christianity, even as we may enjoy with eye-opening amusement the comical prospects for a joyous Christianity.

191. James D. Tracy, "Erasmus among the Postmodernists: *Dissimulatio*, *Bonae Literae*, and *Docta Pietas Revisited*," in *Erasmus' Vision of the Church*, ed. Hilmar M. Pabel, Sixteenth Century Essays and Studies, 33 (Kirksville, Mo.: Truman State University Press, 1997), 37.

192. Kaiser, *Praisers of Folly*, 80–81.

Epilogue

Erasmian Irony and the Courage of Truth

HAVING ENTERTAINED these three meditations and having tasted the irony Erasmus brings to each, what—we should step back and ask—have we learned about ourselves as human beings? What kind of creatures are we, and, again, who is it that we might be? Additionally, who is it that we want to be; and, of course, that we should be? These are the overarching questions that have guided the three meditations with the thinking of Erasmus. At heart, of course, these are questions of self-knowledge. As we saw at the beginning of this work, they are perennial questions; and, to be sure, they are as important as they are demanding. Indeed, the sheer multiplicity of answers offered up over the centuries attests to the fact that these are questions we hold in common; and yet, too, this diversity bears witness to the enormous difficulties they entail. We are, it would seem, and certainly Erasmus would have us see, such utterly fascinating and yet undeniably odd creatures that we have a terrible time coming to terms with the warp and woof of our lives. What a wild theater of folly we perform, and how mad is the life we lead! And it is precisely this folly and this madness that become so prominent when we turn, with the help of Erasmus, to consider the more specific questions concerning human existence—specifically, in his terms, how we handle claims to truth, how we respond to the challenge of peace, and finally, how we chart the quest for happiness.

With this in mind, what have we gathered from these meditations with Erasmus? To be sure, Erasmus offers up plenty of insights, and he puts forward many proposals. But, more importantly, and I suggest the primary step toward understanding Erasmus, and, too, the crucial first step in understanding ourselves in an Erasmian manner, is to deal squarely with the fact that what we are faced with from Erasmus are unsettling proposals. What is so unsettling is, plainly put, the idea that we are all quite mad—somehow beside ourselves, full of folly, even out of our minds, plain crazy. None of this is meant in strictly medical terms, of course, though it is intended to highlight how odd and loopy we are, at least when seen from certain angles; and, indeed, many forms of human madness would be quite pathological—the zeal of the warrior pope, the passion of the crazed lover, the obsession of the miser, or the babbling piety of the charismatic, for instance—if they had not somehow come to seem normal or even noble. Indeed, in Erasmian terms, to be human is to be blessed with a certain form of madness—or, to put it in a more unsettling manner—to be slightly demented in judgment, perhaps vehement in passion, or possibly just happily mindless. We are, to rekindle the examples from *The Praise of Folly*, so full of folly and so wrapped in madness in myriad ways—at once funny, wild, crazed, angelic, romantic, sordid, naive, bored, ecstatic, delusional, treacherous, congenial, and so on. And were someone to suggest—as Horace does in his dialogue with the madman Damasippus—that in his own mind he is sane and sensible—well, then, he deserves (and he in turn receives) a full and frank diagnosis of the "mental disorder" that shapes his life.[1] No one, in the end, is exempt from the madness of humanity—neither Erasmus and his many readers, nor myself and my far fewer readers. But that means, of course, that any account of human life must manage to capture and confront this unsettling quality; and to do this requires that we shift our perspective so that we come to look at ourselves as if from afar, as if from another world, or from the balcony of a theater, such that common assumptions of normalcy—all the ways in which we take ourselves so seriously—are broken and we begin to see ourselves as rather peculiar and just a bit odd, and perhaps, too, as laughable, or possibly despicable, and indeed amazing.

Shifting perspective, however, is just the start to understanding ourselves in an Erasmian manner. We are encouraged, in the second place, to think broadly enough to cope with the unsettled and sometimes conflicting diversity of types of madness. The unsettled truth about our mad existence is that human life, simply put, is never simple, so that to understand anything about who we are and how we live, one must be willing and perhaps also eager to entertain opposing and even contrary versions of our folly, never settling for one-dimensional and hence narrow and partial resolutions. Meeting this challenge, as Erasmus shows us, requires a capacious sensibility, one that is dedicated to entertaining and savoring alternative sides of a single phenomenon. In this regard, oddly enough, Erasmus echoes the ancient sophist Protagoras, who is said (by Diogenes Laertius) to be "the first to say that on every issue there are two arguments opposed to each other."[2] Un-

1. *Horace's Satires and Epistles*, Satires book 2, number 3, line 302, 46. As Damasippus tells it, Horace imitates the wealthy and important, writes worthless poetry, has a "rotten temper," and harbors "mad lusts for a thousand girls, a thousand boys." See lines 305–25.

2. See *The Older Sophists*, 21. The fragment comes from Diogenes Laertius IX. 51:

like Protagoras, however, the Erasmian proceeds not to win an argument (making a bad case look good) and certainly not for profit (as the sophists were reputed to do), but because repeatedly looking at both sides of an issue is the only way of securing a relatively complete understanding of what our lives are like. It is a "quality of mind," as Kaiser puts it so well, "that perpetually perceive[s] the qualifying *but* to any argument," and hence one that insists on giving full due to all sides of a question; and, additionally, it is "an empathy of heart that participate[s] actively in all aspects of being without committing itself exclusively to any one."[3] This is, of course, the very thing—that sense of balance or that hesitant circumspection—that infuriated the opponents and frustrated the friends of Erasmus. But it is also, in a far more positive vein, the quality of mind which prompts us to entertain complexity, to renounce simple answers, and to avoid partisan dogmas; and, just as importantly, it is the empathy which prods us to appreciate the richness of existence and to enjoy the manifold madness of humanity, without recoiling to a simple and privileged sphere.

The Erasmian manner of thinking proceeds from an odd-angled percipience and a capacious sensibility; but on the basis of this perception and by means of this sensibility, it also involves—in the third place—a kind of dialectical agility which gives rise to irony. It is here that the Erasmian manner becomes most interesting; and this is, I suggest, the most significant—and the most intellectually useful—legacy of Erasmian thinking. For as we have seen in the preceding meditations, Erasmus invites us first to think with nuance, treating opposition with flexibility and making space for different sides of issues. The further challenge, however, is to hold the two sides in an odd but provocative tension—as we saw

"[Protagoras] was the first to say that on every issue there are two arguments opposed to each other." See also the fragments from Clement and Seneca, *The Older Sophists*, 13. See Eric MacPhail, "Erasmus as Sophist," 71–88.

3. Kaiser, *Praisers of Folly*, 93.

Erasmus do in the third meditation, with the unusual praise of virginity in marriage; or, more broadly, with the baffling contention that Christians are truly Epicureans; or, more broadly still, where he holds natural felicity and mystical ecstasy in unresolved equipoise. As Kaiser notes, once again, "it is the *coincidentia*—the synthesis, the equipoise, the concord—which produces [this] quality of irony."[4] Or, to be a bit more precise, it is the *unfinished* synthesis, the *tenuous* equipoise, and the *awkward* concord that strikes up the sense of surprise or disarray typical of Erasmian irony, for in each case there is a coinciding of opposites where the opposition remains in play. How awkward that can be and how disconcerting that must feel, as the everyday mind thirsts to break the juxtaposition—insisting, for instance, that married people are *not* celibate, Christians are *not* Epicureans, and mystics *utterly* transcend natural life. But it is exactly this that the Erasmian manner refuses to concede, challenging us instead to come to terms with the dialectically finessed coincidence, and from that recognition to absorb and perhaps even embrace the full impact of the ironic point.

Roughly the same result is produced, but with a more playful agility, where inversions of appearance and reality are tested and pressed to reveal the simple but all-important fact that things are not always as they seem. Indeed, once one begins to distrust appearances, to suspect that there may be something very different beneath the surface than meets the eye, then life is not the same. At that point, as we saw in the first meditation, the door opens to a new view of the world—one that is potentially explosive, as the corrupt are stripped of their artful pretenses and the fraudulent are exposed for the scoundrels that they are; and, too, it is a view that can be revelatory, as the unassuming and unnoticed are heard—surprisingly and perhaps for the first time—as bearing a value never before assumed or a wisdom never noticed. In all

4. Ibid., 24.

of this, things simply are not as they appear to be. Spotting these inversions, however, is the work of a dialectical imagination, one that is agile enough to reverse the twisted reversals of appearance and reality and begin to set the matter straight. As such, it is a way of getting at the truth of our lives, and it is one that is both playful, daring, and thoroughly ironic. At times, however, as we saw in the second meditation, Erasmus prods us to turn up the pressure right at the point of discovery. At these junctures the Erasmian manner is marked by relentless questioning, pushing and prodding to determine whether we really are who we have come to think we are. Perhaps, in fact, we have been deceived by our own appearances, or more specifically by the stories we tell ourselves and others. In response, as we saw especially in the second meditation, the Erasmian proceeds in a bold and daring manner, at once free and unbound, pressing the question to the limit, and thereby confronting us with the unnerving—and deeply ironic—truth about ourselves.

None of this, of course, fits standard models for philosophical reflection on human existence; nor, as Erasmus discovered repeatedly, does it find a place within theological orbits of any sort. Perhaps that is why Erasmus and his irony receive so little attention in either discipline, despite the important work of late in Erasmian studies. Yet, I suggest and I have argued, Erasmian irony—made possible by means of the very specific manner of thinking just outlined—retains the power to prod and prompt fruitful thinking about our lives. And this is—if I may say so—something sorely lacking in current philosophical and theological studies. Indeed, to forfeit the Erasmian manner of thinking diminishes the power of either discipline to deal adequately with human existence, for at the root of Erasmian irony is a peculiar "courage of truth," as Michel Foucault calls it in his lectures on the ancient Cynics. What we have from Erasmus, quite clearly, is not the bold and blunt frankness of a Cynic like Diogenes of Sinope, who—if we are to believe the accounts collected by Diogenes Laertius—made his points by quick repartee, public displays, and an utterly carefree lifestyle. What we receive from Erasmus, instead, is a finely discursive, generously capacious, certainly playful, and frequently round-about manner of conveying the truth. At the same time, however, the Erasmian manner certainly is bold and disruptive in its challenging, questioning, and prodding; and that is, as we have seen, the whole point of Erasmian irony—to tell and receive the truth in such a courageous manner. The final challenge for us, therefore, is to develop and risk a capacity for irony, to learn to look truthfully at ourselves in an ironic manner, and to face the ironic point when it strikes home. Without doubt this is not common. It is rare now and it was rare in the days of Erasmus. And, too, it must be said, that Erasmus does not manage this in every text; indeed, for example, much of the correspondence in his later years is nothing but serious and sober. And yet even in later works there are flashes of that manner of thinking which gives rise to ironic insight; and certainly, too, there are more than enough instances within individual works and in the cross-currents between works to offer us a lasting model—as I have argued throughout these meditations—for anyone willing to risk looking at the truth of our lives with a sense of irony.

So what is the meaning of irony in Erasmian thinking? Quite clearly it is not simply a matter of being clever or witty, though Erasmus could be both. Nor is it identical to being sarcastic, as the word sometimes get used today as an equivalent for irony, though Erasmus was more than capable of tearing a bit of flesh from his adversaries. Nor does irony suggest some kind of philosophical neutrality, hovering above the relative creations of contingent beings, juggling them back and forth, while refraining from any sort of definite commitment—the kind of thing idealized by Rorty as the role of the "ironist" philosopher.[5] Though Erasmus does his fair share of hovering above the fray of fools (we are invited, after

5. See Rorty, *Contingency, Irony, and Solidarity*, 73.

all, to look at human madness from afar) and though he also playfully juggles opposition (we are challenged, quite clearly, to handle difference with playful agility), it is never an idle game, something stripped of commitment, simply for the sake of intellectual amusement. Indeed, as we have seen from Erasmus and as is central to the Erasmian manner of thinking, something only becomes ironic because one cares about or is committed to the matter in question; or, as Lear puts it, the capacity for irony is "partially constituted by an openness to getting rattled by one's own commitments," or I would add, to having one's commitments rattled.[6] True irony always strikes home, to one degree or another; it reverberates throughout one's life, exposing the fragility of the deeply felt set of commitments at stake. But this means, then, that equating irony with cleverness is a trivialization of real irony, and perhaps also an under-estimation of the power of wit; and rejecting irony because it is sarcastic, ruthless, or hurtful is nothing but a defensive resistance to having one's life disrupted. And, too, it means that the image of the philosopher as a "detached" ironist involves a very "thin" view of irony, one that bespeaks a kind of "complacent" gnosticism that wishes to avoid being rattled.[7] In any case, Erasmian irony is something far more and far different from these things. So what, once again, is the meaning of irony in Erasmian thinking?

Erasmian irony has a range of interconnected meanings; and thus, as Lear shows, one can speak of irony in several senses. Most immediately and most recognizably, it is an experience that someone undergoes. In Erasmian terms it springs from a perception that things are not as they appear to be; that the order of things is somehow twisted, backwards, perhaps topsy-turvy, and in any case not the way it was thought to be, or more seriously, not the way it should be. In any case, the perception in turn gives rise to an

6. Lear, *A Case for Irony*, 119; see also 37–39. For Rorty's portrait of the independent and detached ironist, see Rorty, *Contingency, Irony, and Solidarity*, 73.

7. Lear, *A Case for Irony*, 119.

emotive response; and the upshot may be startling, head-turning, surprising, shocking, or deeply disturbing. A whole range is possible—from simple bemusement to devastating shock—but in one way or another the perceived incongruity—things are backwards, the world is upside down, they are not who they appear to be—strikes home, sparking a movement, and eliciting a reaction. It may be a simple head-turning double-take (expressing the startled bemusement that the pretentious abbot is ignorant and the modest lady is learned); or perhaps a wide-eyed smile of surprise (conveying amazed incredulity that Christians really are Epicureans); or, in a more positive vein, a beaming grin of delighted recognition (there is indeed great wisdom hidden beneath the simple visage); or, again, more negatively, a disturbed grimace (so the man of religion has made himself rich by preying on the innocent). But the insight can also strike home in more unsettling ways, leaving us confused, maybe baffled, and certainly less sure of things than we thought. And at its extreme, in fact, one can begin to find basic, everyday assumptions and fundamental beliefs becoming thoroughly unstable and "weirdly unfamiliar."[8] How eerie it is, for instance, to seriously digest the Erasmian questions posed in the second meditation—is it really the "fatal malady" of civilized people to be "quite unable to carry on without wars?" Do we in fact have a secret longing or even a love for warfare? To absorb the impact of these questions without flinching is to undergo an experience of "ironic uncanniness," where the very thing that matters most to us—being civilized, in this case—is deeply unsettled, if not absolutely imploded. It is, as Lear puts it, "like losing the ground beneath one's feet"; or as Kaiser notes, like walking through a "vertiginous semantic labyrinth," where nothing means what it used to mean.[9] In this, the most "robust form of irony," one is left stunned and speechless.[10]

8. Ibid., 16.

9. Lear, *A Case for Irony*, 19; and Kaiser, *Praisers of Folly*, 36.

10. Lear, *A Case for Irony*, 16.

So irony is fundamentally an experience, a form of insight packed with varying degrees and types of emotional punch, often interlaced with a decidedly physical reaction. But in this regard it also—in a certain sense—dwells in the state of things around us. The inversions and coincidences which give rise to the ironic experience, after all, are something that strike us, states of affairs which must be spotted, and things to which we react. None of this can happen, however, without someone having a capacity for irony, as the experience of irony is (as Lear notes) always intensely "first-personal."[11] It is for each person to see through the appearances, contesting their inversions, and digesting the shock of ironic insight; no one can do this for someone else, though the upshot may be shared. A well-developed capacity for irony, however, is quite rare, as most people are not naturally eager to have their lives rattled and their loves disturbed; and social networks of all sorts are not designed to encourage their members to raise and press questions to the point where members are shocked at the specter of the truth, especially if that truth strikes at the heart of the network—that civilized people are savages, that Christ is just a story, that everyone is a liar, and so on. The capacity for irony is unusual, therefore, and consequently it often must be cultivated; to that end, education in irony often is advanced with the help of one whose capacity for irony has become a "human excellence." Such a person—again in Lear's terms—is someone whose very life and existence culminate in "the capacity for deploying irony in the right way at the right time in the living of a distinctively human life."[12] In a word, such a person has the power to engender the experience of irony in others; and the ability to deploy this power has come to define their very existence.[13] Most certainly the authentic sileni encountered in the first meditation embody exactly this kind of ironic existence. And it seems likely that Erasmus lived out such an ironic existence, but

11. Ibid., 9.
12. Ibid., 9; see 119.
13. Ibid., 30.

whether he did or not, or whether he did so consistently, it remains true that many of his writings—certainly *The Praise of Folly*, but many others besides, especially when considered together—bear a kind of ironic existence, and thus maintain the power to challenge us to develop an aptitude for irony.

These meditations, in fact, have banked on the power of Erasmian texts to speak ironically about the madness of our humanity. As we have seen in each meditation, we are challenged to develop just such a capacity for irony. But why exactly is that? Why, in short, is irony good for us, and why is it something we should embrace? The answer, I suggest, is that irony of the Erasmian sort is a manner of thinking especially well-suited for creatures such as ourselves—richly complex and wonderfully odd, yet somehow complacent and at ease with forms of thinking which offer us fixed and settled resolutions. Therefore, where simplified answers reign, the Erasmian offers complexity; where there is one-sided treatment, it demands a capacious sense of breadth; when seriousness grips the mind, it entertains levity; where there is boredom in life, it offers a shock; and should the passions be numbed, it provides surprise. Then, again, when thinking becomes rigid, it demands flexibility; where faith succumbs to dogmatism, it raises doubt; and if skepticism breeds confusion, it offers nuance. Should someone proclaim their sanity, it reveals the extent of their madness; and, of course, if someone has gone mad in an unfortunate way, it prescribes a more pleasant sort of madness.[14] In all of this we have an especially agile "form of truthfulness" that is practically committed to the enhancement of self-knowledge.[15] There is, quite clearly, little interest in strict orthodoxy or rigid ideology, and few concessions are granted to habit

14. Some Erasmian characters do exactly this for a priest they have tricked into becoming insanely possessed with exorcism. Giving him a letter from the spirit he has been bent on helping, they manage to relieve his obsession by giving him a gentler "brand of insanity." "Now he's mad in more pleasant way," one of the characters remarks. See Erasmus, "Exorcism, or The Spectre," CWE 39:541.

15. Lear, *A Case for Irony*, 31.

or convention. Instead, as we have seen, the interest centers on telling the truth about our lives, partly for the immediate effect the text has on readers, but more importantly to prod us to develop our own capacity for sensing the folly and gleaning the madness of our lives. As Lear nicely puts it, "human flourishing … partly consist[s] in cultivating an experience of oneself as uncanny, out of joint."[16] The whole point of Erasmian irony is exactly that—to promote the flourishing of human life by prompting people to cultivate an experience of themselves as full of folly and downright mad. However, no one should be fooled into thinking that this is easy; and, to be sure, no individual and no social network can survive with a sustained experience of irony. And yet without the insight and the experience brought through such irony, one lacks the kind of self-awareness necessary for a full and free life; and thus one becomes vulnerable to narrow and self-satisfied forms of thinking readily available in the worlds in which we dwell.

Equipped with a capacity for irony, however, one can more ably navigate the most basic and most contested questions of human existence—the handling of truth, the challenge of peace, and the quest for happiness. Indeed, as we have seen in the preceding meditations, developing and cultivating such a capacity opens the way to some rich dividends in dealing with these issues. When it comes to how we handle claims to truth, we find Erasmus speaking in an oracular fashion, telling the truth in disguise, posing and dissembling, often playfully and sometimes strategically. He conveys a message, therefore, that can only be told fully with nuance and delicacy, revealing by means of a certain concealment, exposing by way of a playful hiding. By proceeding in this manner, as we have seen, he carves out a narrow space and a distinctive path for speaking the truth, one which rests between those who would skeptically abdicate any interest in truth and those who dogmatically

16. Ibid., 37.

demand (and lay claim to) absolute truths. What we receive in the first meditation, therefore, is a lesson in ironic truth-telling—one which resists the deceivers by insisting on telling the truth, while dissenting from the absolutists by defending honest dissemblance.

When it comes to conflicts between countries and the challenge of peace, we find Erasmus playing the gadfly, assuming an independent tack between those who offer moral justification to warfare and those who renounce war in principle. It is not, however, a compromising middle-ground that Erasmus pursues, but a relentless line of tough questions, wondering whether those who would give moral legitimacy to war are not self-deceived; whether as civilized people they simply cannot live without war; or whether they in fact harbor a deep-seated yet unacknowledged love of war. What we learn in the second meditation, therefore, is a manner of ironic questioning—one which shifts the focus from moral legitimation to questions of sanity and insanity, thereby leaving us with a deeply-disturbing cluster of eerie proposals.

When it comes, finally, to questions of human fulfilment, and thus to debates over the final good of human existence, we find Erasmus performing feats of balance typical of an equilibrist. And, indeed, Erasmus is a master of equipoise, juggling coinciding opposites, and insisting that normally contentious viewpoints be brought together in awkward but interesting conversation. What we learn from the third meditation, therefore, is the ironic art of coinciding opposites—one which challenges both an ascetic and a hedonist account of human life, generously affirming an equipoise of natural and eternal felicity in the ironically formed notion of the Christian Epicurean. On all three scores, I suggest, Erasmian irony at work—at once fiercely independent, capacious in breadth, dialectically agile, and courageous in facing the uncanny—provides helpful guidance in cultivating a capacity for ironic self-knowledge; and, thereby, it contributes mightily to human flourishing.

In the end, Erasmian irony is part and parcel of a humanistic take on the world. In connection with Erasmus, it is true, the word "humanism" takes on a variety of meanings, each of which is important, but only one of which is completely germane to my purposes. Most generally, to speak of Erasmus as a humanist places him historically in a movement of thought which valued literature and rhetoric through the recovery of classic texts and languages. This historical placement, however, entails a second sense of humanism, as it points up the philosophical affirmation of the capacities of human intelligence. While fully acknowledging the weakness and blindness to which the mind is susceptible, the humanist in this sense places what hope we might have in the workings of the human mind. From this follows a third sense of humanism, a theological one that affirms the basic goodness of human nature, albeit weakened, sickened, and distorted to terrible ends; and thus that also insists upon the fundamental integrity of the human will (and, hence, of its desires), despite their distortions and extravagances. Theological humanism, in this Erasmian sense, refuses to participate in the incessant denigration of the human before an all-powerful sovereign; though, to be sure, Erasmus himself—echoing his Augustinian heritage—retained a strong sense of grace and divine majesty. But the humanism of Erasmus includes, as well, an ethical challenge to human action, especially for the poor and maltreated, thereby concentrating attention on care and compassion for other human beings. Each of these forms of humanism contributes to understanding Erasmus as a humanist, and each one helps to give shape to the Erasmian manner of thinking.

More significantly, however, and more germane to the focus of these meditations, is the manner in which Erasmian irony contributes directly to humanistic ends. On this score, consider a comment made by Erasmus in a letter to Erard de la Marck—saying in brief, that "not all who have a tongue have heart and brains."[17]

17. Erasmus, Erasmus to Erard de la Marck, CWE 6:248.

What a remarkably brief yet potent observation, that is. It means, I take it, that a lot of people go about life speaking without a care or a thought; or, more bluntly, they wander about chattering away in a mindless and careless manner. In a word, such people have no idea what their lives are like because they have never—sadly enough—given it much thought. In Erasmian terms, this is not terribly surprising, since all human beings are blessed with a certain folly or madness, and—as *The Praise of Folly* illustrates so well—we fools are notoriously oblivious to our own folly. At the same time, Erasmus reminds us, we human beings also are uniquely capable of self-reflection, of standing back and taking in the shape of our lives, and thereby—just possibly—to marvel at our own condition, finding it funny, or surprising, perhaps shocking, and possibly uncanny. To be human, then, is to be mad, in one way or another; but to flourish as a human being means—among other things—to take stock of this madness, to experience our own folly, to get at the truth of our lives, and to react in a fitting way. In short, to be human in this richer, Erasmian sense means cultivating and practicing a manner of thinking that generates ironic insight; and to manage this with excellence means speaking with both our brains and our hearts, blending agility and capaciousness with generosity, yielding thereby surprising and sometimes unsettling insights as to the shape and quality of our lives. Such is the legacy of Erasmus, and such is this book's invitation to think in an Erasmian manner—to think ironically about the truth of our lives for the sake of enhancing human existence.

Bibliography

Allen, Don Cameron. "The Rehabilitation of Epicurus and His Theory of Pleasure in the Early Renaissance." *Studies in Philology* 41, no. 1 (January 1944): 1–15.

Ambrose. "Concerning Virgins." Translated by H. de Romestin, with E. de Romestin and H. T. F. Duckworth. In *Nicene and Post-Nicene Fathers, Second Series*, vol. 10, edited by Philip Schaff and Henry Wace, 361–87. Grand Rapid, Mich.: Eerdmans, 1955.

———. *Saint Ambrose: Letters 1–91*. Translated by Mary Melchior Beyenka. New York: Fathers of the Church, 1954.

Anselm. *Anselm of Canterbury*. Edited and translated by Jasper Hopkins and Herbert Richardson. 3 vols. Toronto: Edwin Mellen, 1974.

Arieti, James A. *Interpreting Plato; The Dialogues as Drama*. Savage, Md.: Rowman and Littlefield, 1991.

Aristotle. *The Basic Works of Aristotle*. Edited by Richard McKeon. New York: Random House, 1941.

Augustijn, Cornelis. *Erasmus: His Life, Works, and Influence*. Translated by J. C. Grayson. Toronto: University of Toronto Press, 1991.

Augustine. *Concerning the City of God Against the Pagans*. Translated by Henry Bettenson. London: Penguin, 1972.

———. *Saint Augustine: Letters*. Translated by Sister Wilfrid Parsons. Washington, D.C.: The Catholic University of America Press, 1964. First published 1953, Fathers of the Church.

———. *Saint Augustine, Sermons 341–400 (III/10)*, vol. 1. Edited by John E. Rotelle. New York: New City, 1995.

———. *Treatise on Various Subjects*. Edited by Roy J. Deferrari. New York: Fathers of the Church, 1952.

Bailey, F. G. *The Prevalence of Deceit*. Ithaca, N.Y.: Cornell University Press, 1991.

Bakhtin, Mikhail. *Rabelais and His World*. Translated by Helene Iswolsky. Bloomington, Ind.: Indiana University Press, 1984.

Barker, William. "Implied Ethics in the *Adagia* of Erasmus: An Index of *Felicitas*." *Renaissance and Reformation; Renaissance et Réforme* 30, no. 1 (2006): 87–102.

Bense, Walter F. "Paris Theologians on War and Peace, 1521–1529." *Church History: Studies in Christianity and Culture* 41, no. 2 (June 1972): 168–85.

Bernard of Clairvaux. *On the Song of Songs*. 2 vols. Translated by Kilian J. Walsh. Kalamazoo, Mich.: Cistercian Publications, 1976.

Bietenzholz, Peter G., ed. *Contemporaries of Erasmus: A Biographical Register of the Renaissance and Reformation*. 3 vols. Toronto: University of Toronto Press, 1987.

———. "Erasmus, His Mistress Folly, and the Garden of Epicurus." In *Encounters with a Radical Erasmus: Erasmus' Work as a Source of Radical Thought in Early Modern Europe*, by Peter G. Bietenholz, 109–40. Toronto: University of Toronto Press, 2009.

Boyle, Leonard E. *Facing History: A Different Thomas Aquinas*. Textes et études du moyen âge, 13. Louvain-La-Neuve: Fédération Internationale des Instituts d'Études de Moyen Age, 2000.

Boyle, Marjorie O'Rourke. *Erasmus on Language and Method in Theology*. Toronto: University of Toronto Press, 1977.

———. *Christening Pagan Mysteries: Erasmus in Pursuit of Wisdom*. Toronto: University of Toronto Press, 1981.

Brachnin, Pierre. "*Vox Clamantis in Deserto*: Réflexions sur le Pacifisme d'Érasme." In *Colloquia Erasmia Turonensia*, 2 vols., edited by Jean-Claude Margolin, 1:247–276. Toronto: University of Toronto Press, 1969.

Branham, R. Bracht. *Unruly Eloquence: Lucian and the Comedy of Traditions*. Cambridge, Mass.: Harvard University Press, 1989.

Brown, Peter. *The World of Late Antiquity: AD 150–750*. London: Harcourt, Brace, and Jovanovich, 1971.

———. *The Body and Society: Men, Women and Sexual Renunciation in Early Christianity*. New York: Columbia University Press, 1988.

Bultot, R. "Érasme, Épicure et le 'De Contemptu Mundi.'" In *Scrinium Erasmianum*, vol. 2, edited by J. Coppens, 221–26. Leiden: E. J. Brill, 1969.

Burton-Christie, Douglas. *The Word in the Desert; Scripture and the Quest for Holiness in Early Christian Monasticism*. Oxford: Oxford University Press, 1993.

Capps, E., T. E. Page, and W. H. D. Rouse, eds. *The Greek Anthology*. 3 vols. London: William Heinemann, 1915.

Carrington, Laurel. "Erasmus' *Lingua*: The Double-Edged Tongue." *Erasmus of Rotterdam Society Yearbook* 9 (1989): 106–18.

Chapiro, José. *Erasmus and Our Struggle for Peace*. Boston: Beacon Press, 1950.

Chenu, M.-D. *Toward Understanding Saint Thomas*. Translated by A.-M. Landry and D. Hughes. Chicago: Henry Regnery, 1964,

Chomarat, Jacques. *Grammaire et rhétorique chez Erasme*. 2 vols. Paris: Belles Lettres, 1981.

Cicero, Marcus Tullius. *De Officiis*. Translated by Walter Miller. Cambridge, Mass.: Harvard University Press, 1913.

———. *Letters to Atticus*. Translated by E. O. Winstedt. 3 vols. London: William Heinemann, 1912.

———. *The Letters to His Friends*. Translated by W. Glynn Williams. 3 vols. London: William Heinemann, 1927.

———. *On Moral Ends*. Edited by Julia Annas. Translated by Raphael Woolf. Cambridge: Cambridge University Press, 2001.

———. *The Republic*. Translated by Clinton Walker Keyes. Cambridge, Mass.: Harvard University Press, 1966.

Clement of Alexandria. "The Stromata, or Miscellanies." Edited by A. Cleveland Coxe. Vol. 2 of *The Ante-Nicene Fathers*, edited by Alexander Roberts and James Donaldson, 299–556. Grand Rapids, Mich.: Eerdmans, 1951.

Colie, Rosalie L. *Paradoxia Epidemica: The Renaissance Tradition of Paradox*. Princeton, N.J.: Princeton University Press, 1966.

Cowan, Robert. "Introduction." In *Horace's Satires and Epistles*. Oxford: Oxford Univerity Press, 2011.

Cusato, Michael F., and G. Geltner, eds. *Defenders and Critics of Franciscan Life: Essays in Honor of John V. Fleming*. Leiden: E. J. Brill, 2009.

Damian, Peter. *Letters*, vol. 2. Translated by Owen J. Blum and Irven Michael Resnick. Washington, D.C.: The Catholic University of America Press, 1989.

Dealy, Ross. "The Dynamics of Erasmus' Thought on War." *Erasmus of Rotterdam Society Yearbook* 4, no. 1 (1984): 53–67.

Delcourt, Marie, and Marcelle Derwa. "Trois Aspect Humanistes de L'Épicurisme Chrétien." In *Colloquium Erasmianum: Actes du Colloque International réuni à Mons du 26 au 29 octobre 1967*, 119–133. Mons: Centre Universitaire de l'État, 1968.

Derrida, Jacques. *Dissemination*. Translated by Barbara Johnson. Chicago: University of Chicago Press, 1981.

DeWitt, Norman Wentworth. *Epicurus and His Philosophy*. Cleveland, Ohio: Meridian Books, 1967.

Dio Chrysostom. "The Eighth Discourse: Diogenes or On Virtue." In *Dio Chrysostom*, vol. 1. Translated by J. W. Cohoon. London: William Heinemann, 1932.

Diogenes Laertius. *Lives of Eminent Philosophers*. Translated by R. D. Hicks. 2 vols. London: William Heinemann, 1925.

Douglas, A. E. "Erasmus as a Satirist." In *Erasmus*, edited by T. A. Dorey, 31–54. Albuquerque: University of New Mexico Press, 1970.

Drysdall, Denis L. "Erasmus on Tyranny and Terrorism: *Scarabaeus aquilam quaerit* and the *Institutio principis christiani*." *Erasmus of Rotterdam Society Yearbook* 29 (2009): 89–102.

Dunn-Lardeau, Brenda. "Érasme, pédagogue du bonheur, dans les *Colloques*." *Renaissance and Reformation/Renaissance et Réforme* 30, no. 1 (Winter 2006): 103–18.

Epicurus. *The Epicurus Reader: Selected Writings and Testimonia*. Translated by Brad Inwood and L. P. Gerson. Indianapolis, Ind.: Hackett, 1994.

Erasmus, Desiderius. *The Collected Works of Erasmus*. Toronto: University of Toronto Press, 1974–.

———. "Paraclesis: or, An Exhortation." In *The Praise of Folly and Other*

Writings. Translated by Robert M. Adams, 118–27. New York: W. W. Norton, 1989.

———. *The Praise of Folly*. Translated by Clarence H. Miller. New Haven, Conn.: Yale University Press, 1979.

Erler, Michael. "Epicureanism in the Roman Empire." In *The Cambridge Companion to Epicureanism*, edited by James Warren, 46–64. Cambridge: Cambridge University Press, 2009.

Everitt, Anthony. *Cicero: The Life and Times of Rome's Greatest Politician*. New York: Random House, 2003.

Farge, James K. *Orthodoxy and Reform in Early Reformation France: Faculty of Theology of Paris, 1500–1543*. Leiden: E. J. Brill, 1985.

Febvre, Lucien. *The Problem of Unbelief in the Sixteenth Century: The Religion of Rabelais*. Translated by Beatrice Gottlieb. Cambridge, Mass.: Harvard University Press, 1982.

Ferguson, John. "Epicureanism under the Roman Empire." Revised and supplemented by Jackson P. Hershbell. *Aufstieg und Niedergang der römischen Welt: Geschichte und Kultur Roms im Spiegel der neuern Forschung* 2, pt. 36, no. 4:2286–311.

Fernández, José A. "Erasmus on Just War." *Journal of the History of Ideas* 34, no. 2 (April–June 1973): 209–26.

Foster, Kenelm. *The Life of Saint Thomas Aquinas: Biographical Documents*. Baltimore, Md.: Helicon, 1959.

Fukuyama, Francis. *The End of History and the Last Man*. New York: Macmillan, 1992.

Furey, Constance M. "Invective and Discernment in Martin Luther, D. Erasmus, and Thomas More." *Harvard Theological Review* 98, no. 4 (2005): 469–88.

Geroulanos, Stefanos. *An Atheism That Is not Humanist Emerges in French Thought*. Stanford, Calif.: Stanford University Press, 2010.

Gordon, Walter M. *Humanist Play and Belief: The Seriocomic Art of Desiderius Erasmus*. Toronto: University of Toronto Press, 1990.

Gorgias, "Encomium of Helen." Translated by George Kennedy. In *The Older Sophists: A Complete Translation by Several Hands of the Fragments Der Vorsokraticker*, edited by Rosamond Kent Sprague, 50–54. Columbia: University of South Carolina Press, 1972.

Gregory of Nyssa. "On Virginity." Translated by William Moore and Henry Austin Wilson. In *Nicene and Post-Nicene Fathers, Second Series,* vol. 5, edited by Philip Schaff and Henry Wace, 343–71. Grand Rapids, Mich.: Eerdmans, 1955.

Greenblatt, Stephen. *The Swerve: How the World Became Modern.* New York: W. W. Norton, 2012.

Hale, J. R. *War and Society in Renaissance Europe, 1450–1620.* Baltimore, Md.: Johns Hopkins University Press, 1985.

Halkin, Léon-E. *Erasmus: A Critical Biography.* Translated by John Tonkin. Oxford: Blackwell, 1993.

Harrer, G. A. "Cicero on Peace and War." *The Classical Journal* 14, no. 1 (October 1918): 26–38.

Haskins, Charles Homer. *The Renaissance of the Twelfth Century.* Cambridge, Mass.: Harvard University Press, 1933.

Hauerwas, Stanley. *Should War Be Eliminated? Philosophical and Theological Investigations.* Milwaukee, Wis.: Marquette University Press, 1984.

Heath, Michael J. "Erasmus and War against the Turks." In *Acta Conventus Neo-Latini Turonensis*, edited by Jean Claude Margolin, vol. 2, 991–1001. Paris: J. Vrin, 1980.

Horace. *The Complete Odes and Epodes.* Translated by W. G. Shepherd. London: Penguin, 1983.

———. *Horace's Satires and Epistles.* Translated by Jacob Fuchs. New York: W. W. Norton, 1977.

Huizinga, Johan. *Erasmus and the Age of Reformation.* New York: Harper and Row, 1957.

Husserl, Edmund. *Cartesian Meditations: An Introduction to Phenomenology.* Translated by Dorion Cairns. The Hague: Martinus Nijhoff, 1970.

Isocrates. *Isocrates.* Translated by George Norlin. 3 vols. London: William Heinemann, 1928.

Jardine, Lisa. *Erasmus, Man of Letters: The Construction of Charisma in Print.* Princeton, N.J.: Princeton University Press, 1993.

Jerome. "Against Jovinianum." In *Nicene and Post-Nicene Fathers of the Christian Church*, Second Series, vol. 6, edited by Philip Schaff and Henry Wace, 346–416. Grand Rapids, Mich.: Eerdmans, 1954.

John of Salisbury. *Entheticus Major and Minor*, vol. 1. Edited by Jan van Laarhoven. Leiden: E. J. Brill, 1987.

———. *Frivolities of Courtiers and Footprints of Philosophers: Translated*

Selections of the Policraticus of John of Salisbury. Translated by Joseph B. Pike. New York: Octagon, 1972.

Jordan, William Chester. *Louis IX and the Challenge of the Crusades: A Study in Rulership*. Princeton, N.J.: Princeton University Press, 1979.

Jungkuntz, Richard P. "Christian Approval of Epicureanism." *Church History* 31 (1962): 279–293.

Kaiser, Walter. *Praisers of Folly: Erasmus, Rabelais, Shakespeare*. Cambridge, Mass.: Harvard University Press, 1963.

Kant, Immanuel. *Logic*. Translated by Robert S. Hartman and Wolfgang Schwarz. Indianapolis, Ind.: Bobbs-Merrill, 1974.

Kierkegaard, Søren. *Fear and Trembling and The Sickness Unto Death*. Translated by Walter Lowrie. Princeton, N.J.: Princeton University Press, 1954.

———. *Christian Discourses*. Translated by Walter Lowrie. New York: Oxford University Press, 1961.

———. *Kierkegaard's Concluding Unscientific Postscript*. Translated by David F. Swenson. Princeton, N.J.: Princeton University Press, 1968.

———. *Søren Kierkegaard's Journals and Papers*, vol. 4. Translated by Howard V. Hong and Edna H. Hong. Bloomington, Ind.: Indiana University Press, 1975.

———. *The Concept of Irony with Continual Reference to Socrates*. Translated by Howard V. Hong and Edna H. Hong. Princeton, N.J.: Princeton University Press, 1989.

Kojève, Alexandre. *Introduction to the Reading of Hegel: Lectures on the Phenomenology of Spirit*. Translated by James H. Nicols. Ithaca, N.Y.: Cornell University Press, 1980.

Largier, Niklaus. *In Praise of the Whip: A Cultural History of Arousal*. New York: Zone Books, 2007.

Lear, Jonathan. *A Case for Irony*. Cambridge, Mass.: Harvard University Press, 2011.

Leushuis, Reinier. "Dialogue and Intimacy in Erasmus's Matrimonial Writings." *Renaissance Quarterly* 57, no. 4 (Winter 2004): 1287–307.

Lévy, Bernard-Henri. *War, Evil, and the End of History*. Translated by Charlotte Mandell. Hoboken, N.J.: Melville, 2004.

Lucian. *Lucian*. Translated by A. M. Harmon. 7 vols. Cambridge, Mass.: Harvard University Press, 1988.

Lucretius. *On the Nature of the Universe*. Translated by Ronald Melville. Oxford: Oxford University Press, 1997.

Luther, Martin. *Luther's Works: Lectures on Galatians, 1535*, vol. 26. Edited by Jaroslav Pelikan. St. Louis, Mo.: Concordia Publishing, 1963.

———. *Luther's Works: Table Talk*, vol. 54. Edited and translated by Theodore G. Tappert. Philadelphia: Fortress, 1967.

———. *Bondage of the Will*. Edited by Philip S. Watson. Vol. 33 of *Luther's Works: Career of the Reformer*, edited by Helmut T. Lehmann. Philadelphia, Pa.: Fortress, 1972.

Machiavelli. *Machiavelli: The Chief Works and Others*. 2 Vols. Translated by Allan Gilbert. Durham, N.C.: Duke University Press, 1989.

MacPhail, Eric. "Erasmus as Sophist." *Erasmus of Rotterdam Society Yearbook* 26 (2006): 71–88.

Marsh, David. *The Quattrocento Dialogue: Classical Tradition and Humanist Innovation*. Cambridge, Mass.: Harvard University Press, 1980.

Margolin, Jean-Claude. *Érasme: Précepteur de l'Europe*. Paris: Juliard, 1995.

———. "Dire et Ne Pas Dire: La Pratique Érasmienne du Sous-entendu." In *Les Normes du Dire au XVIe Siècle*, edited by Jean-Claude Arnould and Gérard Milhe Poutingon, 125–44. Actes du colloque de Rouen, November 2001. Paris: Honoré Champion, 2004.

Marsh, David. "Erasmus and the Antithesis of Body and Soul." *Journal of the History of Ideas* 37, no. 4 (October–December, 1976): 673–88.

Martin, Terence J. *Living Words: Studies in Dialogues about Religion*. Atlanta, Ga.: Scholars Press, 1998.

McGinn, Bernard. *The Flowering of Mysticism: Men and Women in the New Mysticism, 1200–1350*. New York: Crossroad, 1998.

Miller, Clarence H. "The Logic and Rhetoric of Proverbs in Erasmus's *Praise of Folly*." In *Essays on the Works of Erasmus*, edited by Richard L. DeMolen, 83–98. New Haven, Conn.: Yale University Press, 1978.

Miller, Richard B. "Aquinas and the Presumption against Killing and War." *Journal of Religion* 82, no. 2 (April 2002): 173–204.

Montaigne, Michel de. *The Complete Works of Montaigne*. Translated by Donald M. Frame. Stanford, Calif.: Stanford University Press, 1957.

Nagel, Thomas. *The View from Nowhere*. New York: Oxford University Press, 1986.

Nederman, Cary J. *John of Salisbury*. Medieval and Renaissance Texts and Studies 288. Tempe, Ariz.: Arizona Center for Medieval and Renaissance Studies, 2005.

Niebuhr, Reinhold. *Reinhold Niebuhr: Theologian of Public Life*. Edited by Larry Rasmussen. Minneapolis, Minn.: Fortress, 1991.

Nietzsche, Friedrich. *The Birth of Tragedy and The Genealogy of Morals*. Translated by Francis Golffing. New York: Doubleday, 1956.

———. *Beyond Good and Evil*. Translated by Walter Kaufmann. New York: Random House, 1966.

———. *Twilight of the Idols and The Anti-Christ*. Translated by R. J. Hollingdale. Middlesex, England: Penguin, 1968.

Nussbaum, Martha C. *The Fragility of Goodness; Luck and Ethics in Greek Tragedy and Philosophy*. Cambridge: Cambridge University Press, 1986.

———. *The Therapy of Desire: Theory and Practice in Hellenistic Ethics*. Princeton, N.J.: Princeton University Press, 1994.

Olin, John C. *Six Essays on Erasmus; and a Translation of Erasmus' Letter to Carondelet, 1523*. New York: Fordham University Press, 1979.

Origen. *Origen: An Exhortation to Martyrdom, Prayer and Selected Works*. Translated by Rowan A. Greer. New York: Paulist Press, 1979.

Owens, Joseph. "Aquinas as Aristotelian Commentator." In *St. Thomas Aquinas on the Existence of God: Collected Papers of Joseph Owens, C.Ss.R.*, edited by John R. Catan, 1–19. Albany, N.Y.: State University of New York, 1980.

Pabel, Hilmar M. "The Prince of Peace: Erasmus' Conception of Jesus." In *The Unbounded Community: Papers in Christian Ecumenism in Honor of Jaroslav Pelikan*, edited by William Cafferro and Duncan G. Fisher, 127–48. New York: Garland Publishing, 1996.

Panizza, Letizia. "Valla's *De voluptate ac de vero bono* and Erasmus' *Stultitiae Laus*: Renewing Christian Ethics." *Erasmus of Rotterdam Society Yearbook* 15 (1995): 1–25.

Peter Abelard. *A Dialogue of a Philosopher with a Jew, and a Christian*. Translated by Pierre J. Payer. Toronto: Pontifical Institute of Mediaeval Studies, 1979.

Phillips, Margaret Mann. *The 'Adages' of Erasmus: A Study with Translations*. Cambridge: Cambridge University Press, 1964.

———. *Erasmus and the Northern Renaissance.* New York: Collier, 1965.

———. "Erasmus on the Tongue." *Erasmus of Rotterdam Society Yearbook* 1 (1981): 113–25.

Plato. *The Complete Dialogues of Plato.* Edited by Edith Hamilton and Huntington Cairns. Princeton, N.J.: Princeton University Press, 1973.

Plato. *The Republic of Plato.* Translated by Francis MacDonald Cornford. New York: Oxford University Press, 1945.

Plato. *Symposium.* Translated by Alexander Nehamas and Paul Woodruff. Indianapolis, Ind.: Hackett, 1989.

Plotinus. *Plotinus.* Translated by A. H. Armstrong. 7 vols. Cambridge, Mass.: Harvard University Press, 1984.

Plumer, Eric. *Augustine's Commentary on Galatians: Introduction, Text, Translation, and Notes.* Oxford: Oxford University Press, 2003.

Quinones, Ricardo J. *Erasmus and Voltaire: Why They Still Matter.* Toronto: University of Toronto Press, 2010.

Rebhorn, Wayne E. "The Metamorphoses of Moria: Structure and Meaning in *The Praise of Folly.*" *Publications of the Modern Language Association of America* 89, no. 3 (May 1974): 463–76.

Reese, Alan W. "Learning Virginity: Erasmus' Ideal of Christian Marriage." *Bibiothèque d'Humanisme et Renaissance* 57, no. 3 (1995): 551–67.

Reeve, Anne, ed. *Erasmus' Annotations of the New Testament: The Gospels.* London: Duckworth, 1986.

Riley-Smith, Jonathan. "Crusading as an Act of Love." In *Medieval Religion: New Approaches*, edited by Constance Hoffman Berman, 44–61. New York: Routledge, 2005.

Rorty, Richard. *Contingency, Irony, and Solidarity.* Cambridge: Cambridge University Press, 1989.

Rummel, Erika. *Erasmus' Annotations on the New Testament: From Philologist to Theologian.* Toronto: University of Toronto Press, 1986.

———. *Erasmus and His Catholic Critics, 1523–1536*, vol. 2. Nieuwkoop: De Graaf, 1989.

Ryan, Lawrence V. "*Erasmi Conviva*: The Banquet Colloquies of Erasmus." In *Acta Conventus Neo-Latini Turonesis* 1, 303–14. Paris: J. Vrin, 1980.

Sappho. *The Poetry of Sappho.* Translated by Jim Powell. New York: Oxford University Press, 2007.

Schoeck, R. J. *Erasmus of Europe: The Making of a Humanist, 1467–1500.* Edinburgh: Edinburgh University Press, 1990.

———. "Erasmus and Valla: The Dynamics of a Relationship," *Erasmus of Rotterdam Society Yearbook* 12 (1992): 45–63.

———. *Erasmus of Europe: The Making of a Humanist, 1501–1536.* Edinburgh: Edinburgh University Press, 1993.

"Scholars and Friars: A Chapter in the History of Ecclesiastical Strife." *Macmillan's Magazine, Littell's Living Age* 8, 5th series (1874): 304–12.

Screech, M. A. *Erasmus: Ecstasy and the Praise of Folly.* London: Penguin, 1980.

———. *Laughter at the Foot of the Cross.* Boulder, Colo.: Westview, 1999.

Seneca. *Seneca ad Lucilium Epistulae Morales.* Translated by Richard M. Gummere. 3 vols. Cambridge, Mass.: Harvard University Press, 1934.

Southern, R. W. *Medieval Humanism and Other Studies.* Oxford: Blackwell, 1970.

Spiegelberg, Herbert, ed. *The Socratic Enigma: A Collection of Testimonies through Twenty-Four Centuries.* Indianapolis, Ind.: Bobbs-Merrill, 1964.

Stolz, Anselm. "Anselm's Theology in the Proslogion." In *Many-Faced Argument: Recent Studies on the Ontological Argument for the Existence of God*, edited by John Hick and Arthur C. McGill, 183–206. New York: Macmillan, 1967.

Swain, Barbara. *Fools and Folly during the Middle Ages and the Renaissance.* New York: Columbia University Press, 1932.

Teresa of Avila. "Meditations on the Song of Songs." In *The Collected Works of St. Teresa of Avila*, translated by Kieran Kavanaugh and Otilio Rodriguez, 2:207–60. Washington, D.C.: ICS Publications, 1980.

Tertullian. "To His Wife." Translated by S. Thelwall. Vol. 4 of *Ante-Nicene Fathers*, edited by Alexander Roberts, James Donaldson, and revised by A. Cleveland Coxe, 39–49. Grand Rapids, Mich.: Eerdmans, 1954.

Thomas Aquinas. *Commentary on the Metaphysics of Aristotle,* vol. 2. Translated by John P. Rowan. Chicago: Henry Regnery, 1961.

Thomas Aquinas. *St. Thomas Aquinas on Politics and Ethics.* Translated by Paul E. Sigmund. New York: W. W. Norton, 1988.

Thomas Aquinas, *Summa Theologiae.* 60 vols. Cambridge: Blackfriars, in conjunction with New York: McGraw-Hill, 1964–81.

Torrell, Jean-Pierre. *Saint Thomas Aquinas: The Person and His Work,* vol. 1. Translated by Robert Royal. Washington, D.C.: The Catholic University of America Press, 1996.

Tracy, James D. *The Politics of Erasmus: A Pacifist Intellectual and His Political Milieu.* Toronto: University of Toronto Press, 1978.

———. "Erasmus among the Postmodernists: *Dissimulatio*, *Bonae Literae*, and *Docta Pietas* Revisited." In *Erasmus' Vision of the Church*, edited by Hilmar M. Pabel, 1–39. Sixteenth Century Essays and Studies 33. Kirksville, Mo.: Truman State University Press, 1995.

———. *Erasmus of the Low Countries.* Berkeley, Calif.: University of California Press, 1996.

Trapman, Johannes. "Erasmus on Lying and Simulation." In *Truth and Honesty: Principles and Strategies of Fraud and Deceit in the Early Modern Period*, edited by Toon van Houdt et al., 33–45. Leiden: E. J. Brill, 2002.

Trevor-Roper, H. R. *Men and Events: Historical Essays.* New York: Hippocrene Books, 1977.

Trinkaus, Charles. *In Our Image and Likeness: Humanity and Divinity in Italian Humanist Thought.* 2 vols. Chicago: University of Chicago Press, 1970.

Trivers, Robert. *The Folly of Fools: The Logic of Deceit and Self-Deception in Human Life.* New York: Basic Books, 2011.

Tsakiropoulos-Summers, A. "Horace, Philodemus and the Epicureans at Herculaneum," *Mnemosyne* 51, fourth series, fasc. 1 (February 1998): 20–29.

Valla, Lorenzo. *On Pleasure; De voluptate.* Translated by A. Kent Hieatt and Maristella Lorch. New York: Abaris Books, 1977.

———. *On the Donation of Constantine.* Translated by G. W. Bowersock. Cambridge, Mass.: Harvard University Press, 2007.

Virgil. *The Eclogues and Georgics of Virgil.* Translated by C. Day Lewis. Garden City, N.Y.: Doubleday, 1964.

Weiler, A. G. "The Turkish Argument and Christian Piety in Desiderius Erasmus' 'Consultatio de Bello Turcis Inferendo' (1530)." In *Erasmus of Rotterdam: The Man and the Scholar*, edited by J. Sperna Weiland and W. Th. M. Frijhoff, 30–39. Leiden: E. J. Brill, 1988.

Weisheipl, James A. *Friar Thomas D'Aquino: His Life, Thought, and Work.* Garden City, N.Y.: Doubleday, 1974.

Wippel, John F. *Metaphysical Themes in Thomas Aquinas*. Studies in Philosophy and the History of Philosophy 10. Washington, D.C.: The Catholic University of America Press, 1984.

Wippel, John. "The Five Ways." In *Aquinas' Summa Theologiae*, edited by Brian Davies, 45–110. Lanham, Md.: Rowman and Littlefield, 2006.

Zagorin, Perez. *Ways of Lying: Dissimulation, Persecution, and Conformity in Early Modern Europe*. Cambridge, Mass.: Harvard University Press, 1990.

Index

Truth and Irony: Philosophical Meditations on Erasmus was designed in Minion Pro and composed by Kachergis Book Design of Pittsboro, North Carolina. It was printed on 60-pound House Natural Smooth and bound by Sheridan Books of Ann Arbor, Michigan.